Job Coaches for Adults with Disabilities

of related interest

Autism Equality in the Workplace
Removing Barriers and Challenging Discrimination
Janine Booth
Foreword by John McDonnell MP
ISBN 978 1 84905 678 6
eISBN 978 1 78450 197 6

Helping Adults with Asperger's Syndrome Get & Stay Hired
Career Coaching Strategies for Professionals and
Parents of Adults on the Autism Spectrum
Barbara Bissonnette
ISBN 978 1 84905 754 7
eISBN 978 1 78450 052 8

Employment for Individuals with Asperger Syndrome
or Non-Verbal Learning Disability
Stories and Strategies
Yvona Fast
ISBN 978 1 84310 766 8
eISBN 978 1 84642 015 3

Brain Injury and Returning to Employment
A Guide for Practitioners
James Japp
ISBN 978 1 84310 292 2
eISBN 978 1 84642 111 2

JOB COACHES FOR ADULTS WITH DISABILITIES

A Practical Guide

Edited by Karola Dillenburger, Ewa Matuska,
Marea de Bruijn and Hanns Rüdiger Röttgers

Forewords by Blazej Piasek and Norman Sterritt

Jessica Kingsley *Publishers*
London and Philadelphia

First published in 2019
by Jessica Kingsley Publishers
73 Collier Street
London N1 9BE, UK
and
400 Market Street, Suite 400
Philadelphia, PA 19106, USA

www.jkp.com

Copyright © Jessica Kingsley Publishers 2019
Blazej Piasek foreword copyright © Blazej Piasek 2019
Norman Sterritt foreword copyright © Norman Sterritt 2019

Library of Congress Cataloging in Publication Data
Names: Dillenburger, Karola, 1956- editor. | Matuska, Ewa, editor. | Bruijn,
   Marea de, editor. | R?ottgers, H. R. (Hanns R?udiger), editor. | Piasek,
   Blazej, writer of introduction. | Sterritt, Norman, writer of introduction.
Title: Job coaches for adults with disabilities : a practical guide / edited
   by Karola Dillenburger, Ewa Matuska, Marea de Bruijn, and Hanns R?udiger
   R?ottgers ; forewords by Blazej Piasek and Norman Sterritt.
Description: London, UK ; Philadelphia, PA : Jessica Kingsley Publishers,
   2019. | Includes bibliographical references and index.
Identifiers: LCCN 2018011463 | ISBN 9781785925467 (alk. paper)
Subjects: LCSH: People with disabilities--Vocational guidance--Europe. |
   People with disabilities--Employment--Europe.
Classification: LCC HV1568.5 .J63 2019 | DDC 362.4/0484094--
dc23 LC record available at https://lccn.loc.gov/2018011463

British Library Cataloguing in Publication Data
A CIP catalogue record for this book is available from the British Library

ISBN 978 1 78592 546 7
eISBN 978 1 78450 943 9

Printed and bound in Great Britain

CONTENTS

FOREWORD

Blazej Piasek

When I think of my nephew, a smile of joy and pride appears on my face. For almost 25 years he has faced the challenges of everyday life. First, the struggle for life, heart surgery, cancer, the fear of an inability to move independently, then school education, step-by-step, without any special assistance or treatment. Surrounded by the love and support of his family, each day he moves towards the moment of independence. Yet, unfortunately, this moment seems to elude him, constantly moving further away in time. This is hard to accept, for him and for his family, especially when his brothers are growing up and leaving the family nest.

The urgent need for medical rehabilitation has passed now, and the next step in my nephew's battle for independence is to get a job. But in order to achieve this goal he needs the support of a specialist – someone who is knowledgeable and supportive in the process of social and vocational rehabilitation. That person should be a job coach. The role of the job coach fuses the competences and roles of a consultant, an employment agent, a job instructor, a social worker, and at times, a therapist.

Job coaches work in three stages. The most important first stage is supporting the adult with disabilities in the process of vocational rehabilitation, job searching and gaining employment. The second stage is creating an appropriate job environment, where the job coach works collegially with the employer and the co-workers of the employee with disabilities. The third stage is about taking care of relations with those closest to the adult with disabilities – their family and friends.

In order to better understand the need for and the role of the job coach for people with disabilities we need to first define our understanding of disability. Is it the perception through the prism of our own limitations and imperfections, or perhaps a definition included in legal acts related to medical research, tests and diagnosis?

The World Health Organization (WHO 2017) defines disability as an umbrella term, covering impairments, activity limitations and participation restrictions – impairment, as a difficulty in physical functioning or structure; activity limitation, as a problem encountered in executing a task or action; participation restriction, as a problem experienced by an individual in involvement in social and other life situations.

But a disability is not just a physical health problem. It is a complex phenomenon, reflecting the interaction between features of a person's body and features of the society in which they live. Overcoming the difficulties faced by people with disabilities requires interventions to remove environmental and social barriers. And one of the most important aspects of social inclusion is work employment.

In this book readers will have the opportunity to become familiar with the role of the job coach in the process of vocational rehabilitation. They will learn about formal requirements, the scope of qualifications as well as the practical aspects of this profession. They will learn about different forms of disability and the special kinds of support the job coach can offer. Importantly, readers will hear directly from adults with disabilities who have a job coach, and from job coaches who support these employees, thus reflecting the atmosphere of the profession.

This book brings us closer to the world of people with disabilities and the work of job coaches. It gives us a glimpse of the similarities and differences in life experiences. It gives us a chance to release for a moment from our own virtual reality – understanding others and ourselves better, noticing another human being for who they are, to see something more than disability.

Blazej Piasek, Warsaw, Poland

References

WHO (World Health Organization) (2017) 'Disabilities.' Accessed on 22/02/2018 at www.who.int/topics/disabilities/en

FOREWORD

Norman Sterritt

I have been involved with the development and management of supported employment services in Northern Ireland since the late 1990s, and I am both delighted and honoured to have been asked to compose this Foreword for the book, *Job Coaches for Adults with Disabilities*.

I first met many of the contributors to this book in the autumn of 2016 when I was invited to engage with a group of researchers from across Europe who were meeting at Queen's University Belfast to share and compare their experiences of job coaching within their respective countries. This occasion provided the opportunity to share experiences and knowledge gained over many years in relation to the roles typically performed by job coaches within local, national and international agencies.

Within Northern Ireland the supported employment model has been used successfully by local disability organisations for many years. It is recognised within the *Northern Ireland Employment Strategy for People with Disabilities* as the most appropriate delivery model to improve the job prospects and working careers of people with disabilities.

The job coach role is central to the delivery of the supported employment model, and has existed informally for many years. This book contributes to the recognition of the professionalism of those skilled and dedicated workers who carry out this role.

This book offers a unique combination of expertise and personal experiences from a broad range of stakeholders. This includes supported employees with disabilities, job coach practitioners, researchers and experts across a wide range of disciplines. Each contributor brings a wealth of experience, research, knowledge and examples of best practice approaches, for assisting individuals availing of job coach support.

The structure of each chapter, commencing with a brief overview of the content, provides a quick and easy means for the reader to locate information about their immediate area of interest, for example, the focus on a particular disability or an insight into aspects of the role of job coach itself.

The opening chapter advocates for the recognition and professionalisation of the job coach role, acknowledging the expertise, skills and competences required. Some of the chapters provide specific guidance and examples of interventions and best practice approaches for those working with various disability groups, while others give generic understanding and insight into interventions pertaining to the job coach role. Chapter 9 provides a particularly useful insight to, and analysis of, employers' experiences in this area. The concluding chapter provides a steer for the preparation of job coaches of the future, and outlines the wide-ranging knowledge, skills and competences required for the job within a multidisciplinary context.

For those contemplating a career as a job coach, this book provides a comprehensive overview of the requirements of the role and the values, attributes and competences required and expected of the prospective job coach. Equally, for experienced job coach practitioners, this book brings a depth of understanding of the challenges typically encountered by job coaches as they support jobseekers with disabilities. For those tasked with managing supported employment services, the book contains useful information related to the recruitment and selection of job coaches and guidance that will inform the continuous professional development of the job coach role. The book also provides a comprehensive reference resource for other stakeholders interested in the subject, and represents an invaluable body of work for those researching the topic.

I wholeheartedly recommend this book to all those interested in the subject area of job coaching.

Norman Sterritt DMS, MBA, Progression to Employment Service Manager, Triangle Housing Association and Chair, Northern Ireland Union of Supported Employment

INTRODUCTION

People with disabilities are disproportionately unemployed or under-employed. In other words, their potential to make a living and to contribute economically is not fully utilised, which has negative effects not only on their quality of life, but on society as a whole. It is the role of the job coach to help people with disabilities to find and maintain a job. However, the professional qualifications and training standards for job coaches remain rather unclear in most countries, despite European standards that have been developed (Matuska 2016).

Job coaching is mainly based on the five-stage supported employment model (EUSE 2010), that focuses on the ambitions, strengths and challenges of people with disabilities and includes assessment and relationship building, open labour market research, client–employer matching, on-site training and ongoing support. The involvement of the family support network, friends and any other professionals is also an important prerequisite for successful, sustainable labour market participation. This multidisciplinary approach makes it possible to integrate multiple perspectives in the guidance, and to formulate an appropriate approach with the client.

Adults with disabilities have many skills and talents that can be applied usefully in the open labour market. A strengths-based perspective, such as that taken by the scientific discipline of behaviour analysis (Cooper, Heron and Heward 2007), takes the context in which a person finds themselves fully into consideration. A practical coaching framework is offered by the 5-D cycle of Appreciative Inquiry methodology (Cooperrider, Barrett and Srivastva 2013; Subirana 2016) that focuses on assessing and then reinforcing the positive aspects of organisational and employment contexts: define, discover, dream, design, deliver (see the figure below). Appreciative Inquiry helps the job coach to realise that both the self-fulfilling

11

prophecy (Merton 1948) and learned helplessness (Seligman 1972) prevent adults with disabilities from finding suitable employment.

The 5-D cycle of Appreciative Inquiry
Source: Reprinted with permission from Graham (2017)

The idea for this book was born when the editors and many of the authors met as partners in a European Union (EU)-funded Erasmus+ project called 'Job Coach for People with Disabilities'. This project was led by Anna Block from Grone Schulen, Germany, with partners from France, the Netherlands, Germany, the United Kingdom and Poland (Grone Schulen 2018). The key aim of the project was to develop European standards for job coaches and to share these with practitioners and other stakeholders. In addition to partners from this Erasmus+ project, a number of well-known academics and practitioners in the field of job coaching contributed to this book, widening the international reach to Ireland, Australia, the United States of America and the Czech Republic.

Outline of the book

Chapter 1 defines the role of job coaches and sets the scene for the remainder of the book. The supported employment model is introduced, and standards for the profession of job coaches are explained. Chapter 2 gives a voice to adults with disabilities, most of whom have a mentor or job coach. Their testimonies set the inclusive tone of the book. Chapter 3 is the first of four chapters that focus on specific diagnoses most often experienced by adults who avail of job coaches. It is important that job coaches are familiar with the key issues related to the disability of the employee they support, so, for example, prevalence, aetiology and specific issues are outlined. These four chapters focus on mental health issues (Chapter 3); physical and sensory disabilities (Chapter 4); intellectual disabilities (Chapter 5); and the autism spectrum (Chapter 6). The following chapters then focus on some of the skills necessary for job coaches, with particular attention paid to on-the-job functional assessments (Chapter 7) and dealing with crisis and challenging behaviours (Chapter 8). Chapter 9 identifies the important issues related to collaborating with employers. This chapter is based on an EU-funded project that included partners from the UK, Czech Republic, Finland and Germany (Erasmus+ 2017). Working with employers is an important aspect of job coaching, and it is essential that job coaches understand employers' views – Chapter 10 testifies to the real-life experiences of job coaches. The final chapter, Chapter 11, provides an overview of competences and training for job coaches, and gives some examples of existing training courses.

Acknowledgements

This book was an international collaborative effort. We came together with the aim of offering a practical guide for job coaches, those in training, or those contemplating becoming a job coach, and trainers of job coaches. What we produced is a book that hopefully meets these aims, but that will also be useful for those who avail of the services and support from job coaches.

First and foremost, we acknowledge all the adult employees with disabilities and the job coaches who contributed so generously to this book by sharing their real-life experiences. Most of their names have been changed for reasons of confidentiality, although they will know who they are, and they should know that we are proud of their achievements.

We are also indebted to Professor Emeritus Eric Blyth and Dr Vanessa Blyth, of Premier English Language Editing Services, for their professional services and advice, in light of the fact that many of us are non-native English speakers. That was not an easy job! We also want to express our appreciation to Jessica Kingsley and her team of dedicated editors and producers. As always, they have supported this book project from the start, and ensured a speedy and professional delivery.

Finally, we want to thank our families for their patience during the process of making this book happen. Much like raising a child, it takes a community to produce a book, and we hope that this book will in turn serve many communities, including those of job coaches, employers and adults with disabilities.

References

Cooper, J., Heron, T. and Heward, W. (2007) *Applied Behaviour Analysis* (2nd edn). Upper Saddle River, NJ: Pearson Prentice Hall.

Cooperrider, D.L., Barrett, F. and Srivastva, S. (2013) 'Social Construction and Appreciative Inquiry: A Journey in Organizational Theory.' In D. Hosking, P. Dachler and K. Gergen (eds) *Management and Organization: Relational Alternatives to Individualism* (2nd edn) (pp.157–200). Aldershot: Avebury. Accessed on 07/02/2018 at www.taosinstitute. net/Websites/taos/images/PublicationsWorldShare/ManagementandOrganization. pdf

Erasmus+ (2017) 'SEN Employment Links (SENEL): Working with employers and trainers to support young people with special educational needs/disabilities into employment.' Accessed on 07/02/2018 at http://ec.europa.eu/programmes/ erasmus-plus/projects/eplus-project-details-page/?nodeRef=workspace:// SpacesStore/80ad6f7e-4687-444d-b481-e781929bcb93

EUSE (European Union of Supported Employment) (2010) *European Union of Supported Employment Toolkit.* Accessed on 07/02/2018 at www.euse.org/content/supported-employment-toolkit/EUSE-Toolkit-2010.pdf

Graham, S. (2017) 'Bringing Alternatives to Violence Project workshops to parents and partners.' Sustaining Community. Accessed on 09/02/2017 at https:// sustainingcommunity.wordpress.com

Grone Schulen (2018) 'Job Coach für Menschen mit Behinderungen (Erasmus+).' Accessed on 07/02/2018 at http://ec.europa.eu/programmes/erasmus-plus/projects/eplus-project-details/#project/7a7122ee-ff52-4835-8bc6-3099bb004a5d

Matuska, E. (2016) 'European qualification profile of job coach for people with disabilities.' Accessed on 07/02/2018 at www.cordaan.nl/sites/default/files/downloads/ erasmus_jobcoachproject_samenvatting_korte_versie_ned.pdf

Merton, R.K. (1948) 'The self-fulfilling prophecy.' *Antioch Review 8,* 2, 193–210. Accessed on 18/05/2018 at http://doi.org/10.2307/4609267

Seligman, M.E. (1972) 'Learned helplessness.' *Annual Review of Medicine* 207–412. Accessed on 18/05/2018 at http://doi.org/10.1146/annurev.me.23.020172.002203

Subirana, M. (2016) *Flourishing Together: Guide to Appreciative Inquiry Coaching.* Alresford: O-Books, John Hunt Publishing Ltd.

Chapter 1

WHAT IS A JOB COACH FOR ADULTS WITH DISABILITIES?

Ewa Matuska

This chapter explains the need for formal registering of a new profession – 'job coach for adults with disabilities' – and its eligibility requirements, based on the European standards for the description of the qualifications. It suggests that the job coach occupation should be included in the wide family of occupations in the human resources (HR) development area. This chapter focuses in particular on outlining the detailed job description of job coaches as well as their profile of professional competences.

Why is there a need for job coaches?

The *European Disability Strategy 2010–2020* (European Commission 2010) aims to empower people with disabilities so that they can enjoy their full rights and benefit fully from participating in society and in the European economy, to 'enable many more people with disabilities to earn their living on the open labour market' (2010, p.7). While one of the eight main areas of the strategy is 'Employment', employment rates of people with disabilities are generally low, not only in Europe, but also globally. A significant public health challenge worldwide is to help people with different kinds of disability with their work transition. With the majority of people with disabilities of working age, it is a huge waste of human capital resources to keep them unemployed and not to promote their social inclusion.

According to the United Nations (UN) Convention on the Rights of Persons with Disabilities (CRPD): 'Persons with disabilities include those who have long-term physical, mental, intellectual, or sensory impairments which in interaction with various barriers may hinder their full and effective participation in society on an equal basis with others' (UN 2006, p.4).

Disability, as measured by different clinical symptoms and prevalence, has many faces, but in a majority of cases does not eliminate the person's potential to be socially included via employment or a similar activity. The employment situation of people with disabilities in different European countries is not equal, with differences existing in national laws and regulations regarding supported employment, in business practices and culturally determined family and social surroundings, as well as in behavioural patterns towards employing people with disabilities. Many would like to be employed and to be self-sufficient. They are able to work, but first they have to obtain professional assistance to secure and maintain employment. Many people with disabilities are well educated but have been unable to secure employment. Some acquired professional experience before the onset of their disability, but have become unemployed and discouraged. Usually they are not able to evaluate their own strengths connected to work and to develop the necessary soft or technical skills. They may not know how to move into the labour market, where to find support, or how to negotiate job contracts or salaries.

Today, the labour market is profoundly influenced by technology and automation that is creating new employment chances for people with disabilities, especially those with desirable qualifications. Employers can do much to assist people with a disability in employment if they cooperate with professional work services specialising in the field of the career management of people with disabilities as a particular target group. This provides an opportunity for professional job coaches to intervene, and it is worth pointing out that the demand for this special kind of skilled job coach is growing (Gerhardt 2009).

Currently work assistance for people with disabilities is widely offered within the framework of supported employment, which is recognised as: 'Providing support to people with disabilities or other disadvantaged groups to secure and maintain paid employment in the open labour market' (EUSE 2005, p.13).

While job coaches play a key role here, they are not recognised as professionals acting as part of human resources (HR) development services, but rather, as part of medical or social teams. Usually they perform similar tasks to traditional duties undertaken by social workers who do not necessarily need a wide range of professional skills based on specialised knowledge. However, helping people with disabilities to successfully transfer to the open labour market and maintain employment requires 'work assistants' to undertake much more complex and sophisticated tasks.

What is the new approach to job coaching?

Efficient job coaches should enable a person with a disability to find a suitable job and possibly develop more than one career path, as is frequently the case with people without disabilities. Additionally, a job coach should closely cooperate with employers and be familiar with current labour market issues. Today, job coaches are expected to deliver a personal service to the client in the form of person-centred planning for career development. Job coaching is successful when the client is able to hold a satisfying job position as long as they want and are able to develop professionally.

Hitherto, the role of job coach existed informally. Its occupational status now needs to be confirmed with a formal qualification, meeting Europe-wide training standards for professionals in the field of vocational guidance for people with disabilities, and the European Qualifications Framework (EQF) (European Council 2008) could be used for designing such an internationally recognised formal qualification. The EQF defines expected learning outcomes for every qualification – specifying what a person acquiring a particular qualification will know and will be able to do, as a professional, at the completion of the educational process. In this way the EQF, as an overarching framework, makes it possible to link together the same qualifications of different EU countries. Using the EQF could also facilitate the dissemination of the qualification of 'job coach for people with disabilities' across Europe, hopefully enhancing the employment opportunities of its citizens with disabilities.

European standards adopted for specifying the 'job coach for people with disabilities' as a profession suggest implementing three steps:

- job description

- competence profile

- qualification path.

This chapter discusses the necessary background for the qualification of job coaches for people with disabilities, including the job description and competence profile. In addition, the chapter suggests the appropriate location of the occupation in internationally recognised classifications of professions. More details about a qualification path to 'job coach for people with disabilities' are provided in Chapter 11 of this book.

Occupation of job coach

The general objective of the job coach's work is to offer job coaching to people with disabilities in the wide work context. However, 'job coach' is currently not formally registered as an occupation in the official classification used in the *European Skills, Competences, Qualifications and Occupations* (European Commission 2013), although similar kinds of professions (e.g., job trainer, work assistant, employment support worker) have been included for many years in Europe. In 1998, for example, the Netherlands implemented the (Re)integration of the Work-Disabled Act (REA; European Commission 2017), defining the base for the statutory provision of job coaches. Since that time national legislation in the Netherlands has stipulated that personal support (job coaching) should be provided for workers with disabilities, and the person who implements this provision is called a 'job coach' (BivT 2014). Nevertheless, even in the Netherlands, the profession of 'job coach' is not formally protected and is not a registered profession. Similarly, an International Standard Classification of Occupations (ISCO-8), developed by the International Labour Organization (ILO 2008), does not include an occupation called 'job coach' or 'job coach for people with disabilities'.

The ideal location for the 'job coach for people with disabilities' profession within a comprehensive framework of professions seems to be among the wide group dealing with career development and HR services. After examining the index of existing internationally recognised occupational titles in ISCO-8 (ILO 2008), the 'job coach' occupation could be located in the group of occupations with number 2423: Personnel and careers professionals. ISCO-8 locates occupations in a hierarchical way, adding subsequent numbers when specifying particular occupations and their groups (ILO 2007, p.17), as follows:

- 2 (major group) – professionals
- 24 (sub-major group) – business and administration professionals
- 242 (minor group) – administration professionals
- 2423 (unit group) – personnel and careers professionals.

A similar localisation can be proposed in *European Skills, Competences, Qualifications and Occupations* (ESCO) (European Commission 2013), whose content matches ISCO-8 and clusters occupations or occupational groups with common characteristics. ESCO implements EQF standards and realises the objectives of the *European Disability Strategy 2010-2020* (European Commission 2010), that aims to facilitate internal EU workforce mobility and work transition through ensuring comparison of skills, competences and qualifications obtained in different EU countries. Thus, the ESCO framework could be used to design a new 'job coach for people with disabilities' qualification.

The hypothetical position of the job coach occupation in the ESCO model is presented in Figure 1.1.

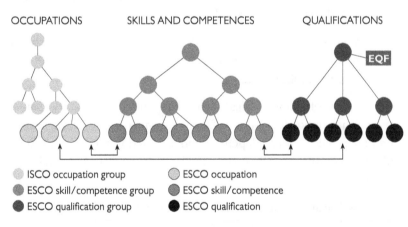

OCCUPATIONS   SKILLS AND COMPETENCES   QUALIFICATIONS

ISCO occupation group   ESCO occupation
ESCO skill/competence group   ESCO skill/competence
ESCO qualification group   ESCO qualification

Figure 1.1: ESCO basic model with the hypothetical position of the occupation 'job coach for people with disabilities'
Source: Author, developed from European Commission (2013, p.6)

Locating the 'job coach for people with disabilities' occupation within the ESCO system and designing the job description and possible qualification path in EQF terms leads to the possibility of disseminating the new qualification in Europe via the constantly broadening ESCO functionalities.

Job description of job coach

The job description specifies the main tasks and responsibilities of the 'job coach for people with disabilities'. There are two main task areas:

- *career counselling:* which represents the interests of jobseekers with disabilities

- *recruitment support:* which represents the interests of employers who seek the best candidate to fill vacancies according to the rules of supported employment.

The work of the job coach for people with disabilities covers two fields of expertise: career counselling to people with special health needs and an HR service to organisations wishing to employ people with disabilities.

The job coach works in the interests of the two main subjects (stakeholders), who are mutually interdependent (Wehman *et al.* 2007):

- *client:* the person with a disability interested in finding/ maintaining employment in the open labour market, as the first level of the job coach's stakeholder

- *employer:* the second-level stakeholder who wants to obtain the valuable HR service of supported employment and to hire competent jobseekers.

The interests of both parties, client and employer, are the same, representing opposite points of views connected with successful recruitment, good work adaptation and satisfaction with work results and work conditions. All of this implies that a job coach (Wehman *et al.* 2007):

- must be able to take an independent position with respect to the employee and the employer

- supports both employee and employer in achieving sustainable employment

- can explain (if necessary) why permanent support is required

- offers judgement based on expertise rather than on their own financial interests or those of the employer

- keeps an optimal balance between the interests of the employee and employer, and cares that the job coaching achieves the best result.

A job coach's work tasks represent a mixture of specialisation, including (Matuska 2017):

- *essential tasks:* first-level tasks, connected with labour market research/personnel marketing and counselling/coaching tasks

- *technical tasks:* secondary tasks, connected with administrative work, documentation or other tasks involving the use of special tools (IT programs, competence tests, HR profiles) and equipment (using a computer, driving a car, etc.).

Essential tasks are aimed at achieving the expected outcomes of job coaching, and include (Matuska 2017):

- identifying the client's job-related strengths and weaknesses and recruitment needs of employer(s)

- delivering adequate training opportunities to the client and employer (co-workers)

- penetrating job market offers and negotiating work conditions with the potential employer

- facilitating the transition from the job training centre (school) to the workplace via providing on-the-job and post-job support and assistance.

The main responsibilities of the job coach as regards the client include (Matuska 2017):

- recognising and adopting the most accurate model of intervention for job coaching, adequate to the client's health *status*

- helping the client to understand how their health may affect their performance while at work

- profiling the client's vocational competences and benchmarking their profile with job offers

- ensuring adequate health and safety conditions are maintained in the work environment

- providing adequate training of technical or soft skills useful in the place of employment

- helping with preparing applications for job offers and for interviews with employers

- collecting proper documentation for the purpose of the client's supported employment

- helping the client to understand their job duties and the employer's policy rules

- helping the client to build and maintain positive relationships with co-workers and customers

- monitoring the work performance of the client and providing them with adequate feedback

- preparing the client for possible job termination and further outplacement proposals

- upholding the quality and ethical standards of the contract with the client.

Further responsibilities are connected with the service to the employer, and include (Matuska 2017):

- knowing and adhering to established useful agency policies, procedures and regulations

- delivering accurate information about supported employment rules, the employer's duties and benefits

- delivering accurate information about the health and life situation of jobseekers

- respecting the employer's organisational structures and values

- negotiating possible job position adaptations with the employer to meet the client's needs

- cooperating with the employer's HR staff and using the employer's templates for completing the client's personnel documentation

- guaranteeing ongoing support to the client in the workplace following employment, including coaching and training

- delivering necessary training for co-workers, promoting the inclusion of clients in project teams, conflict resolution, mediation, mentoring, etc.

- cooperating with the employer in case of necessary job termination and outplacement activities.

The general specification of the tasks for the job coach can also be derived from the description of subsequent stages of supported employment (EUSE 2010, p.7):

- First stage: Assessment and relationship building

  - Creating relationships

  - Assessing abilities

  - Creating the client's vocational profile.

- Second stage: Open labour market research

  - Job finding

  - Job position analysis.

- Third stage: Client–employer matching

  - Direct contact with the employer

  - Work environment adaptation

  - Client's induction.

- Fourth stage: On-site training

  - Workplace introduction

  - Job training.

- Fifth stage: Ongoing support

  - Formal support

  - Off-site support.

However, as already indicated, the job coach for people with disabilities performs much more complex roles and tasks than observed in the traditional supported employment approach, because:

- Their relationship with the client should be based on partnership and use a professional, semi-therapeutic, coaching non-directive approach.

- They are expected to act in parallel in several different roles, as assessor, trainer, counsellor, coordinator, sales person, mentor and negotiator. At the beginning of the coaching process the job coach assists in building the client's motivation to be employed, shapes their vocational profile and orientates them to acquire the necessary new vocational and life skills. Next, they actively seek out available job offers on the open labour market, and later negotiate with the employer the client's best work conditions. Finally, they monitor the client on the job, helping them to find an alternative post, if the client decides to do so, or if the client appears unsuitable to continue in the post. All of this demands a wide range of interdisciplinary knowledge and skills and constant lifelong learning.

- They need to be supervised and supported by experienced professionals who can give them valuable feedback developing their attitudes, skills and knowledge. All this suggests that the job coach for people with disabilities should demonstrate deep interdisciplinary knowledge, well-trained skills, as well as mature and ethical work attitudes. Having recognised the tasks and responsibilities performed by the job coach makes it possible to identify the expected 'learning outcomes' that have to be delivered to trainees together with the proposed new qualification. In this way job coaches should meet the educational requirements defined in terms of 'competences'.

Competence profile of job coaches

The competence profile means the set of knowledge, skills and psycho-social competences that job coaches, as professionals, should acquire during learning for qualification. EQF/ESCO (European Council 2008; European Commission 2013) standards recognise three kinds of expected qualification outcomes:

- *knowledge:* described as theoretical and/or factual

- *skills:* described as cognitive (involving the use of logical, intuitive and creative thinking) and practical (involving manual dexterity and the use of methods, materials, tools and instruments)

- *competence:* described in terms of responsibility and autonomy and interpersonal attitudes specific for the acquired qualification.

The variety of roles played by job coaches also demands a variety of professional competences. The core competences of the 'job coach for people with disabilities' derived from the description of the roles of 'employment support worker' defined in the supported employment concept are illustrated in Figure 1.2.

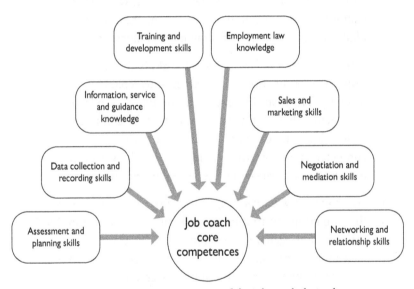

Figure 1.2: Core competences of the job coach derived from the supported employment concept
Source: EUSE (2010, p.122)

As already mentioned, the job description covers a wide range of tasks and responsibilities and fits with a group of professional occupations connected with personnel career counselling and HR counselling, yet dedicated to a special target group – clients with specific kinds of needs and barriers conditioned by their health status. This implies that the job coach competence profile has to be both sufficiently wide and detailed.

The competence profile, conceptualised according to EQF and ESCO rules, and with the aim of being part of the further qualification, has to be created in line with the Knowledge – Skills –Competence (KSC) concept.

ESCO defines the following kinds of KSC terms:

- *Transversal skills (formerly referred to as 'transferable skills')*: the skills individuals have and which are relevant to their jobs and occupations other than the ones they currently have or have recently had. These may also have been acquired through non-work or leisure activities or through participation in education or training. More generally, these are skills that have been learned in one context or to master a special situation/problem and can be transferred to another context. They include, for example, communication, organisation, presentation, teamwork, planning, supervisory and time management, etc.

- *Cross-sector skills and competences*: the skills that can be transferred from one occupation to another, thus enabling occupational mobility. They can be used in a number of similar occupations and sectors, but might require additional training to be used in a new job and/or work environment. Cross-sector skills and competences are of growing importance all over Europe, and are relevant to occupations across several economic sectors.

- *Sector-specific skills and competences*: those skills and competences that are common to a group of similar jobs (job family). They often include 'general job competences' that tend to be required in a number of job families (e.g., partnering), as well as 'job-specific competences' that apply to certain job families more than others (e.g., project management). These tend to be related more to knowledge or skills required for certain types of jobs (e.g., accounting for jobs involving financial administration).

- *Technical/professional competences*: technical/professional competences tend to be specific to roles or jobs within the job family sector and include the specific skills and knowledge (know-how) to perform effectively (e.g., the ability to use particular software; knowledge in particular professional areas such as finance, biochemistry, etc.). These could be generic to a job family as a whole, or be specific to roles, levels or jobs within the family.

- *Occupation (job):* specific competences (functional competences), the competences that are proven to drive high-performance, quality results for a given position. They are often technical or operational in nature (e.g., backing up a database). Job-specific competences are required for success in particular functions or jobs.

Job-specific competences as projected for the role of the 'job coach for people with disabilities' permits a functional approach to its competence profiling to be adopted, based on the previous recognised job description of this profession. This is presented in Figure 1.3.

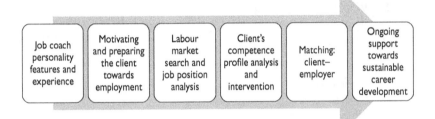

Figure 1.3: Functional approach to the profiling competence of the job coach for people with disabilities
Source: Matuska (2017, p.9)

The starting point in the KSC concept for the job coach is adequate competence (C), defined by the EQF/ESCO as the ability of a person facing new situations and unforeseen challenges to use and apply knowledge and skills in an independent and self-directed way. Obviously the candidate for the 'job coach for people with disabilities' has to be able to act in terms of responsibility and autonomy, which requires demonstration of an adequate personality base (ethical value system, adequate aptitudes) and the acquisition of a set of knowledge (K) and skills (S) defined for the profession.[1]

The 'C' component expected from the job coach includes, as a minimum:

- awareness of personal, professional predispositions and abilities

---

1   It is highly probable that knowledge and skills learned by the person without an adequate personality basis may be used in an inappropriate way in the process of client coaching.

- sensitivity and humanistic orientation towards people

- sense of responsibility

- auto-reflection and orientation on self-development

- stress auto-regulation.

The next parts of the KSC model are built with components of specific knowledge ('K') and skills ('S'), as illustrated in Figure 1.4.

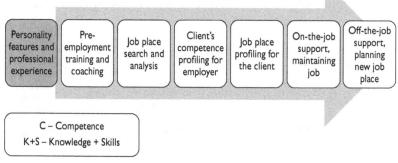

Figure 1.4: Knowledge, skills and competence (KSC)
components of the job coach profile
Source: Author

The job coach for people with disabilities has to demonstrate the necessary skills and knowledge (Röttgers and Metje 2016):

- About the general and professional education system

- About the interaction between (potential) employers and state agencies and bodies supporting employment

- About the respective legal frameworks for unsupported and supported labour

- About common application and placement procedures

- About the conditions for apprenticeships, internships and non-permanent employment

- About work and organisational psychology

- In the fields of the respective job environment

- In conflict moderation and resolutions.

A job coach responsible for the integration of people with disabilities into the open labour market must additionally demonstrate specialised knowledge about the different disabilities and potentials of the target group. They should be able to evaluate in which way and to what extent these disabilities have an influence on the individual perspective for finding a job in the open labour market. In particular, a job coach should have in-depth, specialised knowledge about:

- conditions related to pervasive developmental delay, such as autism spectrum disorders

- intellectual disability

- psychotic disorders such as schizophrenia, major depression and bipolar disorder

- non-psychotic psychiatric conditions like anxiety, obsessive compulsive disorders (OCD), somatoform, eating and personality disorders

- childhood-based behavioural conditions such as attention deficit hyperactivity disorder (ADHD).

Besides this, optionally additional knowledge could be helpful in the following fields:

- sensory disabilities like impaired vision (auditory functions) and blindness (deafness)

- physical disabilities like amputation and paralysis

- physically determined communication problems

- addiction and substance abuse

- childhood-based learning conditions like dyslexia and dyscalculia without cognitive impairments

- inclusion problems of people who have been out of work due, for example, to cancer, back injury/spinal problems etc. or people who have lost touch with the labour market due to lengthy unemployment.

Clustering all knowledge/skills demands, the minimum levels of the knowledge and skills component in the KSC concept required from job coaches for people with disabilities includes those connected with:

- the coaching process oriented towards individually centred career/employment motivating and training, where the client is a person with a disability

- open labour market research and analysis using tools specific for human resources management (HRM)

- profiling the client's competence for the employer – using tools used by the company (HRM) and respecting the client's health situation (the knowledge and skills connected with in-depth awareness of different disabilities, marked as clinical knowledge and skills, 'CKS')

- profiling/adapting the workplace to the client's needs/barriers (HRM) and respecting the client's health situation (CKS)

- support in work adaptation (coaching) and job maintenance by the client (CKS)

- ongoing support in maintaining the client's employment motivation between employment periods (coaching) and respecting the client's health situation (CKS).

The whole spectrum of KSC can be finally clustered into the fifth functional category of competences (knowledge and skills) that are engaged in all stages of the job coaching process. The expertise required of the job coach should cover the following fields (Matuska 2017, p.11):

- training

- coaching

- labour market search and HRM

- behaviour analysis

- task analysis.

The specification of the knowledge and skills that are expected in reference to these functional competences is presented in Table 1.1.

Table 1.1: Core competences of job coaches with reference to science fields

Training	Coaching	Labour market search and HRM	Behaviour analysis	Task analysis
Knowledge about professions and their relationships	Knowledge about employment law, regulations (supported employment) and available financial support sources for the client	Knowledge and understanding of labour market trends, needs and stakeholders (employer organisations, NGOs, etc.)	Observation and functional assessment of client behaviour patterns and reactions	Observation and analysis of work processes and conditions
Knowledge about educational programmes and the skills of adopting programmes to the individual health situation of the trainee	Knowledge about general employment possibilities for the client	Knowledge and understanding of organisational cultures in different job places and employers	Knowledge about disabilities and disorders	Exploration and shaping of client skills
Knowledge and skills of how best to transfer necessary skills to the trainee	Guiding the coaching process in a flexible way, respecting the client's health barriers	Knowledge and understanding of operational work structure and job description on positions	Skills regarding diagnosis of competences of people with disabilities	Discovering client potential and encouraging them re. life change connected with employment decisions
Knowledge about educational and coaching methods and techniques	Coordination and organisational skills, preparing networks and time schedules	HRM basic knowledge and skills (recruitment/job assessment, work career/development planning/organising)	Planning and implementing changes in employment context	Evaluation and stabilisation of the client's developmental processes
Knowledge and skills of vocational guidance	Planning coaching sessions and their objectives	Ability to think in categories of company management and respect employer's personnel needs	General knowledge about competences and understanding professional vocabulary	Knowledge about tools useful for support and adaptation at job place, i.e., developing hierarchy of skills
Manual/technical (instrumental) skills (e.g., to prepare adequate teaching material)	Skills of collecting necessary documentation, preparing reports, monitoring progress of the trainee, etc.	Training company members in disability issues, supporting the client via mentoring		Job place organising in cooperation with a tutor (mentor) from the employer perspective
				On-board support service (stress management, problem solving, etc.)
Pedagogy/counselling	Counselling/social work	HRM/macro-economy	Psychology (clinical, organisational)	Psychology (organisational), ergonomics

Source: Author

The competence component of knowledge and skills (KS) represents the expertise derived for the job coach for people with disabilities from such science disciplines as:

- pedagogy/counselling – knowledge and skills addressed to the:
  - teaching process, its methods and tools
  - coaching process, its models, methods and tools
  - motivating process, its models, methods and tools
  - negotiating methods and tools
  - communication process, its methods and tools
  - vocational guidance.

- counselling/social work – knowledge and skills addressed to:
  - work law regulations (especially addressed to supported employment) and sources of finance support to people with disabilities
  - identifying and organising a suitable support network for clients
  - tailoring the coaching process to the client's individual health profile (using flexible coaching methods and tools)
  - administrative tasks of coaching.

- HRM/macro-economy – knowledge and skills addressed to:
  - labour market trends, needs and stakeholders
  - organisational cultures in different workplaces and employers
  - work structure of tasks (job description) in workplaces
  - HRM basics – using tools for recruitment/job assessment, job description, work career/development planning and organising
  - company management and filling the employer's personnel needs
  - negotiating employment contracts (flexible work forms, remuneration and its components, health protection, etc.)

- engagement methods and techniques (apprenticeships, job sharing, mentoring, interpersonal trainings for co-workers).

- clinical psychology – knowledge and skills addressed to the:

  - characteristic features of the main clinical syndromes, especially about autism spectrum disorders, intellectual disability, psychotic disorders like schizophrenia, major depression and bipolar disorder, non-psychotic psychiatric conditions (like anxiety, OCD, somatoforms, eating and personality disorders), childhood-based behavioural conditions (like ADHD)

  - potentials/barriers faced by people with different disabilities in respect to their employability

  - diagnosis of personality and vocational competences of people with disabilities, preparing profiles and reports

  - adopting suitable communication with the client, tailored to the specificity of their disorder

  - motivating towards employability, respecting the specificity of the client's disorder

  - building a supportive network around the client (with family, friends, NGOs, etc.).

- organisational psychology/ergonomics – knowledge and skills addressed to:

  - determinants and conditions of organisational behaviour (psychological mechanisms of organisational participation; psychological contract, etc.)

  - planning and analysing organisational behaviour

  - analysis of work processes and psycho-physical conditions

  - adaptation of the workplace in respect to ergonomic demands

  - work-related problem-solving

  - coping methods with work-related stress and stress management.

This real 'mixture' of science fields that are incorporated in the qualification process for the job coach suggests that this occupation has to be based on a sufficiently high level of initial education, followed by further specialisation.

The functional approach to job coach competences makes it possible to map them in a form of competence matrix in terms of KSC (Knowledge – Skills – Competence), as recommended by the EQF and ESCO. This concept opens the future possibility of giving legal recognition to the occupation of 'job coach for people with disabilities', both at national and pan-European levels.

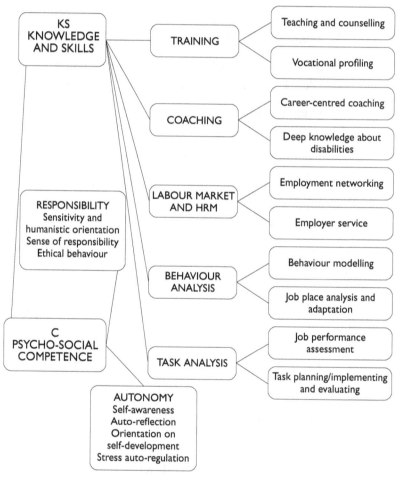

Figure 1.5: Job coach competence matrix in terms of knowledge, skills and competences (KSC)
Source: Matuska (2017, p.13)

The competence profile of the job coach is conceptualised as 'occupation-specific', thus it includes only the main five identified professional and technical competences (see Figure 1.5). These represent competences involved in the whole coaching process offered to individuals with a disability, yet each may be more precisely specified. In the proposed matrix, two sub-competencies were added to each of the main categories. However, a good competence model should not be too detailed, as this can easily result in it losing its clarity and coherence.

Conclusion

The occupation of 'job coach for people with disabilities' is not yet officially registered either in international or in European job classifications, but it should be formalised as the demand for this profession grows. The new occupation of 'job coach for people with disabilities' should be included in the job family of 'personnel and careers professionals' as being dedicated to work with a special target group, that is, people with disabilities looking for employment on the open labour market.

The competence profile presented here is defined in terms of Knowledge – Skills – Competence (KSC), as recommended by the EQF, that facilities the legal recognition and accreditation procedures of the 'job coach for people with disabilities' at both a national and European level.

References

BivT (Beroepsvereniging) (2014) *Code of Ethics for the Profession of Job Coaching*. Version from 30/03/2014.

European Commission (2010) *European Disability Strategy 2010-2020: A Renewed Commitment to a Barrier-free Europe*. COM/2010/0636. Accessed on 18/10/2017 at http://eur-lex.europa.eu/LexUriServ/LexUriServ.do?uri=COM:2010:0636:FIN:en:PDF

European Commission (2013) *European Skills, Competences, Qualifications and Occupations*. Accessed on 22/11/2017 at https://ec.europa.eu/esco/portal/occupation

European Commission (2017) *Employment, Social Affairs and Inclusion*. Accessed on 10/02/2018 at http://ec.europa.eu/employment_social/soc-prot/missoc99/english/socprot/nl.htm

European Council (2008) *European Qualifications Framework for Lifelong Learning: Recommendation of the European Parliament and of the Council of 23 April 2008*. Official Journal C 111, 6.5.

EUSE (European Union of Supported Employment) (2005) *Information Booklet and Quality Standards*. Accessed on 07/02/2018 at www.susescotland.co.uk/media/14715/euse%20information%20brochure%20-%20english.pdf

EUSE (2010) *European Union Supported Employment Toolkit 2*. Accessed on 01/02/2018 at www.euse.org/content/supported-employment-toolkit/EUSE-Toolkit-2010.pdf

Gerhardt, P.F. (2009) *The Current State of Services for Adults with Autism*. Organization for Autism Research. Accessed on 17/05/2018 at www.afaa-us.org/storage/documents/OAR_NYCA_survey_Current_State_of_Services_for_Adults_with_Autism.pdf

ILO (International Labour Organization) (2007) *Resolution Concerning Updating the International Standard Classification of Occupations*. Accessed on 11/10/2017 at www.ilo.org/public/english/bureau/stat/isco/docs/resol08.pdf

ILO (2008) *International Standard Classification of Occupations: ISCO-08*. Accessed on 21/10/2017 at www.ilo.org

Matuska, E. (ed.) (2017) *European Qualification Profile of Job Coach for Persons with Disabilities*. Niedersachsen: Grone Schulen. Erasmus+ project.

Röttgers, H.R. and Metje, C. (2016) *European Quality Standards for the Profession Job Coach for Persons with Disabilities*. Fachhochschule Münster, Niedersachsen: Grone Schulen. Erasmus+ project.

UN (United Nations) (2006) *Convention on the Rights of Persons with Disabilities and Optional Protocol*. Accessed on 25/10/2017 at www.un.org/development/desa/disabilities/convention-on-the-rights-of-persons-with-disabilities.html

Wehman, P., Inge, K.J., Revell, W.G. and Brooke, V. (2007) *Real Work for Real Pay: Inclusive Employment for People with Disabilities*. Baltimore, MD: Paul Brookes Publishing Co.

Chapter 2

HAVING A JOB COACH: INSIDER PERSPECTIVES

Caterina Metje and Lyn McKerr

In this chapter the experiences of adults with disabilities who have worked successfully with the support and encouragement of a professional job coach are explored, although the first author, Caterina, describes her experience of working without such support. In order to help Caterina to learn on the job, she constructed a personal map, which proved useful for understanding and interpreting her learning experiences. Others then describe the support they received from their job coach, and how this enabled them to gain and maintain employment. The personal experiences described in this chapter are not to be viewed as how-to guidelines, but they offer some practical insights, for both employees and job coaches.

Learning within the work environment

Caterina is a researcher at a German university. She is in her early 40s and has Asperger's Syndrome. After completing an apprenticeship and a university degree, she was unemployed for four years. During her studies, when she was 32 years of age, she worked as an assistant in an examination office. Years of freelancing as a journalist followed, before she applied to work for the university and, with the support of one of the professors, was able to secure employment as a researcher. During all this time, Caterina never had a formal job coach.

As part of the Asperger's diagnosis Caterina shares certain characteristics with other people who have autism/Asperger's, but obviously she is an individual, with her own skills, views and challenges. This is *her* story.

— CATERINA'S STORY

As a student I was working in the examination office of another faculty. During my first week there I had to do absolutely trivial work. Work that simply had to be done, but every primary school pupil could have done it as well. I had to sort letters by date of receipt and written tests by name.

Even here it was possible to learn some tricks. One of my workmates recommended that I began by making two piles: first one, A–M, second one, M–Z. I did not listen to her. I struggled hard. Then I did accept her advice – she was right.

I didn't feel downgraded by these humble tasks. They helped me to get used to my new workplace and to get to know my workmates. The head of the office was prudent enough to give me a new task every couple of days. So the scope of my duties increased continuously.

After a couple of months I was capable of doing everything that is done in an examination office. I invited students and lecturers to exams, wrote reminder messages, provided information about the results, filed term papers, scheduled oral examinations, booked rooms and changed addresses. I knew almost anything of relevance about nearly any student. The head of the office even wanted to know my opinion when she had to hold a demanding conversation – a student wanting to leave the university or a student in danger of failing for the third time.

I kept track of what was going on. I was inventive when it came to solving organisational problems. I knew whom to contact for support when needed, and I was always informed about the chief officer's timetable. She was a very nice, intelligent and well-educated lady, but sometimes a bit absent-minded, and non-local in addition, while I had already been a good networker. We split up the tasks so that everyone did what she could do best: I wrote the letters; she made the phone calls.

Here are my experiences:

- Learning by doing is much more effective than learning by lecture.

- It is difficult to identify in advance which skills someone has to acquire to fulfil a job properly – and in which order. Where one workmate is relatively limited, another might experience his or her individual talents. The interplay between the capabilities and impairments of all colleagues determines the distribution of tasks. BUT: You have to be at the workplace to find out the possible weaknesses of your workmates where you could play out your benefits – you can't learn that at the university or in an employment office workshop!

- The best, easiest and most effective way of learning is when you immediately feel the benefit. Imagine yourself on a trip in an unknown city. Within 24 hours you learn so many useful things – where is the hotel, where is the next little kiosk for a bottle of water, where can you quickly get something to eat without spending all your money, where is the bus stop and which line leads to the city centre? Very basic, very easy to learn, just like sorting the letters in the examination office.

  The longer you stay, the more you learn, and the kind of things you have to learn changes too. You will watch out for a supermarket and a grocery store to buy more food and new toothpaste; a cashpoint might become necessary as well. Sooner or later you will need a pharmacy. Little by little your brain creates a mental map. You don't have to force your brain to do that; it does so voluntarily because it's just sensible and pleasant to learn useful things. It simply provides more opportunities. Since you are in a foreign country, you might even learn a new language, and better than intended.

- The more details this map already has, the easier you add new data. The most relevant information that is most commonly used will be the first that you learn. The challenge is you have to place them 'in a vacuum'. Further skills might be a little more demanding, but in return, you can add them to an already established data network. Information can be of varying value for different people – non-smokers will do without the record 'Here is a cigarette machine', for example.

- Successful learning is based on the experience of usefulness and applicability that works as a strong positive reinforcer. The growing capabilities and opportunities reward the effort of learning. Job coaches for people with disabilities should use this strong effect in order to work successfully with their clients. Furthermore, it would be a blessing if the employees could stay at the same workplace for a long time to benefit from what they had already learned. The combination of well-tried 'comfort zone knowledge' and new challenges will increase self-confidence and capabilities, so that both the employer and employee will be satisfied with the working arrangements.

Job coaching in practice

To get an idea of the impact of job coaching on the daily working lives of other adults with disabilities, we developed a set of questions to facilitate their sharing of experiences. The questions were based on Appreciative Inquiry methodology (Cooperrider, Barrett and Srivastva 2013). Appreciative Inquiry facilitates self-determined stakeholder involvement in various management, coaching and employment processes. It is a widely used strengths-based method (Bushe and Kassam 2005), developed at a time when the focus was mainly on a problem-solving approach (Bouwen and Meeus 2011; Subirana 2016). The principles of self-determined change provided an alternative and concentrated attention on the strengths of people and organisations (Cooper, Heron and Heward 2007). The employees who contributed to this chapter provided their comments as an illustration of their personal real-world experiences.

The employees whose views are expressed in the following sections were all actively engaged in the employment market, either as full-time or part-time employees or in work experience. They all received the support of job coaches (EUSE 2010). Their experiences offer an opportunity to discover how organisations can offer a service that improves the life opportunities of people who may otherwise have difficulty finding and maintaining suitable employment. These employees talked frankly about their experiences, and explored issues that were important to them. The names were changed for those who preferred to remain anonymous.

Work settings and colleagues

Adults with disabilities work in many different settings. For many, the support of a job coach is crucial in finding work. Danielle described the importance of her job coach in gaining and maintaining employment when she returned to the workforce after illness. The job coach helped

her re-think her life and career and to take on new responsibilities.
Dylan and Oscar also needed support finding a job:

> It was obvious I couldn't do heavy physical or mental work, but I
> didn't think I was useless. Due to my illness, I do everything slowly.
> Unfortunately, an employer usually does not seem to understand that
> a sick person cannot be as quick and efficient as a person in their
> 20s. Additionally, I feel that the situation in the labour market has
> changed. Currently a cleaner does not only clean up but also does
> the chairman's dishes, brews coffee, serves it, etc. The list of duties
> has lengthened. In the past, it wasn't like that. At the beginning of my
> career, I was a seamstress. It's where my health problems started…
> Thanks to the project, I gained courage to live and faith that I can
> actually manage. Now, I work as a cleaner in a big company co-owned
> by the city council. I have my own floor to manage. I know what should
> be done and I know my responsibilities. I am employed part-time, 20
> hours per week. However, it's not easy to get such a job and for the
> most part, I owe it to my job coach. (Danielle)

> …[the job coach helped in] finding me employment in which I would
> feel most comfortable. A friendly and interesting work environment.
> (Dylan)

> …[the job coach helped me to get] an employment agreement for an
> indefinite period of time. (Oscar)

Depending on their individual interests, for some a job offered the
opportunity to write and research or engage in art or retail, while
others at the start of their career preferred a part-time office-based
position that allowed them to learn new skills and to take on new
challenges:

> I work as an assistant researcher; so far, I have written a lot. (Ashley)

> This is my first job; I didn't have one before. I went to university to
> do computing… I work in [the] housing association…it's just one day
> a week. I put tenant packs together and I do filing, and I do some
> computer work as well. (Mark)

> I am interested in sports; I like spending my free time in the kitchen and please my family and friends with my culinary masterpieces. At present, I learn how to give massages and I work as a sales advisor in one of the shops of [large fashion chain] and I must admit that is fun – fashion is an exciting experience! (Dylan)

A good relationship with work colleagues played an important role in creating fulfilling and enjoyable workplaces:

> I'm a student painter. I can be myself at work. We are with quite a lot of young people. We're having fun and know what's going to happen every day. I learn everything here and we are all equal here. (Cary)

> I value my and other people's time, I am punctual... As a private person, I am into photography, travelling with my family to many different beautiful places. I like sports, among other things, swimming, cycling, horse-riding, ice-skating and dancing. I also like spending time with my wife and daughters creating various artistic works. I work in a large home improvement retailer as a logistician. The work in the warehouse is not a clean one, but despite the fact that it can be hard, it is quite peaceful. (Oscar)

> I think it is important for everyone to be surrounded by nice people at work. And this job provides me with such company. It makes me smile all the time! (Dylan)

Building or maintaining a relationship with family members, where appropriate, is a feature of job coaching that can contribute to employment success (Holwerda *et al.* 2013), although, of course, only at the discretion of the employee.

Relationship with the job coach

The personal and professional relationship between the employee and their job coach is vitally important and valued. The employees interviewed trusted their job coach and had confidence that they could rely on them:

It's a matter of two people getting along. The issue of reaching [out] to a person. This contact is important. Although I have a job, I am still in touch with my job coach. We are in semi-formal contact. We can get to know each other. Group sessions and conversations I had during the meetings gave me a lot. We still meet and talk. My job coach was very receptive. We, old people, demand openness. We can chat not only about work but also about life. Such a rapport with an office worker would not be possible. It's all about getting to know each other, trusting each other and confiding to each other. In my opinion, everyone who finds it difficult to get a job should have a job coach. I'm very happy with my job coach's persistence, and that he is looking for a job for me: if not this one, then something else. And I know that we are picky. It takes us a lot of time to choose a job that would be the one. (Danielle)

That I have always been supported since I began working. She is always there for me. (Ashley)

The best thing about working with my job coach is how well we get on with each other. I've worked with her for about six or seven months now. Well, she's been very pleasant and friendly to me, so she has. (Mark)

Job coaches provided relevant advice and support in the workplace, and worked actively on behalf of the employee to seek out long-term job positions and provide the necessary ongoing support:

It is important that he listens and promotes my interests. (Brett)

At the beginning of my career, I was a seamstress. It's where my health problems started. Poor sight, a handicapped arm and foot. And this work requires constant use of a sewing machine that you need to 'sense/feel'. I broke down both physically and mentally. It was a never-ending stress whether I would manage to sew, whether my foot would let me do it. And there is pressure, a norm that requires you to sew 80–100 pieces, and I know my body will not let me do this much. Now, having worked with a job coach I know that everything will be fine. I will get help and I won't be left to my own devices. (Danielle)

...[the job coach helped with the contract and an] agreement for an indefinite period of time is more favourable, it provides better perspectives in various financial institutions such as banks, financial advisors, credit bureaus. (Oscar)

I think it was important to have somebody like her to help me, and to give me some very important advice in the real job that I will go in to. (Mark)

In addition to the job coach, the input from a multidisciplinary team was appreciated. Danielle explained that the extra time and effort from the job coach helped her explore other avenues of employment support, input that increased her confidence and resulted in a successful outcome:

First and foremost, talks that we had and the support from the psychologist. People who explain to us how the system works, ladies from the Employment Services Office, and lawyers. Training was very important. I got a lot of information there. You could ask questions. I liked this openness for people. The approach represented by my job coach and other people involved in this project was completely different from the one of the office workers. When I visited the local Employment Office, they offered me a job and gave me a phone number. I made a call and all the vacancies had already been filled. The employers ask me: 'How old are you?' and this is the end of the conversation... The officers didn't know me and didn't know what I could or couldn't do. They couldn't match a job to my abilities. Even though a doctor filled in all the documentation, they still couldn't understand what kind of job I was looking for. They still offered me a full-time job, and quite often a physical one. My job coach asked me questions and the Employment Office never does. (Danielle)

For most of the employees, listening to their views and concerns was central to the success of the relationship with their job coach:

Listening to me, understanding that we always have a solution where the problem is or has been. (Ashley)

Listening, understanding and arranging what needs to be done. (Cary)

Getting along with the job coach, trust, engagement. I could always count on help and support in difficult times in terms of relations with the company. [If] I had any questions, she always called me back. Absolute professionalism if it comes to the whole paperwork related to the agency. (Oscar)

Keeping contact with my parents, listening, network capabilities. (Brett)

First of all, his gentle and cheerful approach to other people. For me it was about making sure that I can still do something in my life. That I don't have to stay at home and I am not useless, and this is how I had felt before I got a job coach. (Danielle)

[I appreciate] how much she has tried to help me. How well we get on with each other, and how much she has helped me learn about work. (Mark)

For Danielle, the relationship with her job coach was a 'two-way street'. She felt it was important for her to live up to her job coach's high opinion of her abilities. For many individuals with a disability, previous experiences in education or in the employment market may have been defined by a lack of professional ambition on their behalf (Dillenburger, McKerr and Jordan 2015). Job coaching is different in that expectations are not being limited by perceptions of disability:

I say that I can't, and he says that I can. I say that I can't, and he still says that I can. My job coach represents me as a candidate for a position, so I feel obliged to represent him and be a good employee, because he vouched for me and I don't want to ruin his good name. (Danielle)

The job coach's approachability and warmth of the relationship as well as their expertise and understanding of the employee's individual strengths were most valued. The employees felt that these qualities in their job coach led directly to their own employment success:

Stimulating to work, motivating, and constantly repeating that I will succeed and there are still businesses that would hire me. Now, I just can't imagine looking for a job without a job coach's support. (Danielle)

That she has a lot of understanding. (Ashley)

Openness, being easy going, [job coach] treats me with warmth, I could feel that in our relationship. As an employee, I am valuable to her. (Oscar)

How pleasant and friendly she is. It's a good relationship. (Mark)

The level of motivation and understanding of the individual needs of a client shown by job coaches was greatly appreciated, and at times was in contrast to the limited level of support from non-specialist employment advisors:

At the very thought of visiting the local Employment Services Office I get a twitch. The office workers don't know me, and don't know my needs or my personal situation. They don't have details about my illness. My job coach has all of this information and it's easier for him to match a job offer to my needs and abilities. (Danielle)

Resolving challenging situations

Some employees required support from their job coach during a specific, job-related incident and queries or worries that arose in the workplace. For example, the job coach supported Cary in dealing with unexpectedly changed situations that would have been difficult to manage independently, while Brett and Ashley were supported through conflict situations:

Several times work was arranged, and there was a change to another teacher on the work floor at the moment that it was necessary. [My job coach] made the 'irritation points' so negotiable that we could achieve a good result. I was probably very angry at times. My job coach did not report about it too soon. I always like to try to figure it out myself. But she stayed close and got us all together at the right moment. My job coach listened well to me. (Cary)

[The job coach supported me] when I was in conflict with my employer. (Brett)

She sorts things out when they go wrong and if I have questions, I can always call her. And she takes action right away; I think that is very nice. (Ashley)

My job coach as my employment agent talks to appropriate persons in the HR department to present me in the most favourable light, so that I could achieve my goal in the future. (Oscar)

At first, I had worked as an operator of a machine which crushes cardboard boxes. Nothing special, unpleasant smell and dirt...but well, that's the job. [My job coach] knew that this job wasn't for me, I think she felt it exhausted me mentally. After almost a year, I found out there was a vacancy in a [fashion retail] warehouse and it turned out that we hit the bull's eye. It was worth putting up with the company of cardboard boxes. (Dylan)

High flexibility in solving difficult issues. (Oscar)

Where workplace issues were problematic, it was important for the employee to feel in control of the situation. Not all employees require advocacy, and some prefer their job coach not to be an active advocate. They prefer that the job coach remains neutral, perhaps worrying that their input could escalate potential conflict (Metje 2018). Where the issues cannot be resolved, the job coach is needed to find a new job:

...[my job coach] intervened by ending the contract and found a new assignment. (Brett)

The switch from my teacher on the work floor has created a break-through. My job coach got me around the table with the secretary and the planner of the work. My job coach told them what was important for me and asked for a solution. I got a new teacher on the work floor. (Cary)

That she came into action right away with the [Institute for Employee Insurance]. (Ashley)

The resolution of challenges is helpful for both employer and employee. Some employees have difficulties 'reading' the social behaviour of others (Metje 2018), while others struggle with new routines. The job coach can help develop precise and practical guidelines when expected and unexpected situations arise:

> Conversations and encouragement on the part of the job coach when I feared new challenges, such as logistics. (Oscar)

> Really just how clear and concise she has been. (Mark)

> My barrier is a visual impairment. It is difficult to find oneself a job these days when computers, which destroy my optic nerves, are used almost everywhere. And at work, I work as everyone else [except] I do not operate a computer or cash register. Instead I have other, interesting, activities. (Dylan)

While many conflicts can be resolved quickly, in some cases the intervention of the job coach needed to be more long term. This was the case when building relationships in the workplace to help the employee feel included and motivated. As Danielle explained, it was not always easy to go back into employment and to get to know new colleagues. Entering a new working environment after a lengthy absence, perhaps having been socially isolated as a result, can be a challenge that needs to be overcome:

> It's mostly about contact with people. When you stay at home, you just watch TV or do some cleaning. And in the project, you are immediately in contact with people and you get to know new persons. It's not easy to leave home and meet someone new just like that. I won't go out and just approach some stranger and I won't say: 'Good morning, I'd like to get to know you.' In my new job I've got great colleagues, terrific women. Very likeable. These girls assured me that I would manage; they motivated me to work. Such [an] atmosphere at work is just great. Everywhere should be like this. It was fine thanks to my job coach and his support. It would be hard just on my own. At the beginning it was tough, but after a couple of days I knew it would be fine. I felt as if I had been working there for years. (Danielle)

Recognising success

The most positive indicator of the success of a job coach is when employees have jobs they enjoy:

> The job coach knew what I wanted and thanks to him I met many valuable people, and above all, I got a job. I really appreciate the assistance offered by my job coach. Only positives. He motivated me and what I heard all the time was that I would manage, and I could make it and I was good. (Danielle)

> When she hears that I am praised for something. I work in a great place where I find fulfilment, the management is satisfied as well. That is our shared success! (Dylan)

> In all the results we have had until now. She acts very quickly. I'm very happy with her. (Ashley)

> I've learned new skills. For instance, my job coach has helped me learn how to scan documents with the photocopier. I want to get more skills, so I'm taking an Excel spreadsheet class on Mondays. I think the most successful part in working with a job coach is the job satisfaction that I've got. (Mark)

> When I manage to reconcile my work with family life, in situations [that are] difficult for me thanks to the job coach – I see it as a great success of the cooperation. (Oscar)

For Cary, this practical help was in resolving issues with the employer that could otherwise have had negative consequences, while for Brett, when circumstances at work meant the position became unsuitable, a better alternative was found:

> That my job coach sees what I want and what will be accepted by an employer and that she is able to find the middle way in which it works for both of us. (Cary)

> When things did not go well we found a new (and better suited) assignment. (Brett)

Suggestions for others working with a job coach

Danielle was particularly encouraging, emphasising the positive outcomes of an open relationship with her job coach:

> They should be more open, without reservations, say everything, as it's obvious that all will be fine, you will be understood, and it will only get better. I always recommend this sort of cooperation to everybody. If I could, I would start this adventure again. (Danielle)

> I can recommend it to everyone. As a young person, it is very nice to get help, for example, with an employer. (Cary)

> Based on my few years of experience, I would recommend cooperation with a job coach, that gives a feeling of security and protection, and inner peace. (Oscar)

> To be honest, and that there is no such thing as a 'stupid question'. (Dylan)

> Always be polite, and friendly and pleasant. You need to ask plenty of questions and pay close attention to what the job coach is telling you. (Mark)

Conclusion

In this chapter employees with disabilities have given an 'insider view' of their experiences with job coaching and the support they received in overcoming challenges that affected their employment. For Caterina, this was a journey she accomplished by setting her own goals and strategies, as job coaching was not available to her at the start of her career; in effect, she became her own job coach. The others had the support and encouragement of a professional, who acted as advisor, mediator and coach.

The thread that runs through all of their experiences is that a successful job placement requires a good match between the employee's talents and the job specifications and employment context. The role of the job coach is to ensure that this match is tailored to the individual. It requires a significant amount of preliminary work to build up the necessary skills and confidence or achieve a shift in perspective, to facilitate the career path of employees with disabilities, but ultimately, having the right job coach benefits both employees and employers:

> Recently my job coach checked up something in the internet for me and I am not able to do it myself. This is what a job coach is for, to help me ask questions and find things out so that I wouldn't go astray. Openness and sincerity; we trust each other. I know that my issues will remain confidential. I can ask any question and I will get a true and fair answer. In my opinion, everyone who finds it difficult to get a job should have a job coach. (Danielle)

References

Bouwen, G. and Meeus, M. (2011) *Vuur Werkt. Met Talent Toekomst Maken.* Houten, NL: Lannoo Campus.

Bushe, G.R. and Kassam, A.F. (2005) 'When is appreciative inquiry transformational? A meta-case analysis.' *Journal of Applied Behavioral Science 41*, 2, 161–181. http://doi.org/10.1177/0021886304270337

Cooper, J., Heron, T. and Heward, W. (2007) *Applied Behaviour Analysis* (2nd edn). Upper Saddle River, NJ: Pearson Prentice Hall.

Cooperrider, D.L., Barrett, F. and Srivastva, S. (2013) 'Social Construction and Appreciative Inquiry: A Journey in Organizational Theory.' In D. Hosking, P. Dachler and K. Gergen (eds) *Management and Organization: Relational Alternatives to Individualism* (2nd edn) (pp.157–200). Aldershot: Avebury.

Dillenburger, K., McKerr, L. and Jordan, J.-A. (2015) *Helping the Most Vulnerable Out of the Poverty Trap and Reducing Inequality: Policies, Strategies and Services for Individuals with Autism Spectrum Disorder, including Intellectual and Neurodevelopmental Disabilities*, BASE Project (Vol. 5). Belfast: Queen's University Belfast. Accessed on 10/02/2018 at www.qub.ac.uk/research-centres/CentreforBehaviourAnalysis/filestore/Filetoupload,620594,en.pdf

EUSE (European Union of Supported Employment) (2010) *European Union of Supported Employment Toolkit.* Accessed on 01/02/2018 at www.euse.org/content/supported-employment-toolkit/EUSE-Toolkit-2010.pdf

Holwerda, A., van der Klink, J.J., de Boer, M.R., Groothoff, J.W. and Brouwer, S. (2013) 'Predictors of sustainable work participation of young adults with developmental disorders.' *Research in Developmental Disabilities 34*, 9, 2753–2756.

Metje, C. (2018) *Survey.* Erasmus+. Accessed on 07/02/2018 at http://ec.europa.eu/programmes/erasmus-plus/projects/eplus-project-details-page/?nodeRef=workspace://SpacesStore/7a7122ee-ff52-4835-8bc6-3099bb004a5d

Subirana, M. (2016) *Flourishing Together: Guide to Appreciative Inquiry Coaching.* Alresford: O-Books, John Hunt Publishing Ltd.

Chapter 3

JOB COACHES FOR ADULTS WITH MENTAL HEALTH CONDITIONS

Hanns Rüdiger Röttgers

This chapter focuses on the support necessary for employees who have mental health-related diagnoses. Central aspects of specific mental health conditions, such as prevalence, aetiology, specific symptoms and behaviour, treatment strategies and job-related issues, are outlined. The role and tasks of job coaches who work with this particular population are described, clarifying specific issues and sharing some suggestions for best practice.

Introduction

In most Western countries, mental health-related diagnoses regarding psychiatric disorders (these terms can be used as synonyms) seem to have become more frequent; this is true for published prevalence levels, the number of inpatient and outpatient cases treated and above all, for the numbers of people who retire early due to health issues, thus ending their professional life. In Germany and Austria, mental health-related issues have even taken over the lead from orthopaedic conditions and cancer as the most important reason for early retirement (Czypionka *et al.* 2016; Deutsche Rentenversicherung Bund 2017; Gesundheitsberichterstattung des Bundes 2017). Furthermore, the average age of people who retire early due to psychiatric diagnoses is gradually decreasing, and is much lower than the average age of people retiring early due to other healthcare issues. So the impression is given of a rising epidemic affecting the mental health of more and more younger working people.

These data are misleading, however: there is no evidence supporting the view that psychiatric disorders are becoming more frequent; earlier diagnoses, more inclusive healthcare and less stigmatisation of mental health issues merely make these existing issues more visible (Richter and Berger 2013).

While there is no cause for alarm, these data do indicate that the participation of people with psychiatric disorders in the labour market needs to be improved as early retirement typically indicates that the specific needs of a working person have not been addressed successfully. This is even more likely with diagnoses like dementia and schizophrenia. However, these diagnoses only play a small but significant part in early retirements, whereas affective disorders, such as anxiety, dissociative, stress-related somatoform and other non-psychotic mental disorders (WHO 1992) are the largest cause of early retirement, and their prevalence continues to increase. This is even more regrettable as these conditions generally respond well to treatment. In contrast to psychotic disorders, they leave cognitive functioning and sense of reality intact, so they should generally not be an obstacle for a work career, especially if support mechanisms such as job coaching are available.

As there are too many mental health-related diagnoses or psychiatric disorder classifications, according to the *International Statistical Classification of Diseases and Related Health Problems* (ICD; WHO 1992) or *Diagnostic and Statistical Manual of Mental Disorders* (DSM; APA 2013), to be covered in a short chapter, we decided to focus on four groups of diagnoses here: These are:

- schizophrenia

- affective disorders

- anxiety disorders

- obsessive compulsive disorders (OCD).

Of course, other mental health problems do also have an impact on the health, quality of life and occupational situation of those affected. Interested readers are referred to the extensive literature in the field (see, for example, Bamford 2006; Lauber and Kawohl 2013; Tölle and Windgassen 2014). While these and many other scientific books are excellent resources, the quality of information on the internet and in popular literature varies considerably, and poor quality advice may actually cause harm (Lilienfeld 2007).

The diagnoses covered in this chapter were chosen because job coaches are frequently employed to support employees with diagnoses such as affective disorders, anxiety and OCD. Other disorders have at least a potentially lifelong impact on the individual's private and professional life. This is especially true for schizophrenia. In the past, most people who experienced chronic psychiatric disorders were excluded from professional life in general. This led to isolation, discrimination and poverty, and a drastically reduced life expectancy for those without family or other informal support. While the implications are most severe in many poor countries without extensive social security systems, and those governed without respect for human rights, even in affluent Western democracies a 'benevolent exclusion' and restriction to sheltered workplaces can be observed. The growing influence or personal choice/autonomy-centred ethical positions and national legislation derived from the United Nations (UN) Convention for the Rights of Persons with Disabilities (CRPD; UN 2006), however, supports the idea of mainstream labour market inclusion, 'place and train' strategies using job coaching being one of the most important and helpful instruments (Eikelmann *et al.* 2005).

In spite of massive public awareness, information and anti-stigmatisation campaigning in most Western countries, there are still common misunderstandings about effective interventions and the potential outcomes of psychiatric conditions (Lilienfeld 2007). Scientifically sound knowledge will not only be in the best interests of employees, but also of vital importance to colleagues and employers. Of course, it is important to remember that a job coach is neither a psychiatrist nor a therapist. The task of job coaches is to offer support and to enable employees to find and keep a job.

The information in this chapter focuses on general knowledge and on symptoms or behaviours that either:

- have a direct impact on the job situation or employability

- need specific support or intervention in a workplace situation or

- indicate a change in the course of the psychiatric condition, so that an employer, colleague or job coach may refer the employee to the relevant professional.

In the context of this book, we assume that a job coach is informed about the diagnosis and medical background of the employee they support. From a professional perspective, knowing the medical background is a sine qua non for the best possible support. In reality, the availability of information depends on national, local and company data protection regulations and personal preference regarding disclosure of diagnosis of the employee. If job coaching is paid for by public institutions, the employee's approval to share information with the job coach might be required by law, although the extent to which this is mandatory differs. The abstract knowledge of, for example, a hospital-based diagnosis itself, is not very helpful if, in everyday contact, the employee does not inform the job coach about acute symptoms and problems. So the quality of the personal relationship between job coach and employee plays a decisive role. In all circumstances, the autonomy of the employee has to be respected. Only if the employee views the support of the job coach as important, a positive element for their employment situation, will they not only share crucial third-hand personal information but also regard the job coach as a person of trust.

Depending on the social security system and personal constellations, individuals may be seeking to claim disability pensions on the grounds of mental ill health, so any attempt by a job coach to promote reintegration to work is likely to be futile. Job coaches should be open to recognise such tendencies and, in case of doubt, seek professional supervision or exchange. Generally, these tendencies are more frequent in the 'less severe' diagnosis groups, whereas individuals with severe psychiatric disorders tend to make admirable efforts to regain stability and work.

Schizophrenia

Schizophrenia and related disorders tend to be long-term, recurrent and/or chronic conditions that have a lifelong impact on the occupational situation of the individual. Job coaches with detailed knowledge who ensure well-adapted workplaces and an accepting, non-stigmatising atmosphere will contribute to successful placements as a crucial element for quality of life and personal autonomy.

According to ICD-10 diagnostic criteria, individuals diagnosed with schizophrenic disorders experience disrupted thought processes and sensory disturbances. These 'positive symptoms' (Tölle and Windgassen 2014; Velligan and Alphs 2008) can include episodes of more or less intense hallucinations in the form of hearing voices, delusional misinterpretation of reality and thought processes that are difficult or impossible to understand for others and (in hindsight, after the acute episode has subsided) for the afflicted person as well. Schizophrenic disorders can be limited to a single episode, typically lasting weeks when treated or months in case of non-treatment, but in the majority of cases episodes are recurrent even if prophylactic measures are taken. Thus, they tend to progressively limit employment prospects. As every psychotic episode has the potential to worsen cognitive functions, early diagnosis of relapses and rapid intervention is crucial.

With a prevalence of approximately 1 per cent among the general population, schizophrenia is one of the most common mental illnesses. Given that the symptoms are difficult to comprehend for those unaffected, schizophrenia tends to shape the image of and prejudices regarding mental illnesses in general.

Schizophrenic disorders occur in all cultures, social status groups and geographic regions. However, the risk of developing schizophrenia is much higher in some families – many 'risk genes' are under suspicion, but there is no clear evidence of inheritance. Despite the potential of genetic vulnerabilities, ultimately external stress factors lead to the development of the condition. Recent research has identified 'urbanicity', the fact of living in densely populated, culturally heterogeneous and socially fragmented surroundings, as an important stress factor (Heinz, Deserno and Reininghaus 2013). Another key factor for initial manifestation and relapse is cannabis use (Schöler et al. 2016) during youth and college years. Typically, the onset of schizophrenia occurs between 20 and 30 years of age and generally, men tend to be affected at a younger age than women. Thus, schizophrenic disorders affect people at the beginning of their vocational or academic training, with adverse impacts on their entire career and working life.

Treatment is predominantly based on pharmacotherapy with so-called neuroleptics, in most cases prescribed initially for one to two years; in cases with recurrent episodes even longer. Neuroleptics have been used since the late 1950s and enable the individual to re-establish a stable view of reality and undisturbed thought processes. Thus, long-time hospitalisation, a typical fate of people with schizophrenia in the past, can be avoided in most cases. However, this kind of medication comes with varying, sometimes severe, adverse effects, so that compliance with the medication regime can be volatile. Non-adherence to the prescribed medical regime is one of the key risk factors for relapse, while the use of un-prescribed psychoactive substances also poses major risks. Whereas medication is clearly the responsibility of the prescribing medical professional, usually a psychiatrist, it is important that job coaches cooperate closely and encourage employees to adhere to prescribed medication schedules.

Chronic symptoms of schizophrenic disorders, also called 'negative symptoms' (Tölle and Windgassen 2014; Velligan and Alphs 2008), can continue after the acute symptoms have subsided and have long-time detrimental impacts on working life. Negative symptoms include lack of or deficits in drive and motivation, but also neuropsychological deficits in executive functions (planning, initiating and executing actions and reviewing the results). There are a number of workplace-related arrangements that can alleviate high risks and that can therefore be considered preventative factors:

- Most individuals affected by schizophrenic disorders benefit from a regular day-night rhythm, so that night and (alternating) shift work should be avoided.

- Social stress factors can also play a role. Settings like open-space offices contain the risk of becoming a stressor. Individual workstations and possibilities to retreat for privacy should be provided as an option.

Therefore, for individuals with schizophrenic disorders, a skills assessment and/or functional assessment prior to commencement of employment, or prior to any planned change in the job profile, helps to avoid situations that may become stressful or overwhelming. A job coach who supports an individual affected by a schizophrenic disorder can prepare employees and employers by asking the following questions:

- What was the formal educational and professional qualification before the onset or first episode of schizophrenia?

- What was the level of performance prior to the onset of schizophrenic disorder?

- Is there a stable or declining development of skills and performance?

- What are the specific symptoms for this individual, and how pronounced are any 'positive' or 'negative' symptoms'?

- Does the employee experience neuropsychological deficits and are they experiencing recurring episodes?

- Is the employee undergoing psychiatric treatment, that is, do they have prescribed medication, and if so, are they taking it regularly?

- Is there a supportive private network of family or other people of trust who can be helpful in crisis situations?

- Is there a legal proxy instrument, such as a guardianship, that has to be taken into account for decision-making?

- What are the typical early or preliminary symptoms that precede a relapse or episode? And what are the contingency plans for such situations?

- Are there additional stress factors such as changing work hours, loud/disturbing environments, night or shift work, and how can they be managed?

- Are the employer, supervisors, occupational health service and co-workers informed about the specific arrangements for this employee, and if yes, to what extent are special arrangements in place?

Affective disorders

Affective disorders, also known as 'affective psychoses' or 'manic depressive disorders', are associated with emotional, mood and drive symptoms, and manifest in diametrically opposed emotional/affective states, from high or manic affect to low and depressive/melancholic symptoms. For most individuals affected by affective disorders, general motivation and psychological drive changes in parallel to shifts in mood. They are reduced during depression and enhanced during mania, that is, the general level of activity is elevated in the latter case. They progress in chronological phases that usually completely remit (that is, there can be decade-long 'healthy' intervals without any symptoms), and are prone to recurrences without causing any significant personality changes or chronic deficits. Additionally, thought processes and the reference to reality are only affected/distorted by mood and drive, but not disrupted. In this respect, the symptoms differ from schizophrenic disorders. So the objective of any supportive measure should be no less than a complete restitution of the personal and professional situation before the first episode.

The term 'affective disorder' was coined to avoid the negative connotations of the older term 'manic depressive illness'. The majority of cases show a 'unipolar' progression: in this case, all phases of the condition in one person are either depressive (quite common) or manic (less common). Accordingly, progression of the condition with both manifestations is referred to as 'bipolar' disorder or 'bipolar affective psychosis'.

Different so-called severity levels are distinguished in the respective phases ('mild', 'moderate', 'severe' episode); if delusions co-occur, the phase is classified as an 'episode with psychotic symptoms'. While during mild and, depending on motivation and environmental factors, also during moderate episodes the ability to work is essentially preserved, a severe episode is not compatible with working life and often needs to be treated in an in-patient setting. About 10 per cent of people with known depressions commit suicide, so any suicidal statements and impulses have to be taken extremely seriously and can be a cause for hospitalisation. People with manic disorders usually do not perceive themselves as 'ill'. They regard themselves as particularly active, creative and productive, even though this is objectively not the case, and the condition often leads to serious adverse financial and personal decisions. In the workplace, this is a frequent cause of conflicts – colleagues need to be informed that logical reasoning is not generally helpful once a severe manic episode has developed. Hospitalisation cannot be avoided in the majority of cases. However, without the individual's consent, treatment is legally not possible, or only possible under certain circumstances in Western democracies, which can lead to extreme stress situations for families, and also for co-workers. What is important to point out, after the symptoms have subsided, is that the behaviours were caused by the condition and the individual cannot be held accountable for them. Nevertheless, even if financial issues caused in acute mania can be settled in some situations, this is not necessarily true for personal offences and slights.

Affective psychoses occur at about similar rates in all ethnic groups, societies and social status groups. The prevalence (all forms included) is rated at 0.5 to 2 per cent, and the lifetime risk is at about 1 per cent. In general, more women are affected. This imbalance is due to the more frequent depressive phases while manic phases are as frequent in men as they are in women. A clear genetic impact is certain; there are some families where affective disorders occur much more frequently than in others, and patterns of affective disorders can be observed across generations.

The onset of the condition is usually in the third or fourth decade of life. If the first phase is a manic phase, the onset is earlier on average; bipolar disorders also have a tendency of an earlier onset and can occur before the age of 20. In these cases, as in schizophrenia, early interruptions to and dropouts from school and professional education are frequent, and have more severe long-term effects on an employment career than the typical manifestation in later life, when a secure occupation and workplace experience have already been acquired. Trigger events for a relapse can only be identified in some cases; other than psycho-reactive or stress disorders, affective disorders often progress according to their own biological laws.

Treatment for mild to moderate depressive episodes is mainly psychotherapy. Cognitive behavioural therapy and its methodical variants are the 'gold standard'. During moderate episodes, additional anti-depressive medication can be helpful. Personal preferences and prior experiences will guide a psychotherapeutic and/or medication-based treatment strategy; during severe depression medication is mandatory for fast recovery, accessibility for psychotherapy and suicide prevention.

Family physicians and general practitioners tend to issue sick notes that are necessary in severe cases, even for mild and moderate forms. Though the notion of 'relief' from workplace obligation appears obvious, sick notes promote further isolation and withdrawal; furthermore, the individuals miss out on social contact, and the feeling of purpose and success in the workplace. In psychotherapy, this is known as loss of positive reinforcement. So sick notes issued without due consideration of the circumstances are often well intentioned but carry negative long-term consequences. After severe episodes during which the individual was unable to work, however, an individualised return process, with gradually increasing demands ('progressive reintegration'), can be helpful.

Acute manic phases are mainly treated pharmacologically with neuroleptics; there is no motivation for psychotherapy in the narrow sense during acute manic phases.

Since both depressive and manic disorders are prone to recurrence, 'phase prophylaxis' medication with substances from the 'mood stabilisers' group is recommended on top of the acute treatment after recurring episodes, depending on the individual progression, and has proven to be of great value in many cases. The first of these substances, Lithium, was introduced shortly after neuroleptics in the mid-20th century, and has, in many cases, successfully prevented relapses over decades in people who experienced a rapid succession of severe episodes before treatment.

It has to be stressed that none of the medication groups mentioned – antidepressants, neuroleptics or mood stabilisers/phase prophylactics – carry any risk of creating addiction. This widespread but definitely unfounded concern of individuals and their families or friends frequently leads to discontinuation of treatment; all professionals should work as trustworthy advisors in this field.

The following aspects are important for job coaches who support people with an affective disorder.

Regarding the disorder:

- Is it a recurring disorder and were there depressive, manic or both manifestations in the past?

- Is the person in their care undergoing psychiatric treatment?

- How do friends and family react to the condition and how supportive is the social network?

- Is the prescribed medication taken regularly and is psychotherapeutic treatment attended regularly?

- Are there typical early or preliminary symptoms that preceded a relapse or recurrence in the past?

- Is there a 'contingency plan' for such events?

- Is there a legal proxy instrument, such as a guardianship, that has to be taken into account for decision-making in case of an acute relapse?

Regarding the work routine:

- What was the level of performance prior to the condition?

- Which specific aspects of work have been reinforcing and motivating?

- Are there experiences as to neuropsychological deficits in the recovery/convalescence period after an acute episode?

- How can a progressive reintegration be structured after an acute episode has subsided?

- Are there additional stress factors such as changing work hours, loud/disturbing environments, night or shift work?

- Are there hazardous situations specific in the work routine to the disorder, such as suicidal tendencies or risks during a manic episode?

- Are the employer, supervisors, occupational health service and co-workers informed about the condition, and if yes, to what extent?

Anxiety disorders

Together with addiction and affective disorders, anxiety disorders are the most common psychological disorders. Three main types are distinguished here:

- *Phobias* are clearly defined object-related or situational anxieties. Well-known examples are phobias triggered by living or inanimate objects (spiders, syringes) or situations (fear of heights, social situations).

- In the case of *generalised anxiety disorders*, no specific triggers can be identified; rather, the individual experiences fear of many situations or even 'everything', and this can also present as 'fear of fear itself'.

- The third group is *panic disorders*. Acute onset of anxiety leads to heart attack-like situations during which the individual feels in mortal danger or even dying. Prior to identifying these attacks as an anxiety disorder, suspicions of, for example, cardiovascular or metabolic diseases must be excluded by medical examination. (In Western countries, emergency rooms and advanced medical services are readily available.) In many cases, people with panic disorders are strongly unsettled by their symptoms and tend to seek assurance by repeated tests and hospital stays. Here, a very sensitive psycho-educational approach is required to prevent 'iatrogenic', medical care system-induced chronification.

People with anxiety disorders typically react with avoidance behaviour, that is, they try to avoid situations where they have experienced anxiety in the past. This can expand to complete isolation and withdrawal. Another risk is that of developing an addiction – undiagnosed and/ or untreated individuals affected by anxiety try to numb or prevent unpleasant or unbearable sensations with legal (alcohol, tranquilisers) or illegal drugs.

Anxiety disorders are essentially treatable, and no deficits or long-term impairments should remain after successful treatment. In the majority of cases, psychotherapy, in the form of cognitive behavioural therapy, makes quick and long-time recovery possible. In the case of phobias, confrontation techniques have proved to be most effective. Here, individuals receive extensive psycho-education and cognitive preparation before moving on to real-life exposure to the anxiety-provoking stimuli.

In some cases, added antidepressant medication can be supportive, although it must be stressed that these substances do not carry any risk of provoking an addiction.

So, if the medical and psychotherapy service system provides state-of-the art treatment, a job coach should not be necessary for the individual affected by anxiety disorders. In reality, however, we find various maintenance factors that abet a chronification and even expansion of anxiety disorders. Paradoxically, some of these factors can be found in the care system itself (lack of qualified psychotherapists and psychiatrists or uncritical prescription of tranquilisers by general practitioners – drugs generally offer immediate relief but frequently lead to addiction within a very short time, so any prescription longer than a week can be dangerous). Other maintenance factors also often occur in the individual's personal life when families and friends try to support the individual by taking over obligations and responsibilities. This reaction is well intended but likely to cause chronification and increases in avoidance behaviour. Some people will no longer consider the family circle usually perceived as 'safe'. Although this effectively avoids anxiety-inducing situations, thus reinforcing avoidance behaviour, the individual loses the opportunity to have corrective experiences and to find out that allegedly dangerous objects and/or situations are not actually a hazard. Additionally, the mechanism characterised by loss of positive reinforcement opportunities, described above in relation to affective disorders, may propagate depressive developments.

In the working environment, anxiety disorders can lead to prolonged absenteeism and work interruptions that, inadvertently, can be reinforced by benevolent employers and ostensibly supportive co-workers. Tolerating an untreated anxiety disorder is equivalent to propagation. In terms of learning psychology, this positively reinforces avoidance behaviour while promoting further development of the anxiety symptoms.

When people with long-term anxiety disorders return to the workplace, the underlying principle is that of normality. Anxiety disorders do not cause long-term damage or limitations of capability; there are no particular professional activities that are excluded for individuals who were formerly affected by anxiety.

If a job coach were installed as a personal assistant in the working life in such cases, they should try to make themselves dispensable as soon as possible. This is done by active support in the search of a qualified therapist. Any permanent assistance on the grounds of an anxiety disorder is counterproductive. Therefore, for job coaches who support individuals affected by anxiety, the following aspects are important.

Regarding the disorder:

- Were there complicating factors in the past, for example, substance addiction?

- Is the person in their care undergoing psychiatric and/or psychotherapeutic treatment?

- Are there typical avoidance behaviours?

- Is the individual claiming disability pension?

Regarding the work routine:

- Are there factors at the workplace that have triggered anxiety in the past?

- Can the individual be transferred to a position without known trigger factors until the condition as such is treated?

Obsessive compulsive disorders

Obsessive compulsive disorders (OCD) are also among the more common mental disorders, and have many parallels to the anxiety disorders discussed above. A common feature of all OCDs is that the individuals are aware of the nonsensical nature of the specific thought or impulse, yet the compulsions are upheld by a fear that is powerful, even if it is perceived as completely irrational.

Typical foci are cleanliness (for example, fear of disease and infection) and control (for example, the danger of fire if household appliances are not switched off or risking burglary by leaving the door open).

Three main manifestation types of OCD are distinguished that, respectively, are defined by obsessive-compulsive thoughts, impulses and acts:

- Obsessive-compulsive thoughts that exist exclusively in the individual's imagination, such as obsessive counting and magical thoughts that are difficult to let go, and therefore have an impact on, for example, everyday routines or workplace processes.

- Obsessive-compulsive impulses that have an imperative component. Frequently, individuals experience impulses to perform aggressive actions against other people, even members of their own families. The moral and legal implications are known and the impulses exist regardless of the individual's better judgement. In the vast majority of cases, these impulses are never realised, that is, a bystander cannot see anything 'objectively'. However, they can cause feelings of guilt and severe depressive developments.

- Obsessive-compulsive acts that manifest in observable motor movements. They can be anything from short tic-like movements to extensive rituals.

Compulsive acts that are motivated by issues of cleanliness and fear of contamination/infection, in particular, have dire consequences for structuring everyday activities and quality of life. There are individuals who shower for hours and perform their personal hygiene in a strictly set routine, and even the slightest deviation forces them to start over again.

Similarly, rituals around the issue of 'safety and security' can be very extensive and time-consuming. For example, this can encompass repeated checks of all doors and windows, heat sources and electrical appliances – such acts can delay leaving the house in the morning and the way to work for hours.

People with OCD are usually embarrassed by their own actions because they are aware that 'it's nonsense', although they are unable to abolish them without professional help; therefore, the problems are often kept secret or 'covered up' with great effort.

OCDs are essentially well treatable. As with anxiety disorders, there are no deficits or long-term impairments after successful treatment. However, even after years there can be relapses, possibly with a different 'topic'. Psychotherapy treatment, similar to the anxiety disorders in the form of cognitive behavioural therapy, is successful in most cases. The most effective method is exposure with the relevant stimulus and consequent prevention of the OCD-motivated behaviour. For example, individuals are supposed to not give in to the impulse of excessive washing and disinfection after touching a door knob or using a public toilet; they may have to take the bus from their home to work without checking the stove again, etc. The anxiety caused by this and its physical symptoms will then physiologically subside so that the catastrophic cognitions and expectations lose their influence. Certain antidepressants have been successful for many people with a more chronic or very severe obsessive-compulsive perception or behaviour.

As with anxiety disorders, with OCD there are factors that abet chronification or expansion of the symptoms. Again, there are deficiencies in the care system (lack of qualified psychotherapists, use of unsuitable forms of therapy) as well as maintenance factors in the individual's personal life. Since the OCD symptoms are 'controlled by fear', therapy is not 'attractive' for every individual; treatment offers are often foregone. Unlike individuals affected by anxiety, individuals affected by OCD usually hide their problems and often drift into isolation. In severe cases, OCD can lead to long leaves of absence and work interruption; simply 'sitting out' a leave of absence does not lead to an improvement of the situation but risks it becoming chronic.

When a person with OCD returns to the workplace the underlying principle, as with anxiety disorders, is that of normality. OCDs do not cause long-term damage or limitations of capability; there are no particular professional activities that are excluded for individuals previously affected by OCD.

If a job coach was employed as a personal assistant in the workplace, they should therefore strive to make themselves 'redundant', as permanent assistance on the grounds of OCD is as counterproductive as in the case of anxiety disorders. A well-informed job coach can, however, play an important role for the employer and the co-workers by – in coordination with the individual – pointing out the workplace-related factors on the one hand, and specific needs for assistance on the other, or developing such means of assistance. If an individual affected by OCD has trouble completing a work process, it can be helpful to have external limits on the processing time or an active 'intervention', removing the process from the individual's responsibility.

Therefore, for job coaches supporting individuals affected by OCD, the following aspects are important.

Regarding the disorder:

- Is the person in their care undergoing psychiatric and/or psychotherapeutic treatment?

- Which interventions have been successful in the past?

- Is there a tendency of symptom worsening/expanding rituals?

Regarding the work routine:

- Are there factors at the workplace that caused or triggered compulsive thoughts, impulses or acts in the past?

- Can the individual be transferred to a position without known trigger factors until the condition as such is treated?

- Do OCD symptoms have a direct impact on the work routine, for example, is the individual unable to complete a process because they have to check repeatedly for errors and mistakes?

- Are the employer, supervisors, occupational health service and co-workers informed about the condition, and if yes, to what extent?

Conclusion

In this chapter a number of mental health conditions have been discussed and issues identified that are important for job coaches. Prevalence, aetiology, specific symptoms and behaviour, treatment strategies and job-related issues were outlined for schizophrenia, affective disorders, anxiety disorders and OCD. It is important that job coaches have a good understanding of the conditions of the employees they support. The chapter clarified diagnosis-related issues and has fostered understanding of best practice.

References

APA (American Psychiatric Association) (2013) *Diagnostic and Statistical Manual of Mental Disorders – Fifth edn* (DSM-5). Accessed on 01/11/2017 at www.psychiatry.org/psychiatrists/practice/dsm/feedback-and-questions/frequently-asked-questions

Bamford, D. (2006) *Bamford Review of Mental Health and Learning Disability.* Accessed on 01/06/2018 at www.health-ni.gov.uk/articles/bamford-review-mental-health-and-learning-disability

Czypionka, T., Lappähn, S., Pohl, A. and Röhrling, G. (2016) 'Invaliditätspension aufgrund psychischer Erkrankungen' ['Early retirement due to psychiatric disorders in Austria']. Pressekonferenz am Institut für Höhere Studien [Press Conference, Austrian Institute for Advanced Studies]. Vienna, Austria, 22 February.

Deutsche Rentenversicherung Bund (2017) 'Deutsche Rentenversicherung in Zeitreihen' ['German state pension system statistics']. *DRV-Schriften 22*, S. 104–106. Berlin.

Eikelmann, B., Zacharias-Eikelmann, B., Richter, D. and Reker, T. (2005) 'Integration Psychisch Kranker: Ziel ist Teilnahme am "Wirklichen" Leben' ['Integration of mentally ill persons: Participation in "real life" has to be the objective']. *Deutsches Ärzteblatt 102*, 16, A-1104/B-929/C-876.

Gesundheitsberichterstattung des Bundes (2017) 'Rentenzugänge wegen verminderter Erwerbsfähigkeit in der Gesetzlichen Rentenversicherung im Laufe des Berichtsjahres (Anzahl und je 100.000 aktiv Versicherte).' Gliederungsmerkmale: Jahre, Region, Zugangsalter, Geschlecht, 1. Diagnose (ICD-10). ['German Federal Medical Statistics: Disability Pensions Due to Medical Conditions in 2016.']

Heinz, A., Deserno, L. and Reininghaus, U. (2013) 'Urbanicity, social adversity and psychosis.' *World Psychiatry 12*, 187–197.

Lauber, C. and Kawohl, W. (2013) 'Supported Employment.' In W. Rössler and W. Kawohl (eds) *Soziale Psychiatrie* (pp.129–137). Stuttgart: Kohlhammer.

Lilienfeld, S.O. (2007) 'Psychological treatments that cause harm.' *Perspectives on Psychological Science 2*, 1, 53–70. Accessed on 18/05/2018 at http://doi.org/10.1111/j.1745-6916.2007.00029.x

Richter, D. and Berger, K. (2013) 'Nehmen psychische Störungen zu? Update einer systematischen Übersicht über wiederholte Querschnittsstudien' ['Are mental disorders increasing? Update of a systematic review on repeated cross-sectional studies']. *Psychiatrische Praxis 40*, 176–182. Accessed on 18/05/2018 at http://dx.doi.org/10.1055/s-0032-1333060

Schöler, T., Petros, N., Pingault, J.B., Klamerus, E., *et al.* (2016) 'Association between continued cannabis use and risk of relapse in first-episode psychosis.' *JAMA Psychiatry* *73*, 11, 1173–1179. doi:10.1001/jamapsychiatry.2016.2427

Tölle, R. and Windgassen, K. (2014) *Psychiatrie. Einschließlich Psychotherapie* (17th edn). Berlin: Springer.

UN (United Nations) (2006) *Convention on the Rights of Persons with Disabilities and Optional Protocol.* Accessed on 11/02/2018 at www.un.org/development/desa/disabilities/convention-on-the-rights-of-persons-with-disabilities.html

Velligan, D. and Alphs, L. (2008) 'Negative symptoms in schizophrenia: The importance of identification and treatment.' *Psychiatric Times,* 1 March. Accessed on 01/11/2017 at www.psychiatrictimes.com/schizophrenia/negative-symptoms-schizophrenia-importance-identification-and-treatment

WHO (World Health Organization) (1992) *International Statistical Classification of Diseases and Related Health Problems: 10th Revision* (ICD-10). Accessed on 01/11/2017 at http://apps.who.int/classifications/icd10/browse/2016/en

Chapter 4

JOB COACHES FOR ADULTS WITH PHYSICAL AND SENSORY DISABILITIES

—— *Trish MacKeogh and Marcia J. Scherer* ——

A disability employment gap is evident across the globe, with lower employment rates for individuals with disabilities than those without (WHO 2011). Creating an inclusive environment, building skills and providing support is essential if people with disabilities are to have an equal opportunity to enter employment. For people with physical disabilities, a job coach provides an essential support to ensure that the employee understands the responsibilities of the employment and the employer understands the needs of the employee and possible adaptations to the working environment that may be needed. Universal design provides a framework to design-inclusive workplaces, and assistive technology provides the means to customise applications to suit the individual needs of people within employment situations. This chapter outlines how a job coach can support a person with a physical disability, and the role that universal design and assistive technology can play in the accommodation of the needs of employees to ensure they can successfully deliver their work.

Introduction

The importance of employment to people with disabilities is the same as with the wider population. Employment is valued in society as it increases social status and provides greater opportunities for choice and quality of living. The International Labour Organization (ILO 2015) estimates that the exclusion of people with disabilities from the labour market represents a significant waste of potential labour and an estimated loss of 3–7 per cent GDP. Moreover, a high rate of unemployment for people with disabilities increases a country's expenditure on social welfare and prevents social inclusion and economic self-sufficiency (Burkhauser and Daly 2011). According to World Bank figures (Raja 2016) one billion people, or 15 per cent of the world's population, have some form of disability. An estimated 630 million people have a physical limitation, which includes 70 million with a mobility impairment, 240 million with a visual impairment and 300 million with a hearing impairment. The report for 51 countries shows employment rates of 52.8 per cent for men with disabilities and 19.6 per cent for women with disabilities, while those for men and women without disabilities were 64.9 per cent and 29.9 per cent, respectively. This makes the work of a job coach all the more invaluable.

Important role of the job coach

Although many employers have successfully employed people with disabilities, it is often lack of information and a fear of the unknown that prevents more people with disabilities becoming employed (NDA 2014). Misconceptions by employers that people with disabilities are less productive than non-disabled potential employees and lack of knowledge about available adjustments to work arrangements often limit employment opportunities. Attitudes of employers can also affect job opportunities available for people with disabilities. International research shows that employees and employers may have biased or wrong perceptions of the performance and social skills of employees with disabilities, and under-estimate their capacities (Vornholt, Uitdewilligen and Nijhuis 2013). Moreover, according to Liz Sayce, Chief Executive of Disability Rights UK (cited in O'Mahony 2017), for people with disabilities, '[i]f the company is viewed as non-diverse and inflexible, with no evidence of employing disabled people, the anxiety about whether you will be accepted is magnified.' In fact, Sayce says: 'The experience of disability, in particular, often means people develop resilience, problem solving, empathy and creativity' – and these are important attributes in today's work environment.

A job coach can allay such misconceptions through the provision of information for both the employer and the employee, looking for and providing solutions that will make appropriate adjustments to the workplace for an employee with disabilities. For people with physical disabilities, they may already have achieved the skills needed for employment, and once physical adaptions are made, can easily fit into the company or organisation. A crucial element for the job coach is to ascertain what those requirements are, and to ensure that the client is able to access the support they need.

A survey of people with disabilities (Watson and Nolan 2011) identified a number of key factors that would increase successful employment, including flexible work arrangements, wage subsidies and accessibility modifications. While adaptations can support the physical needs of the employee and employer, there could also be cultural and attitudinal changes that may need to be challenged. De Jonge, Scherer and Rodger (2006) highlight in their publication, *Assistive Technology in the Workplace*, some of the difficulties that both employees and employers can have when a person with disabilities is employed. The following quote summarises some of the stresses and difficulties of a person starting in a new job and not wanting to 'make too many waves':

> You see that's why I feel very vulnerable because… I'm always terrified of telling my boss of what needs I have…because I have to compare with a person who is capable… (quoted in de Jonge *et al.* 2006, p.171)

A quote from the employer sums up the importance of information and the key role a job coach can play in the process:

> People don't recognise the possibilities if they're not aware of the assistive aids that people might access, then they're not going to be able to explore those with the particular employee, so you need to have some sort of knowledge of all the possibilities. (quoted in de Jonge *et al.* 2006, p.171)

Policy changes in Europe with respect to people with disabilities have moved from a medical model that emphasised health issues within the person with a disability to a focus on the disabling environment, putting the onus on removing barriers that prevent people from engaging in all aspects of life, including employment. Assistive technology is centrally important within disability policy, as it is one of the more concrete ways that barriers to participation in the workplace can be overcome for people with disabilities. There has been a significant push internationally by the World Health Organization (WHO) towards better provision of assistive technology, which has resulted in the GATE (Global Cooperation on Assistive Technology) initiative, launched in 2017. GATE defines assistive technology as:

> Any external product (including devices, equipment, instruments or software), especially produced or generally available, the primary purpose of which is to maintain or improve an individual's functioning and independence, and thereby promote their well-being. (WHO 2014)

WHO (2014) estimates that there will be 2 billion people with a need for assistive technology by the year 2050. It considers assistive technology, universal design and information and communication technology (ICT) as interlinked and preconditions for mainstreaming disability in the development of inclusion and equal opportunities for people with disabilities.

A recent study on assistive technology argued that it is important to take into account its potential to deliver substantial value for money in better educational and labour market outcomes for its users (Cullen *et al.* 2012). A job coach provides an important role as a conduit of information for both employees and employers in regard to disseminating information on accessibility.

A European Union (EU) Directive prohibits direct and indirect discrimination in the field of employment on a number of grounds, including disability. The Directive applies to various areas including selection criteria, guidance, training, employment and working conditions. Importantly, the Directive states that 'reasonable accommodation' shall be provided, that is, that employers are to take appropriate measures, where needed, to enable a person with a disability to have access to, participate in, or advance in employment, or to provide training, unless such measures would impose a 'disproportionate burden' on the employer (EU 2000). However, the ILO (2015) points to a lack of accommodation as one of the most frequent reasons for workplace exclusion.

Many countries now provide a range of grants for the employment of people with disabilities, adaptation of the workplace (including alteration and access) or an allowance for additional expenditure on work tools required on account of employing a person with a disability. Wage subsidies are also provided in a number of countries, which provide a percentage of the wage if there is a productivity difference in the work of the person with a disability (EU 2000). In France the law requires that companies with a workforce of more than 20 employees must ensure at least 6 per cent of their personnel are people with disabilities. A number of other European countries use a similar quota system including Germany, Italy and Spain (Cuppage 2013). If the employer fails to comply with the quota, they are required to pay a monthly penalty. In the UK, the Access to Work programme provides support with travel costs, special equipment or adaptations and access to specialist assessment services. The Job Accommodation Network in the US (JAN 2018) provides resources for both employees and employers and a phone and online consultancy service. In the Republic of Ireland, the comprehensive Employment Strategy sets out a ten-year approach to supporting employment for people with disabilities, including equipment and adaptation grants and salary top-ups so that employers are not out of pocket (NDA 2014).

Assistive technology in the workplace

The World Bank Group identifies technology as a key driver for the successful employment of people with cognitive and physical disabilities due to the proliferation of technology in the world of employment. ICT has changed how people build their skills, how they search for work, how they do their work, how they interact with co-workers and clients, and how they receive and use benefits in the workplace (Raja 2016). Email, websites, social media and web-enabled multimedia content and communication are commonplace in work situations, and the use of online applications, cloud-based content management and video conferencing are increasing accessibility. Information and computer technology, computerised applications and systems, and internet-based applications have become ubiquitous features of office-based work. These technological advances and solutions have greatly improved the work environment and offer many solutions to adapt the situation to the needs of people with disabilities.

However, advancements in technology alone are insufficient to bridge the gaps – successful inclusion is dependent on people's knowledge and awareness of the technology solutions available, laws and policies, and the capacity to support accessible technology services. A job coach can have a significant impact on bridging the gap between technology advancements, availability and providing information for both employers and employees. It is good practice to ascertain the needs of a range of expected users in a workspace or public building at an early stage of development, and to check the practicality and usability of the environment with a diverse range of employees and users.

A growing number of mainstream technologies, such as mobile devices, tablet, laptop and desktop computers, provide functionalities that facilitate accessibility for people with disabilities (see 'Glossary on assistive technology' at the end of this chapter). Features such as text to speech and voice recognition, ability to change contrast and colour schemes, touch and gesture input screens and screen magnification that previously required specialised standalone software and hardware are now freely available on technology devices. Multimodal technologies allow access to information in a way that is easily accessible to people with disabilities. A person with mobility impairments can use voice recognition to operate and navigate their digital device, while the provision of lifts and ramps removes barriers from their environment. A person with visual impairments can use speech to text software or a screen magnification system to enlarge text and graphics on a computer screen, and simple design modifications will help them to negotiate their surroundings. A person with a hearing impairment can use instant text messaging to communicate, and can be facilitated within the workplace through text-based communication systems. Video modelling or virtual reality can help a person to understand what the work environment might be like and an alternative means to learn job-related skills and follow instructions.

Universal design in the workplace

The rapid rate of deployment of mainstream technologies is enabling people with physical disabilities to overcome challenges in the environment, and the gap is narrowing between a universal design approach that focuses on universal access through mainstream and assistive technologies (Craddock 2015) to ensure the emerging design of the environment meets the needs of diverse populations – proper signage for those with a visual impairment, loop systems for those with a hearing impairment, accessible buildings for those with a physical impairment accommodates both employees and customers. Universal design eliminates or reduces the need for expensive changes or retro fits to meet the needs of particular groups at a later stage. It makes good business sense to have accessibility built into the environment of the workplace, facilitating a wide range of users. Both Microsoft Windows and Mac OS come with in-built accessibility settings that a user can activate including text to speech, voice recognition, preferences for mouse and keyboard navigation, contrast settings and magnification.

In assessing the work environment for a person with a physical or sensory disability, there are a number of useful websites, for example, with information on modifications of the build environment on the Centre for Excellence in Universal Design website[1] (NDA 2014); this provides a range of free guides and advice on designing environments and engaging with people with disabilities including toolkits and videos that all employees can easily access (see Figure 4.1).

Figure 4.1: Building for everyone: A universal design approach
Source: Centre for Excellence in Universal Design

For full integration of a person with a disability in the workplace, other employees should be given information on how they can ensure that their fellow employees are fully included. Moreover, many jobs necessitate engaging with clients and customers, meeting diverse people, so it is in the best interests of a company that their employees understand and feel at ease with people with disabilities. A job coach can find many useful guides and toolkits on disability equality eLearning (NDA 2014).

---

1   See http://universaldesign.ie

Assessment of the workplace for assistive technology

An essential role for a job coach is to assess the overall needs of the employee, the employer and the workplace environment to accommodate and ensure employees can perform their work duties. Assistive technology can play a key role in the adaptation of the workplace, but it is crucial that the assistive technology matches the needs of the person and can be applied to the work situation with the employer's support and approval. The most frequent reason cited for not using assistive technology devices was a poor fit between the user, the technology and the environment (de Jonge *et al.* 2006). Approximately one-third of all assistive technology devices prescribed to adults are abandoned because the users did not participate in the prescription process (Scherer and Craddock 2002). An understanding of the person with a disability, their environment and the technology is essential, and it is therefore strongly recommended that if the job coach does not have specific skills with technology, that a qualified assistive technology adviser or ergonomic specialist is called to assess the employee's needs and abilities. Technology can be expensive and a bad match of technology can waste both time and money and put both employer and employee in an unnecessarily stressful situation (de Jonge *et al.* 2006).

Assistive technology is a term used to describe a wide range of tools that can support the functional needs of people who have disabilities. One of the most widely used definitions is the International Organization for Standardization (ISO 2011):

> Any product (including devices, equipment, instruments and software), especially produced or generally available, used by or for persons with disability: for participation; to protect, support, train, measure or substitute for body functions/structures and activities; or to prevent impairments, activity limitations or participation restrictions.

Assistive technology, which supports access to the environment, is also called environmental control. It can range from remote control devices to specialised apps to integrated systems that allow a person to control their environment, such as checking or answering the front door, opening doors within a building, turning on the lights, opening or closing window blinds or turning on electrical appliances or heating systems.

There are a number of assessment tools that can guide a job coach to determine the needs of people with both cognitive and physical disabilities and how they can be accommodated within a working environment. The Matching Person & Technology (MPT) model focuses on three primary areas: the environment and factors influencing technology use; consumer personal characteristics, needs and preferences; and functions and features of the most appropriate technology that will match a user's needs. The *Workplace Technology Predisposition Assessment* (Institute for Matching Person and Technology 2018) provides an assessment format for job coaches, employers and vocational counsellors. There are two assessment tools, one designed for the employer, trainer or teacher, and a second for the technology user. A job coach can use the tools to ascertain the needs of both the employer and the employee. The tools are quick and easy to use, and were developed from the experiences of both users and non-users of technology through participatory action research to ensure that employers and employees could work together to achieve a good match within the workplace environment. The tools also assess the person's experience with technology and an overview of their technology use and experience. A post-assessment tool analyses and provides useful information about the successful or unsuccessful use of the technology. A review of how the employee and employer are achieving their goals is important to both this situation and other employment situations.

Understanding the nature of disability and how it affects a person's access to the environment can help employers to understand the accommodations that are necessary to include people with disabilities. Selecting an assistive technology device is not only about the most appropriate piece of technology, but it may also entail an understanding of a person's life and their interaction with personal assistants, friends or work colleagues. It is critical for professionals such as job coaches to work in partnership with both the employee and employer. This approach leads not only to greater control on the part of the end user, but also better technology outcomes and more cost-effective results (Andrich and Besio 2002). Abandonment may result when the process fails to take account of individual abilities or needs, where there is a lack of participation of the person in the choice, or insufficient funding to acquire the correct technology. There are also other important details that need review to ensure that the assistive technology is working and is reliable – an employee under pressure to produce work should not have to contend with a faulty or unreliable device. It is important when obtaining new devices that technical support is available and easily contactable, that the employee and technical support are trained in the use of the device, and it is advisable that a service agreement is put in place.

As outlined above, many countries offer workplace adaptation grants and provide a range of information and advice to support people with physical disabilities. Examples of adaptations for which a grant may be given are:

- minor building modifications such as ramps or modified toilets

- alarm systems with flashing lights

- equipment adaptation such as voice synthesisers for computers or amplifiers for telephones

- assistive technology devices.

Depending on the disability, a number of changes to the workspace can be undertaken, and these are outlined below.

Sensory disabilities

When employing a person with sensory disabilities there are number of changes to their workspace and environment that can provide a more inclusive environment. It is important to discuss with the employee their difficulties and to determine what affect their condition has on their ability to do the work. Common disorders are briefly discussed below, but every individual will have individual differences and needs, and so it is vital that a job coach understands these individual needs and abilities, and directs the employee and employer to the appropriate assistive technology or environmental controls that can amend the workplace to suit the employee's needs.

Visual disabilities

A person is termed legally blind when their visual acuity (sharpness of vision) is 20/200 or worse after correction, or when their field of vision is less than 20 degrees in the best eye after correction. Low vision includes problems (after correction) such as dimness of vision, haziness, film over the eye, foggy vision, extreme near- or farsightedness, distortion of vision, spots before the eyes, colour distortions, visual field defects, tunnel vision, no peripheral vision, abnormal sensitivity to light or glare and night blindness. Visual impairment represents a continuum, from people with very poor vision to people who can see light but no shapes to people who have no perception of light at all. Different eye conditions can create barriers to employment.

Simple adaptations in the workplace for people with visual disabilities are critical, including signage, evenly distributed lighting, adjustable arm lamps or stick-up and clip-on lighting. Task lighting can help to put the light exactly where it is needed so that an employee can see enough to carry out a task safely and independently.

Hearing impairment

Hearing loss can range from a mild reduction in hearing to profound deafness, and can mean any degree and type of auditory disorder. Deafness means an extreme inability to discriminate conversational speech through the ear. Deaf people are those who cannot use their hearing for communication. People with a lesser degree of hearing impairment are called hard of hearing. Usually a person is considered deaf when sound must reach at least 90 decibels (5 to 10 times louder than normal speech) to be heard, and even amplified speech cannot be understood.

The primary difficulty for individuals with hearing impairment in using standard products is in receiving auditory or aural information, but this can be compensated through presenting information in a visual and/or tactile form. Another alternative solution is a mechanism such as a jack, which allows the user to connect alternative output devices. Increasing the volume range and lowering the frequency of products with high-pitched auditory output would be helpful to some less severely impaired individuals. Even with a good acoustic environment, hearing-impaired people have difficulty in hearing at a distance from the source of the sound. Alternative communication systems such as sign language at events, conferences and work meetings, hearing loop systems throughout the building or infrared and radio systems can support inclusion in the workplace. Moreover, people with a hearing loss can be at an increased risk if spoken announcements and warnings are not loud or intelligible enough for them, or if frequencies are too high to detect.

Physical disabilities

A person with a disability that results in losing their control of either their upper or lower body or both will have issues in accessing most environments unless they are adapted to their needs or assistive technology solutions are put in place. If a person has lost their hand function, there are a number of alternative options to control their environment, such as mouth sticks, eye gaze, sip-and-puff or switch access. For a person with a physical disability, it is about providing the means to access their work, and there are thousands of pieces of both mainstream technology and assistive technology that will provide easy access. It should also be noted that there is a wide range of accessible ICT products, for instance, in voice recognition, and it is now considered that voice input has the potential to be the most efficient form of computing – people can speak 150 words per minute on average, but can only type 40. This technology also fits with the Internet of Things-connected devices such as Amazon Echo or the Apple Watch – 65 per cent of smartphone users reported using 'voice assistants' on their phones (Townsend 2016).

There is a range of assistive technology websites that can be used depending on your country. In America, AbleData (2018) provides comprehensive information on products, solutions and resources. EASTIN (2018) provides a list of assistive technology devices in Europe and access to several national databases with translation into a number of languages. All products and associated information in the EASTIN databases are classified according to the ISO 9999 international standard on assistive products, and include a section on 'Assistive products for persons with disability' (ISO 2011). This provides details on products intended to aid a person in engaging in all aspects of a job, trade, occupation or profession, including vocational training. Included, for example, are machines, devices, vehicles, tools, computer software, production and office equipment, furniture and facilities and materials for vocational assessment and training.

Conclusion

The United Nations Convention on the Rights of Persons with Disabilities (CRPD; UN 2006) has 160 signatories. In Article 27 it:

> ...recognizes the right of persons with disabilities to work, on an equal basis with others; this includes the opportunity to gain a living by work freely chosen or accepted in a labour market and work environment that is open, inclusive and accessible to persons with disabilities.

There are very few jobs that cannot be performed by someone with a physical or sensory disability. Similar to all potential employees, abilities are matched to the requirements of the job and given the right support, adaptations and an inclusive environment, there is no valid reason for a person with a disability to be excluded. Yet the figures show that people with disabilities have significantly fewer opportunities then abled-bodied people and lower employment rates.

A job coach can have a significant role in reversing many of the myths and misconceptions that exist amongst employers about employing a person with a disability. They also play a central role in allying the fears of people with disabilities engaging in the workplace, and an essential role in ensuring that the workplace has the essential supports and adaptations that will allow a person to participate on an equal footing in employment. The complexity of the role of the job coach for people with physical or sensory disabilities is sketched out in Figure 4.2.

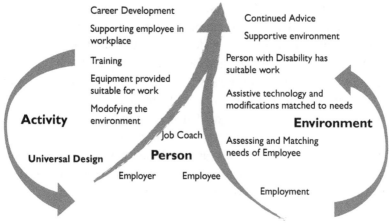

Figure 4.2: The supportive employment model
Source: Adapted from BASE (2011)

References

AbleData (2018) 'Tools & Technologies to Enhance Living.' Accessed on 10/02/2018 at www.abledata.com

Andrich, R. and Besio, S. (2002) 'Being informed, demanding and responsible consumers of assistive technology: An educational issue.' *Disability and Rehabilitation 24*, 1–3, 152–159.

BASE (2011) *Supported Employment and Job Coaching: Best Practice Guidelines.* London: Central Government. Accessed on 15/05/2018 at www.base-uk.org/knowledge/supported-employment-and-job-coaching-best-practice-guidelines

Burkhauser, R.V. and Daly, M.C. (2011) *The Declining Work and Welfare of People with Disabilities: What Went Wrong and a Strategy for Change.* Washington, DC: AEI Press.

Centre for Excellence in Universal Design (2016) *Building for Everyone.* Accessed on 01/06/2018 at http://universaldesign.ie/Built-Environment/Building-for-Everyone

Craddock, G. (2015) 'A National Perspective: Education Viewed through a Universal Design Lens.' Association for Higher Education Access & Disability (AHEAD) Conference, Dublin. Accessed on 10/02/2018 at www.ahead.ie/conference2015

Cullen, K., McAnaney, D., Dolphin, C., Delaney, S. and Stapleton, P. (2012) *Research on the Provision of Assistive Technology in Ireland and Other Countries to Support Independent Living across the Life Cycle.* Dublin: Work Research Centre and National Disability Authority. Accessed on 10/02/2018 at nda.ie/File-upload/Research-on-the-provision-of-Assistive-Technology1.pdf

Cuppage, J. (2013) 'The World and Disability: Quotas or No Quotas?' iGlobal Law, 11 December. Accessed on 10/02/2018 at www.igloballaw.com/the-world-and-disability-quotas-or-no-quotas

de Jonge, D., Scherer, M. and Rodger, S. (2006) *Assistive Technology in the Workplace.* Maryland Heights, MO: Mosby. Accessed on 10/02/2018 at https://evolve.elsevier.com/cs/product/9780323041300?role=student

EASTIN (European Assistive Technology Information Network) (2018) Accessed on 10/02/2018 at www.eastin.eu/en/searches/products/index

EU (European Union) (2000) *Code of Good Practice for Employment of People with Disabilities.* Accessed on 10/02/2018 at http://ec.europa.eu/employment_social/soc-prot/disable/codehaen_en.htm

Institute for Matching Person and Technology (2018) *Workplace Technology Predisposition Assessment.* Accessed on 10/02/2018 at matchingpersonandtechnology.com

ILO (International Labour Organization) (2015) *Decent Work for Persons with Disabilities: Promoting Rights in the Global Development Agenda.* Accessed on 10/02/2018 at www.ilo.org/skills/pubs/WCMS_430935/lang--en/index.htm

ISO (International Organization for Standardization) (2011) ISO 9999:2011, 'Assistive products for persons with disability – Classification and terminology.' Accessed on 10/02/2018 at www.iso.org/standard/50982.html

JAN (Job Accommodation Network) (2018) Accessed on 10/02/2018 at https://askjan.org

NDA (National Disability Authority) (2014) 'eLearning.' Accessed on 10/02/2018 at http://nda.ie/Resources/eLearning

O'Mahony, H. (2017) 'Disabilities in the workplace: Are we failing our disabled workforce?' *The Guardian*, 17 April. Accessed on 10/02/2018 at https://jobs.theguardian.com/article/disabilities-in-the-workplace-are-we-failing-our-disabled-workforce-

Raja, D.S. (2016) *Bridging the Disability Divide through Digital Technologies.* The World Bank Group. Accessed on 10/02/2018 at http://pubdocs.worldbank.org/en/123481461249337484/WDR16-BP-Bridging-the-Disability-Divide-through-Digital-Technology-RAJA.pdf

Scherer, M.J. and Craddock, G. (2002) 'Matching Person & Technology (MPT) assessment process.' *Technology & Disability, Special Issue: The Assessment of Assistive Technology Outcomes, Effects and Costs 14*, 3, 125–131.

Townsend, T. (2016) 'Mary Meeker says voice search is going to be huge.' *Internet Trends*, 1 June. Accessed on 10/02/2018 at www.inc.com/tess-townsend/mary-meeker-says-voice-search-is-going-to-be-huge.html

UN (United Nations) (2006) *United Nations Convention on the Rights of Persons with Disabilities*. Accessed on 27/06/2014 at www.un.org/development/desa/disabilities/convention-on-the-rights-of-persons-with-disabilities.html

Vornholt, K., Uitdewilligen, S. and Nijhuis, F.J.N. (2013) 'Factors affecting the acceptance of people with disabilities at work: A literature review.' *Journal of Occupational Rehabilitation 22*, 4, 463–475.

Watson, D. and Nolan, D. (2011) *A Social Portrait of People with a Disability in Ireland*. Dublin: Economic and Social Research Institute (ESRI) and Department of Social Protection.

WHO (World Health Organization (2011) *World Report on Disability*. Accessed on 27/06/2014 at www.who.int/disabilities/world_report/2011/report.pdf

WHO (2014) *Global Cooperation on Assistive Technology (GATE)*. Accessed on 27/06/2014 at www.who.int/phi/implementation/assistive_technology/en

Glossary on assistive technology

Accessibility features are various options that exist within products that allow a user to adjust the settings to their personal needs. Products can come with various accessibility features that can adjust to the individual's visual, mobility, hearing, language and learning needs.

Accessible inbuilt utilities – software programs that modify the standard keyboard for users with access issues, replace the mouse, substitute visual cues for sound signals or add sound cues to keystrokes. Many basic modifications can be made through software that already exists on the computer such as the altering of font size, colour contrast, etc.

Adjustable workstations allow height adjustment for users who cannot access a standard computer workstation. Models include movement mechanisms to include: crank, spring-assisted and electronic. Electronic models are most ideal from an access standpoint as a user can adjust the height independently.

Alternative access/input device allows individuals to control their computers using tools other than a standard keyboard or pointing device. Examples include alternative keyboards, electronic pointing devices, sip-and-puff systems, wands and sticks, joysticks and trackballs.

Alternative format refers to the transcription of books or other content (such as notes or newspapers or magazines) into a format other than standard print, that is, large print, HTML Braille, audio and talking books.

Alternative keyboards – alternative keyboard layouts and other enhancements allow people who experience difficulty with conventional keyboard designs to use computers. The products available range from key guards that prevent accidental key activation to alternative keyboards with differing layouts, sizes, etc. for people who have specific needs, to alternative input systems that require other means/methods of getting information into a computer.

Alternative pointing devices, trackballs and keypads are used to replace the traditional computer's mouse.

Assistive listening devices (ALDs) are used to aid individuals with hearing impairments to hear more clearly in public situations. The system can be set up to amplify things such as televisions, radios, doorbells and PA systems. The Springfield system is commonly used in schools. ALDs can be used with or without hearing aids.

Augmentative and Alternative Communication (AAC) system – an AAC system is one that increases or improves the communication abilities of individuals with receptive or expressive communication impairments. It can include sign language, graphical symbol systems, synthesised speech, dedicated communication devices and computer applications. AAC technology spans a wide range of products, from low-tech picture boards to high-tech speech recognition programmes.

Braille is a raised dot printed language used by many people with visual impairments. Each raised dot arrangement represents a letter or word combination.

Braille embosser or translator is a hardware device for 'printing' a hard copy of a text document in Braille. A Braille translation software program is required to translate the text from the computer into Braille. Most Braille translation software programs can translate material into several grades or versions of Braille.

Captioning is a text transcript of the audio portion of multimedia products, such as video and television, which is synchronised to the visual events taking place on screen.

Electronic pointing devices allow the user to control the cursor on the screen using ultrasound, an infrared beam, eye movements, nerve signals or brain waves. When used with an onscreen keyboard, electronic pointing devices also allow the user to enter text and data.

Eye gaze systems are eye-operated communication and control devices designed for use by children and adults with multiple disabilities. Users make selections by looking at keys displayed on the screen for a fraction of a second (eye gaze). A small camera mounted under the eye gaze screen takes 60 pictures per second of the user's eye. Those images are analysed by a processor that interprets where the user is looking. Users generate speech by using an onscreen keyboard or pre-programmed phrases.

Environmental control (EC) enables individuals to control electronic devices in their environment through a variety of alternative access methods, such as switch or voice access. ECs can control lights, televisions, telephones, music players, door openers, security systems and kitchen appliances.

Ergonomic keyboards address the positioning of the user to allow for more neutral arm, wrist and hand positioning. Most address wrist deviation and some address pronation.

FM systems are assistive listening devices that are worn by the speaker to amplify their voice and transmit it directly to the listener's ears via an electronic receiver and special earphones or the listener's own hearing aids; the Springfield system is an example of such a device. It reduces the problem of background noise interference and of distance between the speaker and hearing-impaired listener.

Joysticks are alternative input devices that can be plugged into the computer's mouse port to control the cursor on the screen. Other joysticks plug into game ports and depend on software that is designed to accept joystick control.

Onscreen keyboards are software-generated images of a standard or modified keyboard placed on the computer screen. The keys are selected by a mouse, touch screen, trackball, joystick, switch or electronic pointing device.

Screen magnification software enlarges the information on the screen and can magnify the full screen, parts of the screen or provide a magnifying glass view of the area around the cursor or pointer. These software programs also often allow for inverted colours, enhanced pointer viewing and tracking options.

Screen magnifier is a hardware device that is placed externally on a monitor to enlarge the image on the screen. It will only allow one to two times enlargement of the original. Some of these also incorporate anti-glare features. Some users complain of distortion.

Screen readers are software programs that use synthesised speech to 'speak' graphics and text aloud. These types of programmes are used by people with limited vision or blindness or with a print disability such as dyslexia. Hardware and software produce synthesised voice output for text displayed on the computer screen, as well as for keystrokes entered on the keyboard.

Speech or voice recognition programmes are software applications that convert words that are spoken aloud to text. Voice recognition may be used to dictate text into the computer or to give commands to the computer (such as opening application programs, pulling down menus or saving work). Continuous speech voice recognition applications allow a user to dictate text fluently into the computer. Speech recognition is designed to respond to a wide range of voices, without prior 'training' of the software. Voice or speaker recognition involves the training of a device to recognise a specific individual's voice. Both speech and voice recognition programs may be used to create written documents without the use of a keyboard, to control specially adapted equipment and to operate telephone, mobile phone and other applications.

Switches and switch software offer an alternative method of providing input to a computer when it is not possible to use a standard keyboard or mouse. Switches come in various sizes, shapes, methods of activation and placement options. Some software programs have been developed specifically for use with a switch and can employ onscreen scanning.

Text to speech software programs convert written text, including Word documents, web pages, PDF files and emails, into audio files that play on a computer, CD-ROM player, MP3 device, iPod or other digital audio playback equipment. Developed for individuals with low vision or blindness, text to speech technology has improved greatly, with natural sounding voices, greater conversion speed and improved ease of use.

Touch screens are devices that are placed on or built into the computer monitor that allow direct activation of the computer, or selection of a program, through a touch on the screen.

Universal design refers to the design and composition of an environment so that it can be accessed, understood and used to the greatest extent possible by all people, regardless of their age, size or disability.

Video modelling can be an effective tool to use for teaching a variety of skills. It simply entails a videotape of a model (it could be the individual or a model) doing the task or skill that the student can watch and follow.

Virtual reality is a computer-generated scenario that simulates a realistic experience. The immersive environment can be similar to the real world in order to create a life-like experience of a situation or environment.

Voice output communication aid is an electronic device that generates spoken language for individuals who are unable to use natural speech to express their needs and to communicate with others during a conversation. These devices are intended solely for communication purposes.

Word prediction programmes allow the user to select a desired word from an onscreen list located in a prediction window. The computer-generated list predicts words based on the first or second letter(s) typed by the user. The word may then be selected from the list and inserted into the text by typing a number, clicking the mouse or scanning with a switch.

Chapter 5

JOB COACHES FOR ADULTS WITH INTELLECTUAL DISABILITIES

Ewa Matuska

This chapter focuses on the support necessary for employees with intellectual disabilities. First, issues related to intellectual disabilities, such as prevalence, aetiology, specific issues etc., are outlined, and then the role and tasks of job coaches who work with this particular population is described, clarifying specific issues and sharing some best practice.

Definition and description of intellectual disability

The term 'intellectual disability' generally refers to significant limitations in the cognitive performance and adaptive functioning of a person, caused by a variety of factors during their developmental period, and even pre-natal issues. Cognitive ability influences overall psychological, social, emotional and economic functioning of the person, including their potential employability.

The World Health Organization (WHO) identifies intellectual disability to be 'a condition of arrested or incomplete development of the mind, which is especially characterized by impairment of skills manifested during the developmental period, which contribute to the overall level of intelligence, i.e., cognitive, language, motor, and social abilities' (WHO 1992).

Clinically, intellectual disability is recognised on the basis of diagnostic criteria that are formulated in two parallel systems of classification of mental disorders, namely, the WHO *International Classification of Diseases,*

10th revision (ISD-10) (WHO 1992) and the American Psychiatric Association *Diagnostic and Statistical Manual of Mental Disorders, 5th edition* (DSM-5) (APA 2013). It is worth noting that ICD-10 still uses the outdated term 'mental retardation' and there is a section entitled 'Mental retardation' (codes F70–F79). In the upcoming revision, ICD-11 is expected to replace this term with either 'intellectual disability' or 'intellectual developmental disorder'. DSM-5 already uses these terms, and we use them in this chapter as they focus on the support necessary to maximise an individual's skills rather than on the description of barriers and limitations in the functioning of a person with intellectual disabilities.

DSM-5 identifies three types of neuro-developmental disorders including: intellectual disabilities; intellectual disability (intellectual developmental disorder) and global developmental delay/unspecified intellectual disability (intellectual developmental disorder). For the purposes of this chapter, the general term 'intellectual disability' is used that covers all subtypes mentioned above.

The American Association on Intellectual and Developmental Disabilities (AAIDD 2013) indicates three main diagnostic criteria of intellectual disability:

- significant limitations in intellectual functioning, for example, reasoning, learning and problem solving

- significant limitations in adaptive behaviour, that is, conceptual, social and practical skills in everyday life

- onset in childhood, that is, before the age of 18.

Individuals with intellectual disabilities are a very heterogeneous group and their communication skills can vary due to the severity level, co-occurring conditions and other behavioural, emotional and social factors. Intellectual disability is usually categorised according to three severity levels: mild (IQ scores between 55 and 70), moderate (IQ scores between 30 and 55) or severe and profound (IQ scores of 30 and below). Limitations in adaptive functioning in specific skill areas are a necessary criterion for diagnosis under the AAIDD and DSM-5 definitions (APA 2013). The categories are based on evaluations of adaptive functioning of the person in three main areas: conceptual, social and practical.

- *The conceptual area* includes skills in language, reading, writing, maths, reasoning, knowledge and memory. Possible clinical signs and symptoms in this domain include slow language development (children learn to talk later, if at all), slow development of pre-academic skills, difficulties in academic learning (reading, writing, maths), difficulty understanding concepts of time and money, problems with abstract thinking (concrete approach to problem solving), difficulties in executive function (i.e., planning, strategising, priority setting, cognitive flexibility), problems with short-term memory and difficulties with functional use of academic skills, such as money management and time management.

- *The social area* refers to empathy, social judgement, interpersonal communication skills and the ability to make and retain friendships. Clinical signs and symptoms in this domain may include lack of imitations in language and communication skills, more concrete and less complex spoken language (if used), limited vocabulary and grammatical skills compared with peers, receptive language that may be limited to the comprehension of simple speech and gestures, communication that may occur through non-spoken means only, such as gestures, signs, facial expressions and other forms of augmentative and alternative communication (AAC). Clinical signs and symptoms deficits in the area of social skills may include immature social judgement and decision-making, difficulty understanding peers' social cues and social rules and emotional and behavioural regulation difficulties that may adversely affect social interactions.

- *The practical area* centres on self-management in personal care, job responsibilities, money management, recreation and organising school and work tasks. Clinical signs and symptoms in this domain demonstrate that a person with intellectual disabilities requires different levels of support for daily life activities, such as personal care, more complex tasks (e.g., shopping, transportation, care organisation, meals, money management) and employment, healthcare and legal decisions, household tasks, etc.

The adaptive behaviour on all three of the above areas determines how well the individual copes with everyday tasks, especially in the practical domain. This is why, when diagnosing intellectual disability, the clinical assessment of adaptive functioning is considered most important. Secondary consideration is the IQ psychological test score that has to be at least two standard deviations or more below the general population, that is, an IQ score of 70 or below. A thorough and detailed assessment of the adaptation across all three domains (i.e., conceptual, social and practical) is the basis for the development of an individual intervention and development plan.

Intellectual disability is lifelong and often co-occurs with different mental health conditions, such as depression, anxiety disorders, attention deficit hyperactivity disorder (ADHS) and autism (APA 2013). High prevalence physical health conditions in individuals with intellectual disabilities include hearing loss, heart conditions, obesity-related problems, seizure activity and visual impairment. In addition, people with intellectual disabilities tend to have more physical health problems than the general population, yet these are usually a result of inadequate healthcare, limited access to quality services (Krahn, Hammond and Turner 2006) and communication problems (Gentile, Cowan and Smith 2015). However, providing adequate healthcare and training can significantly improve quality of life and increase the longevity of individuals with intellectual disabilities.

Epidemiology and economic cost

Intellectual disability is the most common developmental disability. The prevalence (number of cases of a disorder based on the population at the time) of intellectual disability is estimated between 1 and 2.5 per cent, and the incidence (number of new cases per year) is estimated to be around 1.8 per cent. This means that as many as about 200 million people worldwide are diagnosed with intellectual disabilities. In Europe, about 4.2 million people have an intellectual disability (McKenzie et al. 2016), but there are big differences between countries. Generally, indexes of intellectual disability prevalence are lower in Western Europe, while the opposite trend is seen among regions with low- to middle-range incomes (Maulik et al. 2011). Social and environmental risk factors include alcoholism, lead exposure, iron deficiency, malnutrition, peri-natal problems and other non-genetic conditions (Bertelli *et al.* 2009).

A high percentage of people diagnosed as having an intellectual disability receive social welfare benefits or pensions, which obviously increases the financial burden on a country. The economic cost of intellectual disability is estimated on the basis of expenses to society in the form of different resources (financial, medical, psychological, etc.) to provide adequate services to people with intellectual disabilities. This calculation does not usually include direct non-medical costs due to the disability, such as the extra resources needed in educational and social service sectors, and neither does it include indirect costs in terms of lost productivity. A 2010 study (Olesen *et al.* 2012) dedicated to estimating the cost of brain disorders in Europe calculated that the total annual cost of intellectual disability ('mental retardation' in ICD-10) was €43.3 million. The earlier benchmark European study (Wittchen *et al.* 2011) showed similar results. Considering that the employment rate is very low among individuals with intellectual disabilities and that intellectual disability is usually associated with significant health problems, such as multiple disabilities and other medical conditions, the total economic cost of this diagnosis is even higher. These costs could be minimised if people with intellectual disabilities could find adequate employment.

The working environment

In most cases, the level and scope of intellectual disability determines the educational and vocational career of the person with intellectual disabilities. When 'school readiness' is assessed before children are sent to primary school (usually when they are five to six years of age, depending on the particular country), any indication that the child may have an intellectual disability may be confirmed (or disconfirmed) through detailed psychological assessment and diagnosis.

The level of educational attainment determines the employment opportunities of people with intellectual disabilities (as is the case for everyone), but also important are individual characteristics of communication and adaptive skills as well as the individual's general physical and mental health. People with mild intellectual disabilities are likely to be hired in the open market, for example, by community grocery stores, garden centres or small businesses. There are many companies that offer jobs for people with intellectual disabilities at a variety of levels, from cleaning or landscape services, to commercial services and businesses, including production, packaging and distribution. There are some very good examples, such as the employment of individuals with Down syndrome in the care and support of older people or in the retail industry. Most people with moderate intellectual disabilities can work in more supported employment systems or in sheltered workshops, usually carrying out relatively simple tasks under supervision. Sheltered workplaces, including copy centres or packing facilities, often focus on simple product assembly or the performance of relatively basic tasks, such as bulk mailing.

On-the-job training becomes an important factor to promote employability. The advantage for employers is that individuals with intellectual disabilities tend to be stable and consistent in their performance, as long as they receive adequate training and support. Job coaches should seek to support all people with intellectual disabilities to find employment that is most suitable for their skills levels and interests, rather than being restricted by the label of intellectual disability or the clinical assessment of severity.

Employment statistics

Employment rates of people with disabilities are generally low in Europe, and the situation for people with intellectual disabilities is even worse, with rates varying from 18 to 30 per cent. For example, in Scotland, of the 26,786 adults with an intellectual disability known to local authorities, only 1782 were listed as 'in employment', with only 875 in open-market, paid employment (Stuart and McKeown 2014).

In Northern and Western European countries, the employment rate appears higher due to the provision of sheltered workplaces. However, in the majority of cases these workers do not have a full employee status. In Southern, Central and Eastern Europe people with intellectual disabilities usually remain unemployed, although some public and non-governmental institutions have some notable initiatives to engage this group vocationally.

According to Inclusion Europe (2015), the most significant barriers to employment for people with intellectual disabilities include:

- *Outdated legal capacity legislation:* in many European countries people with intellectual disabilities cannot be employed legally because they are not considered to have the capacity to sign work contracts. Furthermore, if they live in residential institutions or work in sheltered workplaces, they often do not earn a real salary or the institution keeps their salary.

- *Common indirect discrimination* against people with intellectual disabilities in recruitment includes the fact that school leaving certificates are requested even if there is little or no connection to the job in question. Thus, people with intellectual disabilities who may not have received a school leaving certificate are excluded from jobs they could perform with little or no support. This is increased by lack of knowledge about reasonable accommodation measures and a lack of support services. Even where job coaches or other support services exist, they are mostly unknown to potential employers.

- *The benefits trap* means that frequently legislation regarding social benefits does not allow people to return to a disability benefits scheme after they have worked in open employment. This creates a huge barrier for people with intellectual disabilities who may want to try working in the open labour market.

- *Lack of appropriate skills training for people with intellectual disabilities.* For the smooth transition from school to working life, the acquisition of professional and social skills is important. This is frequently not the focus of schools or in transition planning.

- *Lack of accessible workplaces.* Some employers are reluctant to employ people with intellectual disabilities, even if they are offered financial support or the benefits of a supported employment policy.

- *Pay gaps* remain in place between people with intellectual disabilities and other workers.

Interventions

The main goal of interventions for people with intellectual disabilities is to minimise the effects of existing impairments as well as an improvement in their adaptive skills and behaviour. Usually life skills and functioning can be expanded if appropriate personalised support is provided and maintained (AAIDD 2013). As communication skills are a key competence in the case of people with intellectual disabilities (Sevcik and Romski 2016), different levels of communication skills training can be very useful. For example, some people may require support with basic language, while others need interventions to support functioning in more advanced areas related to communication, including cognitive level, speech production skills and emotional status. Interventions always should consider coexisting strengths and challenges in all areas to ensure individualised support is provided. Communication interventions should focus on the context of interactions that people with intellectual disabilities encounter in their day-to-day lives.

Job coaches can support therapists by providing ample opportunities for communication that incorporate a variety of language functions (e.g., greeting, commenting, describing, requesting); multiple partners and varied communication contexts (e.g., home, educational, recreational, vocational, community settings) to safeguard the generalisation of new skills; and different forms and modalities of speech to ensure comprehensive communication repertoires.

The variety of interventions used for people with intellectual disabilities utilise information technology-based support systems in conjunction with functional communication and social skills training, including the following:

- *AAC devices*, such as the iPod, or various 'tablets' with AAC applications (apps), offer technology-based supplements that can be used in the absence of natural speech and/or writing skills, with aides such as picture communication symbols, line drawings, Blissymbols and tangible objects (Beukelman and Mirenda 2013).

- *Activity schedules and visual supports* include objects, photographs, drawings or written words that act as cues or prompts to help individuals complete a sequence of tasks and activities, attend to instructions, transition from one task to another or behave appropriately in various settings, and to initiate or sustain interaction. Scripts promote social interaction and can be used in a classroom or work setting to facilitate academic interactions and social or work-related engagement (Hart and Whalon 2008).

- *Computer-based instructions* include the use of computer technology (e.g., iPad) and/or computerised programs to teach communication, work and social skills directly (Neely *et al.* 2013).

- *Video modelling* incorporates video recordings of desired behaviours, either performed by a model or therapist or by another service user who is able to engage in the target behaviour competently (Anderson *et al.* 2016; Nikopoulos and Keenan 2004).

Many other behavioural technology-based interventions, for example, various kinds of differential reinforcement, prompting, fading and modelling (Cooper, Heron and Heward 2007) designed to reduce problem behaviours and teach functional alternative behaviours utilise the basic principles of behaviour change discovered through the science of behaviour analysis. The application of this science, Applied Behaviour Analysis (ABA), employs principles of learning to bring about meaningful and positive change in behaviour. ABA-based behavioural technology can be developed to help build a variety of skills such as communication, social skills, self-control and self-monitoring (Spreckley and Boyd 2009).

Transition planning is used to prepare young people and adults with intellectual disabilities for the next phase in their career, for example, successfully moving from school to post-secondary education/training programmes, progress to employment settings, transition between various social and employment situations or to relocate from home to independent living. It is important that transitions are well planned and the necessary skills are learnt before, during and after a transition has taken place.

Job coach assistance

The job coach support necessary for a person with intellectual disabilities depends on their functional and communication skills levels that were achieved during school education and the professional preparedness of the employer. At times, the job coach needs to intervene to support either the employee or the employer with regards to these skills. In such cases, the assistance of a job coach is crucial as there is much scope through setting up adequate supports as well as skills training to enable individuals with intellectual disabilities to find work and become valued employees, especially since many individuals with intellectual disabilities are particularly motivated and hard working.

Furthermore, job coaches can be involved in a person's transition planning, especially when the individual is moving between jobs. This may also involve identifying other supports that are necessary. For ageing adults with intellectual disabilities special support may be needed to facilitate continued levels of maximum independent functioning. It is important to note that ageing in these cases is not necessarily linked to chronological age, as the ageing process of people with intellectual disabilities may be premature when compared with the general population (Lin *et al.* 2011). For example, individuals with Down syndrome are at relatively high risk for early onset dementia (Burt *et al.* 2005), and even without a diagnosis of dementia, speech and language skills may begin to decline in adults with intellectual disabilities from about the age of 50 (Roberts, Price and Malkin 2007).

Some adults with intellectual disabilities, particularly those with psychomotor or feeding and swallowing impairments, may experience dysphagia-related problems as they age (Lazenby-Paterson and Crawford 2014). Interventions designed to enhance peer interactions in the settings in which adults live, work or socialise have shown that continued support can lead to enriched social functioning; for example, job coaching, partner training and social facilitation can improve the interactions of these individuals in the workplace (Mautz, Storey and Certo 2001).

General guiding principles for job coaches who support and advocate for individuals with intellectual disabilities include:

- use family-centred and culturally appropriate practices

- form collaborative teams

- follow a strengths-based perspective

- maximise self-sufficiency

- recognise individual variability

- foster a community environment of respect and inclusion

- use natural environments

- involve peers as communication partners.

Conclusion

For individuals with intellectual disabilities well-delivered assistance by job coaches is necessary and usually very welcome. Increasingly, organisations are recognising the value of employees with intellectual disabilities and consequently developing non-discriminatory recruitment and employment methods. In a labour market where dedicated workers for relatively basic tasks are increasingly difficult to find, the job market for individuals with intellectual disabilities looks promising. It is therefore essential to reconsider legal capacity legislation that hinders access to employment, and to contest any direct or indirect discrimination against people with intellectual disabilities.

References

AAIDD (American Association on Intellectual and Developmental Disabilities) (2013) 'Definition of Intellectual Disability.' Accessed on 16/02/2018 at www.aaidd.org

Anderson, A., Furlonger, B., Moore, D.W., Sullivan, V.D. and White, M.P. (2018) 'A comparison of video modelling techniques to enhance social-communication skills of elementary school children.' *International Journal of Educational Research 87*, 100-109. http://doi.org/10.1016/j.ijer.2016.05.016

APA (American Psychiatric Association) (2013) *Diagnostic and Statistical Manual of Mental Disorders, 5th edition (DSM-5)*. Washington, DC: APA.

Bertelli, M., Hassiotis, A., Deb, S. and Salvador-Carulla, L. (2009) 'New contributions of psychiatric research in the field of intellectual disabilities.' *Advanced Psychiatry 3*, 37–4.

Beukelman, D.R. and Mirenda, P. (2013) *Augmentative and Alternative Communication: Supporting Children and Adults with Complex Communication Needs*. Baltimore, MD: Brookes.

Burt, D., Primeaux-Hart, K., Loveland, K., Cleveland, L. *et al.* (2005) 'Aging in adults with intellectual disabilities.' *American Journal on Mental Retardation 110*, 268–284.

Cooper, J.O., Heron, T.E. and Heward, W.L. (2007) *Applied Behavior Analysis*. Upper Saddle River, NJ: Pearson Prentice Hall.

Gentile, J.P., Cowan A.E. and Smith, A.B. (2015) 'Physical health of patients with intellectual disability.' *Advances in Life Sciences and Health 2*, 1, 91–102.

Hart, J.E. and Whalon, K.J. (2008) 'Promote academic engagement and communication of students with autism spectrum disorder in inclusive settings.' *Intervention in School and Clinic 44*, 3, 116–120.

Inclusion Europe (2015) *Inclusion Europe's Contribution to the Mid-Term Review of the European Disability Strategy*. Accessed on 18/10/2017 at http://inclusion-europe.eu/wp-content/uploads/2015/03/IE_submission_EDS_final1.pdf

Krahn, G.L., Hammond, L. and Turner, A. (2006) 'A cascade of disparities: Health and health care access for people with intellectual disabilities.' *Mental Retardation and Developmental Disabilities Research Reviews 12*, 70-82. doi:10.1002/mrdd.20098

Lazenby-Paterson, T. and Crawford, H. (2014) 'Aging in adults with intellectual disabilities.' *Perspectives on Gerontology 19*, 36–43.

Lin, J.D., Wu, C.L., Lin, P.Y., Lin, P.L. and Chu, C.M. (2011) 'Early onset ageing and service preparation in people with intellectual disabilities: Institutional managers' perspective.' *Research in Developmental Disabilities 32*, 188–193.

Maulik, P.K., Mascarenhas, M.N., Mathers, C.D., Dua, T. and Saxena, S. (2011) 'Prevalence of intellectual disability: A meta-analysis of population-based studies.' *Research in Developmental Disabilities 32*, 419–436.

Mautz, D., Storey, K. and Certo, N. (2001) 'Increasing integrated workplace social interactions: The effects of job modification, natural supports, adaptive communication instruction, and job coach training.' *Journal of the Association for Persons with Severe Handicaps 26*, 257–269.

McKenzie, K., Milton, M., Smith, G. and Ouellette-Kuntz, H. (2016) 'Systematic review of the prevalence and incidence of intellectual disabilities: current trends and issues.' *Current Developmental Disorders Reports 3*, 104. Accessed on 21/05/2018 at https://doi.org/10.1007/s40474-016-0085-7

Neely, L., Rispoli, M., Camargo, S., Davis, H. and Boles, M. (2013) 'The effect of instructional use of an iPad on challenging behaviour and academic engagement for two students with autism.' *Research in Autism Spectrum Disorders 7*, 4, 509–516.

Nikopoulos, C.K. and Keenan, M. (2004) 'Effects of video modeling on social initiations by children with autism.' *Journal of Applied Behavior Analysis 37*, 93–96. Accessed on 21/05/2018 at http://doi.org/10.1901/jaba.2004.37-93

Olesen, J., Gustavsson, A., Svensson, M., Wittchen, H.U. and Jönsson, B. (2012) 'The economic cost of brain disorders in Europe. CDBE2010 study group; European Brain Council.' *European Journal of Neurology 19*, 1, 155–162. doi:10.1111/j.1468-1331.2011.03590.x

Roberts, J.E., Price, J. and Malkin, C. (2007) 'Language and communication development in Down syndrome.' *Mental Retardation and Developmental Disabilities Research Reviews 13*, 1, 26–35.

Sevcik, R.A. and Romski, M.A. (eds) (2016) *Communication Interventions for Individuals with Severe Disabilities: Exploring Research Challenges and Opportunities.* Baltimore, MD: Brookes.

Spreckley, M. and Boyd, R. (2009) 'Efficacy of applied behavioural intervention in preschool children with autism for improving cognitive, language, and adaptive behaviour: A systematic review and meta-analysis.' *The Journal of Paediatrics 154*, 338–344.

Stuart, C. and McKeown, A. (2014) *Learning Disability Statistics Scotland: A National Statistics Publication for Scotland.* Accessed on 17/02/2018 at www.scld.org.uk/wp-content/uploads/2015/08/Learning-Disability-Statistics-Scotland-2014-report.pdf

Wittchen, H.U., Jacobu, F., Rehm, J., Gustavsson, A., *et al.* (2011) 'The size and burden of mental disorders and other disorders of the brain in Europe 2010.' *European Neuropsychopharmacology 21*, 655–679.

WHO (World Health Organization) (1992) *The International Classification of Diseases, 10th Revision (ICD-10).* Geneva: WHO.

Chapter 6

JOB COACHES FOR ADULTS ON THE AUTISM SPECTRUM

—— Lyn McKerr and Karola Dillenburger ——

This chapter focuses on the support necessary for employees with autism. Issues related to autism, for example, prevalence, aetiology, specific issues etc., are outlined, and then the role and tasks of job coaches who work with this particular population are described, clarifying specific issues and sharing some best practice.

Definition of autism spectrum disorder

Autism spectrum disorder (ASD), also known as autism spectrum condition (ASC), is a pervasive developmental disorder that affects many aspects of an individual's development, and is diagnosed when persistent social communication and repetitive/restricted behaviour issues are observed (APA 2013). It is recognised as a 'spectrum condition' because the severity of these issues and individual support needs vary widely (NIMH 2016).

There are two main diagnostic systems used to confirm an autism diagnosis – the *International Classification of Diseases, 10th revision (ICD-10)*[1] (WHO 1992) and the *Diagnostic and Statistical Manual of Mental Disorders, 5th edition* (DSM-5) (APA 2013). Although ICD-10 is the instrument most widely used in European countries, most of the published research internationally is based on the diagnostic definitions within DSM-5 (Dillenburger, McKerr and Jordan 2015). Examples of

---

1   In 2019, the ICD-11 will replace ICD-10 as the diagnostic manual (World Health Organization 2018). Rather than a separate diagnostic category, ICD-11 will include Asperger's Syndrome along with Childhood Disintegrative Disorder and other generalised developmental disorders within the diagnosis of 'Autism' (Autism Europe 2018).

behaviours relevant to a diagnosis of autism (Dillenburger, McKerr and Jordan 2015) are shown in Table 6.1.

Table 6.1: Examples of behaviours that need to be observed over a prolonged period for autism diagnosis

Social interaction and communication difficulties	Restricted and repetitive behaviours
• Difficulties in initiating or sustaining a conversation • Difficulties in reading facial expressions accurately • Difficulties in building and maintaining peer relations • Developmental delay in language	• Repetitive behaviours • Restricted interests (and in some cases, special abilities) • Inflexible adherence to routines • Sensory issues, e.g., sensory overload or distortion • Difficulties with perspective taking

Following the American Psychiatric Association (APA) DSM-5 guidelines, ASD is currently diagnosed according to three levels of support needs (APA 2013):

• Level 1: Requiring support

• Level 2: Requiring substantial support

• Level 3: Requiring very substantial support.

Asperger's Syndrome is a diagnostic category used in ICD-10 and *DSM-IV* (an earlier version of the DSM, in use until 2013), but not *DSM-5*. Asperger's Syndrome is characterised by average or above-average intellectual ability, with significant social and communication difficulties (despite possession of functional speech and language capabilities) and restricted/repetitive behaviours. Even though the diagnostic category has been removed from clinical contexts, many people previously diagnosed with Asperger's Syndrome continue to identify with it, and some view it as a 'fundamental aspect of their identity' (NAS 2016a).

There are currently no reliable biological or neurological indicators for autism (APA 2013), although genetics of autism is an area of intense research interest. A diagnosis of autism is confirmed by 'specialist and interdisciplinary clinical judgement' (Elsabbagh and Johnson 2010, p.82) based on direct behavioural observations by professionals with the use of validated assessment tools, for example, the Autism Diagnostic Observation Schedule (ADOS) (Lord *et al.* 2000), together with reports from others who are closely involved with the individual, such as parents/guardians (the Autism Diagnostic Interview) (Lord, Rutter and Couteur 1994).

Recent advances in research support the existence of multiple impairment models of autism (Bedford *et al.* 2014), and it seems increasingly unlikely that a single causative factor underlies the condition (Boucher 2012; Elsabbagh and Johnson 2010). There is some evidence that autism may have a genetic origin (Elsabbagh and Johnson 2010; Elsabbagh *et al.* 2012; Szatmari *et al.* 2007; Zhao *et al.* 2007), although a broad range of environmental factors may also impact on pre- and post-natal development (MRC 2001; Rutter 2011). Andrew Wakefield's now retracted 1998 study linked the mumps, measles and rubella (MMR) vaccine to rising rates of autism (Wakefield *et al.* 1998), but these findings have been discredited (Dyer 2010). An association between autism and vaccinations remains purely speculative (DeStefano *et al.* 2004; Doja and Roberts 2006; Rutter 2011), and has never been supported by any valid causation models or epidemiologic studies. A recent large-scale US study ($n=95,727$) determined that the MMR vaccination was not associated with any increased risk of autism, even for children who had an older sibling diagnosed with the condition (Jain *et al.* 2015).

The role of the mercury-based vaccine preservative thimerosal has also been discussed as a possible causative factor, but no substantive evidence has been found (Doja and Roberts 2006). However, the presence of industrial chemicals in the environment has been linked with developmental neurotoxicity (Rutter 2011), that is, exposure before birth or during childhood can lead to problems with the development of the nervous system (including the brain), and may be linked to neurodevelopmental disorders such as autism (Grandjean and Landrigan 2014). However, at present, no specific factor linked to autism has been confirmed.

Many individuals with autism may also have a range of debilitating co-occurring ('co-morbid') conditions (Kielinen *et al.* 2004; Mannion, Leader and Healy 2013). These can include overall developmental delays or disabilities (83%), psychiatric conditions, reported to be 10 per cent of the population (Levy *et al.* 2010), and epilepsy, that has been reported to affect between 5 and 40 per cent of people with autism (Amiet *et al.* 2008; Canitano, 2007; Mannion *et al.* 2013; Tuchman and Rapin 2002). This figure varies depending on age, co-occurring conditions and gender, that is, it seems that individuals who also have intellectual disabilities, or females, had a greater risk of epilepsy (Amiet *et al.* 2008). Other co-occurring medical conditions include motor difficulties, sensory impairment, Down syndrome and cerebral palsy (Kielinen *et al.* 2004; ONS 2005).

There is some evidence that gastrointestinal problems are relatively common among individuals with autism (Mouridsen, Rich and Isager 2010; Wills and Evans 2016). This can include the presence of harmful gut bacteria, such as *Clostridium bolteae* (Pequegnat *et al.* 2013), and more general dietary issues, with many parents surveyed reporting significant problems both with food intake (76%) and with gastrointestinal symptoms such as bloating (72%) (Wills and Evans 2014). Mannion *et al.* (2013) and Mannion and Leader (2013a) found that children with sleep problems were more likely to demonstrate gastrointestinal symptoms, and these were more common in participants without intellectual disabilities. There is currently no evidence to show that dietary restrictions or supplements have a beneficial effect with respect to autism.

Although intellectual disability is not a diagnostic feature of autism (Matson and Shoemaker 2009), between 50 and 70 per cent of individuals with autism are so affected, many with severe intellectual disability, that is, an IQ of less than 70 (Baio 2012). Those who have both learning disabilities and autism frequently have other co-occurring conditions, including epilepsy (Amiet *et al.* 2008; Smith and Matson 2010a) and challenging behaviours (Smith and Matson 2010b), with more than a quarter engaging in self-injurious behaviour (Soke *et al.* 2016). If not addressed early, challenging behaviours continue throughout the life course (Richards *et al.* 2016; Shattuck *et al.* 2007). In the UK, the National Institute for Health and Care Excellence (NICE) guidelines for the management of challenging behaviours recommends 'personalised interventions for children, young people and adults that are based on behavioural principles and a functional assessment of behaviour, tailored to the range of settings in which they spend time' (NICE 2015, para.1.7.5).

Although not a diagnostic feature, mental health problems such as depression and anxiety also frequently co-occur with autism (Matson and Shoemaker 2009; Rosenblatt 2008), with males more frequently experiencing anxiety disorder and those with gastrointestinal symptoms more commonly experiencing depression, as well as avoidance and conduct disorders (Mannion and Leader 2013b). Women and girls with autism, in particular, may be given a mental health diagnosis rather than an autism diagnosis (Gould and Ashton-Smith 2011), and conversely, a number of parents worried that the diagnosis of autism 'overshadowed' other medical and behavioural conditions that were not being treated appropriately (Wills and Evans 2016).

Epidemiology

The prevalence rates for autism diagnoses have risen steadily – from 1 in 110 in 2006 (CDC 2017) to 1 in 50 for children in 2016 (CDC 2016) – and there is no evidence of geographic, ethnic or socioeconomic differences, although there are limitations of existing data sets, particularly in developing countries (Elsabbagh *et al.* 2012). In some places, estimated prevalence rates are even higher; for example, in South Korea prevalence is reported to be 1 in 38 (Kim *et al.* 2011). In the UK, a secondary analysis of the Millennium Cohort Study (n=18,000+ children born in 2000) reported rising prevalence rates over time, that is, 0.9 per cent when the children were aged five, rising to 3.5 per cent when the children were aged 11 (Dillenburger, Jordan and McKerr 2014). In Northern Ireland, the annual School Census revealed that in 2016 2.3 per cent of school-aged children were diagnosed with autism (Waugh 2016). It is unclear if the rising prevalence rate is due to an increase in diagnostic procedures, earlier referrals or broader inclusion criteria (Blumberg *et al.* 2013; King and Bearman 2009) or, in fact, represents real epidemiological change.

Accurate prevalence estimates for adults are not presently available (Dillenburger, McKerr and Jordan 2016); in the UK, the National Health Service (NHS) uses the Adult Psychiatric Morbidity Survey to estimate adult autism prevalence to be between 0.5 and 1.3 per cent (NHS Digital 2016). While it is generally agreed that males outnumber females (by a ratio of approximately 1 to 4), there are increasing concerns about the impact of gender on prevalence estimates. It is suggested that standard diagnostic tools may miss females with autism, who are likely to be diagnosed later and where more severe impairments are identified (Gould and Ashton-Smith 2011; Dworzynski *et al.* 2012). Some work has been undertaken by clinicians on a revised Autism Spectrum Screening Questionnaire (ASSQ-REV) to address this issue (Kopp and Gillberg 2011), but it seems possible that a substantial number of girls and women with autism remain undiagnosed, with their social and emotional difficulties attributed to other causes, for example, mental health issues (Gould and Ashton-Smith 2011).

The cost of autism

Although there is no centralised database, some European and other countries have collected data on the cost of autism. Estimates of the economic costs of autism in the UK and the US (Buescher *et al.* 2014) indicate that the additional lifetime expenditure for support needed by an individual on the autism spectrum (without an intellectual disability) is £0.92 million (€1.03 million), and for an individual with a co-occurring intellectual disability, it is up to £1.5 million (€1.67 million). In the UK, this represents an annual cost of around £29–31 billion (€32.4–34.6 billion);[2] of this estimate, around 42 per cent is due to lost employment opportunities for adults with autism (Buescher *et al.* 2014).

In Germany, the economic cost is thought to be around 70 per cent of that in the UK, with lifetime costs for a person with autism (without an intellectual disability) around €766,865 (Bachmann 2013). A study from the Netherlands estimated that €109.2–€182 billion is spent on autism annually (Peters-Scheffer *et al.* 2012). Costs were incurred in providing special education, childcare and therapy allowances, employment support and specialised provision in accommodation, and the authors concluded that this could be off-set by approximately €1,103,067 for each individual with autism, if early intensive behavioural interventions (EIBIs) were put in place. There is increasing evidence of the effectiveness of EIBIs in improving outcomes (including, in due course, employment prospects) for children with autism (Reichow *et al.* 2014).

At the time of writing, the organisation Autism Spectrum Disorders in the European Union (ASDEU)[3] is conducting a wide-ranging study that includes prevalence and economic costs within 12 European

---

2   Dependent on the variation in estimated prevalence figures for co-occurring intellectual disability (40–60% respectively); the figure does not include social security benefits, which the authors deem 'transfer payments and not real societal costs'; see Buescher *et al.* (2014, p.724). Cost equivalents £/€ correct as of October 2017.

3   For details of the programmes and funding, see www.autismeurope.org/files/files/09h35-joaquin-fuentes.pdf

countries (2015–18). When published, this study will provide more complete statistics and employment profiles for adults with autism; it will also put forward policies for 'harmonised support' across member states in Europe.[4]

Intervention strategies

Interventions for most adults with autism focus on adaptive behaviour and many are based on assistive technology, augmentative communication or Applied Behaviour Analysis (ABA)-based interventions (Anderson *et al.* 2018) to enhance skills and reduce challenging behaviours (Research Autism 2016). In the UK, the National Institute for Health and Care Excellence (NICE 2012) has produced clinical guidance that recommends a number of interventions. These include psychosocial therapies such as adaptive life skills training, anger management and job support, as well as pharmacological, physical and dietary interventions.

There is a statistically significant relationship between early intensive ABA-based interventions and 'optimal outcomes' for children with autism, including a significant reduction in symptoms such as restricted and repetitive behaviours (MacDonald *et al.* 2014; Troyb *et al.* 2014); in turn, this can lead to improved chances of employment and reduced care needs for adults (Fein *et al.* 2013; Orinstein *et al.* 2014). Conversely, lack of appropriate EIBIs has been linked with very poor long-term outcomes (Howlin *et al.* 2004, 2014), and some parents have successfully sued for damages, citing lack of these kinds of intervention (SEN Advocates 2018). ABA-based interventions are considered gold standard or 'treatment as usual' in most of North America and Canada (Keenan *et al.* 2014), and have been linked to significant cost savings (Motiwala *et al.* 2006).

Employment statistics for autism and the workplace

Although EU-wide employment figures for adults with autism are not available, the Academic Network of European Disability (ANED) has indicated that in general the proportion of people with disabilities not participating in the labour market is at least twice as high as that of

4   For full details, see http://asdeu.eu

other EU citizens (European Commission 2014a). ANED published country-specific reports in 2011 (ANED 2017), and between 2011 and 2013, the European Commission funded a number of pilot employment projects for individuals with autism in Bulgaria, Germany, Denmark, Poland and Italy (European Commission 2014b).

Accurate employment figures for adults with autism in the UK are not presently available, largely because the existing government employment data sets do not differentiate between autism spectrum disorders and more general disability categories (Dillenburger *et al.* 2014). A survey of 1179 adults with autism in England for the National Autistic Society (NAS) suggested that only 15 per cent of adults with autism were in full-time employment (Rosenblatt 2008). Another survey of over 2000 people with autism by NAS (2016b)[5] indicated that this figure has changed very little, with only 16 per cent in full-time paid work; 32 per cent were defined as being in 'some kind of paid work (full and part-time combined)', which compares to official figures of 47 per cent for people with disabilities and 80 per cent for those who do not have a disability. Under-employment of adults with autism is an acknowledged problem worldwide (Chen *et al.* 2015).

Autism and the working environment

It seems obvious that many adults on the autism spectrum are not fulfilling their employment potential. However, some employers are already aware of the advantages of recruiting people with autism, particularly (but not exclusively) in the information technology (IT) sector. For example, the German IT firm Systems Applications Products (SAP) introduced a scheme in 2013 to specifically recruit adults with autism, and an Autism at Work scheme was established in India, Ireland, Canada, the US, Germany, the Czech Republic and Brazil, with the aim of having 1 per cent of its workforce comprised of people on the autism spectrum by 2020 (Florentine 2015). The company values the potentially enhanced abilities that could be offered by some individuals with autism. In Ireland, SAP has entered into partnership with the Danish not-for-profit organisation Specialisterne,[6] that selects and trains adults with autism for employment in 17 countries worldwide.

---

5   Source for these figures quoted by NAS (2016b): ONS (2016) Dataset: A08: Labour market status of disabled people (20 July 2016).

6   See http://specialisternefoundation.com

Given the behaviours associated with a diagnosis of autism, that is, adherence to inflexible routines, sensory issues and difficulties with perspective taking, it is not surprising that some individuals on the spectrum may have difficulties adjusting to life in the workplace. They may be unable to interpret colleagues' feelings or expressions, and thus appear insensitive or are thought to behave inappropriately; others may have difficulty coping with changes to a routine or environment, organising work, planning or predicting outcomes of their actions (Hendricks 2010). These are issues that can and should be addressed by adequately informed employers with the support of job coaches and can make working life easier for colleagues as well as the employee and family members:

> ...[name] was stacking shelves somewhere and halfway through the job someone asked him to change and wipe the floor, and that was just a nightmare. In the work placements, I think there could have been better autism awareness training around what stresses out people on the spectrum. (Parent of a young adult with autism and intellectual disability; Dillenburger *et al.* 2015, p.88)

Others may find that employers under-estimate their capabilities and do not offer employment that makes full use of their abilities because of misconceptions about autism:

> ...[I was working in] a laptop repair shop... I'm very interested in the technical spec of things... I like to work with an open source system, something called Linux [but]...people see computers like a black box...they just want to push the buttons...and the way they speak to me... "No [name]...brush the floor"... I'm probably exaggerating, but... (Adult with Master's degree; Dillenburger *et al.* 2015, p.101)

Public opinion has a very positive role in increasing expectations for employment, as it can shape employers' marketing strategies and encourage more diversity in the workplace. For example, the Northern Ireland Life and Times Survey included a designated autism module in 2012 that canvassed the views of 1209 respondents. Overall, the public expressed positive views about education and daily living, and about working with adults with autism. In terms of supporting diversity in the workplace, 12 per cent of respondents said they would be prepared to give more business to firms with an active policy of employing adults with an autism spectrum condition (Dillenburger *et al.* 2013). For employers, employing a person with autism (with appropriate support and guidance) could represent a sound financial investment, as well as demonstrating a 'commitment to equality and diversity and a positive attitude to disabled people' (NAS 2016c).

If employers make reasonable adjustments for the needs of individuals on the autism spectrum, it will enable them to become 'effective and highly valued employees' who can excel at their job (Hendricks 2010). This need not necessarily involve expensive alterations or the provision of continuous specialised support. For example, for farmers engaged in food production, work patterns are seasonal and weather-dependent, and in most areas of Western Europe, there is no guarantee of a fixed daily routine. Advance planning that builds in adjustments to changes in routine will be a great advantage, and this should include contingencies for any unexpected activities that could arise. For example, if the power or water goes off, employees should know their options will be to go home early, or to move to another work site with the necessary facilities. Experienced job coaches who know their clients will have helped develop communication strategies suitable for the needs of employees with autism, and will recognise individuals with autism may need extra time or additional instruction to cope with changes, at a level that meets their abilities:

> And in the morning, too, to help the people with autism, we'd have a white board, so you would write down, structure…what they're doing today…you know, in this climate sometimes it rains… You can clearly score it out, "we are unable to do that because of the weather" and if they can't read you can draw wee symbols, it's raining, cloud, and that helps to de-stress…because things do change. (Business owners offering work placements; Dillenburger *et al.* 2015, pp.145–146)

For some adults with autism, self-employment can offer a creative and fulfilling environment that they can tailor to meet their own needs. In cases like this, the job coach role may be to help negotiate suitable premises, perhaps to 'signpost' the client to suitable advice on obligations such as insurance or to offer support in sorting out financial matters such as organising accounts, sending out and paying bills.

Finding the right solution in self-employment, if appropriate, offers a great deal of personal satisfaction and independence for individuals with autism:

I basically found a job where people would tell me what they want…and then they would leave me alone…and I could get on with it [laughs]. So, doing [craft] is very good, you know, I'm an expert in it…it's all controlled and I don't get any paradoxical situations… I like the fact that I'm in control, with it, and it's definable, and then occasionally… you get a moment where what you do far surpasses what people expect, and they come in and go "Wow" and then, that's great. (Self-employed craftsman and artist; Dillenburger *et al.* 2015, p.102)

Some practical advice for employing adults with autism

Everyone with autism is first and foremost an individual, and employment support should be specifically tailored for each person, designed with the expectation that over time, support needs will change. While job coaches work closely with their clients and prospective employers to ensure that the working environment remains as positive as possible, some general guidelines can help employers understand that adjustments do not necessarily entail radical changes in the workplace. NAS offers a series of 'top tips' for employers that include:

- being clear about the expectations of the job (including workplace etiquette)

- providing structured training and monitoring – consider one-to-one rather than group training

- making sure instructions are concise and specific – use plain language/written as well as oral directions

- ensuring the working environment is well structured (e.g., functional assessments and task management) and routines are clearly signposted

- holding regular reviews

- giving sensitive but direct feedback

- providing reassurance/contingency planning in potentially stressful situations, such as IT failures

- exploring sensory adaptations, if needed, such as low noise/ extra privacy in the working area

- raising staff awareness (with consent from the employee with autism).

Conclusion

The low employment rates identified for adults with autism do not reflect a lack of willingness to work; although an estimated 15–16 per cent of people with autism are in some form of employment, some 79 per cent of individuals with autism surveyed said they want to work (Redman *et al.* 2009). It is clear that many people with autism are keen to take up employment, and the initial role of the job coach will be to match the skills of the client with prospective jobs. However, it needs to be remembered that obtaining a job is only the start of a process, and the job coach role should be flexible to accommodate the challenges and rewards that employment can bring. As well as needing a structured environment, and learning to cope with the unexpected, people with autism may face additional barriers to maintaining a job, such as discrimination and/or bullying in the workplace. Consequently, after having found a job, an estimated 43 per cent of adults with autism resign or are made redundant (Bancroft *et al.* 2012).

People with autism are most likely to succeed in employment when they have less severe intellectual disabilities and are able to communicate effectively, without marked language impairments (Holwerda *et al.* 2012). People who have consistent levels of family support, independent living skills and a positive social attitude are also more likely to enjoy a better working outcome (Holwerda *et al.* 2013). On the more negative side, co-occurring conditions may place additional stresses on an individual with autism. These can include mental health problems, coexisting medical conditions, maladaptive behaviours or intellectual disabilities, and may raise significant barriers to gaining and maintaining employment, and that will need ongoing support (Baio 2012; Kielinen *et al.* 2004; Matson and Shoemaker 2009; Rosenblatt 2008). Guidelines related to these issues should be considered in conjunction with the autism guidelines.

References

ANED (Academic Network of European Disability) (2017) 'Employment.' Accessed on 11/10/2017 at www.disability-europe.net/theme/employment

APA (American Psychiatric Association) (2013) *Diagnostic and Statistical Manual of Mental Disorders, 5th edition (DSM-5)*. Washington, DC: APA.

Amiet, C., Gourfinkel-An, I., Bouzamondo, A., Tordjman, S., Baulac, M., Lechat, P., *et al.* (2008) 'Epilepsy in autism is associated with intellectual disability and gender: Evidence from a meta-analysis.' *Biological Psychiatry 64*, 7, 577–582.

Anderson, A., Furlonger, B., Moore, D.W., Sullivan, V.D. and White, M.P. (2018) 'A comparison of video modelling techniques to enhance social-communication skills of elementary school children.' *International Journal of Educational Research 8*, 100–109. Accessed on 21/05/2018 at http://doi.org/10.1016/j.ijer.2016.05.016

Autism Europe (2018) *World Health Organization updates classification of autism in the ICD-11*. Accessed on 17/10/2018 at www.autismeurope.org/blog/2018/06/21/world-health-organisation-updates-classification-of-autism-in-the-icd-11

Bachmann, C. (2013) 'Autism costs in Germany: Scarce data.' [Blog post.] Health and Social Care, London School of Economics and Political Science. Accessed on 10/02/2018 at http://blogs.lse.ac.uk/healthandsocialcare/2013/10/08/autism-costs-in-germany-scarce-data

Baio, J. (2012) 'Prevalence of autism spectrum disorders – Autism and developmental disabilities monitoring network, 14 sites, United States, 2008.' *Surveillance Summaries 61*, 1–19.

Bancroft, K., Batten, A., Lambert, S. and Madders, T. (2012) *The Way We Are: Autism in 2012*. London: National Autistic Society.

Bedford, R., Pickles, A., Gliga, T., Elsabbagh, M., Charman, T. and Johnson, M.H. (2014) 'Additive effects of social and non-social attention during infancy relate to later autism spectrum disorder.' *Developmental Science 17*, 4, 612–620.

Blumberg, S.J., Bramlett, M.D., Kogan, M.D., Schieve, L.A., Jones, J.R. and Lu, M.C. (2013) 'Changes in Prevalence of Parent-reported Autism Spectrum Disorder in School-aged US Children: 2007 to 2011–2012.' *National Health Statistics Reports 65*, 20 March. Accessed on 10/02/2018 at http://njintouch.state.nj.us/health/fhs/sch/documents/changes_in_pre.pdf

Boucher, J. (2012) 'Putting theory of mind in its place: Psychological explanations of the socio-emotional-communicative impairments in autistic spectrum disorder.' *Autism 16*, 3, 226–246. doi:10.1177/1362361311430403

Buescher, A.V.S., Cidav, Z., Knapp, M. and Mandell, D.S. (2014) 'Costs of autism spectrum disorders in the United Kingdom and the United States.' *JAMA Pediatrics 168*, 721–728. doi:10.1001/jamapediatrics.2014.210

Canitano, R. (2007) 'Epilepsy in autism spectrum disorders.' *European Child and Adolescent Psychiatry 16*, 61–66.

CDC (Centres for Disease Control and Prevention) (2016) 'Autism Spectrum Disorders. Data and Statistics: Prevalence.' Accessed on 10/02/2018 at www.cdc.gov/ncbddd/autism/data.html

CDC (2017) 'Autism Spectrum Disorder: Data and Statistics. Identified Prevalence of Autism Spectrum Disorder, ADDM Network 2000–2012.' Accessed on 10/02/2018 at www.cdc.gov/ncbddd/autism/data.html

Chen, J.L., Leader, G., Sung, C. and Leahy, M. (2015) 'Trends in employment for individuals with autism spectrum disorder: A review of the research literature.' *Journal of Autism and Developmental Disorders 2*, 115–127. doi:10.1007/s40489-014-0041-6

DeStefano, F., Bhasin, T.K., Thompson, W.W., Yeargin-Allsopp, M. and Boyle, C.(2004) 'Age at first measles-mumps-rubella vaccination in children with autism and school-matched control subjects: A population-based study in metropolitan Atlanta.' *Pediatrics 113*, 2, 259–266.

Dillenburger, K., Jordan, J.-A. and McKerr, L. (2014) *BASE Project: Secondary Data Analysis* (Vol. 3). Accessed on 10/02/2018 at www.qub.ac.uk/research-centres/CentreforBehaviourAnalysis/filestore/Filetoupload,463790,en.pdf

Dillenburger, K., McKerr, L. and Jordan, J-A. (2015) *BASE Project: Qualitative Data Analysis* (Vol. 4) Accessed on 10/02/2018 at www.qub.ac.uk/research-centres/CentreforBehaviourAnalysis/filestore/Filetoupload,620592,en.pdf

Dillenburger, K., McKerr, L. and Jordan, J.-A. (2016) *BASE Project: Final Project Report* (Vol. 5) Accessed on 10/02/2018 at www.qub.ac.uk/research-centres/CentreforBehaviourAnalysis/filestore/Filetoupload,620594,en.pdf

Dillenburger, K., Jordan, J-A., McKerr, L. and Keenan, M. (2015) 'The Millennium child with autism: Early childhood trajectories for health, education and economic wellbeing.' *Developmental Neurorehabilitation 18*, 37–46. doi:10.3109/17518423.2014.964378

Dillenburger, K., Jordan, J-A., McKerr, L., Devine, P. and Keenan, M. (2013) 'Awareness and knowledge of autism and autism interventions: A general population survey.' *Research in Autism Spectrum Disorders 7*, 12, 1558–1567. doi:10.1016/j.rasd.2013.09.004

Doja, A. and Roberts, W. (2006) 'Immunizations and autism: a review of the literature.' *Canadian Journal of Neurological Science 33*, 4, 341–346.

Dworzynski, K., Ronald, A., Bolton, P. and Happe, F. (2012) 'How different are girls and boys above and below the diagnostic threshold for autism spectrum disorders?' *Journal of the American Academy of Child and Adolescent Psychiatry 51*, 8, 788–797.

Dyer, C. (2010) 'Lancet retracts Wakefield's MMR paper.' *BMJ 340*, c696.

Elsabbagh, M. and Johnson, M.H. (2010) 'Getting answers from babies about autism.' *Trends in Cognitive Sciences 14*, 2, 81–87.

Elsabbagh, M., Divan, G., Koh, Y.J., Kim, Y.S., Kauchali, S., Marcin, C., *et al.* (2012) 'Global prevalence of autism and other pervasive developmental disorders.' *Autism Research 5*, 160–179.

European Commission (2014a) 'World Autism Awareness Day: EU projects help people with autism get a foothold on the employment ladder.' Accessed on 11/10/17 at http://europa.eu/rapid/press-release_MEMO-14-253_en.htm

European Commission (2014b) *Results of Four Pilot Projects on Employment of Persons with Autism.* Accessed on 11/10/17 at http://ec.europa.eu/justice/discrimination/files/report_pilot_projects_empl_autism_2014_en.pdf

Fein, D., Barton, M., Eigst, I.M., Kelley, E., Naigles, L., Schultz, R.T., *et al.* (2013) 'Optimal outcome in individuals with a history of autism.' *Journal of Child Psychology and Psychiatry 54*, 2, 195–205. doi:10.1111/jcpp.12037.

Florentine, S. (2015) 'How SAP is hiring autistic adults for tech jobs.' 9 December. Accessed on 24/01/18 at www.cio.com/article/3013221/careers-staffing/how-sap-is-hiring-autistic-adults-for-tech-jobs.html

Gould, J. and Ashton-Smith, J. (2011) 'Missed diagnosis or misdiagnosis? Girls and women on the autism spectrum.' *Good Autism Practice 12*, 1, 34–41.

Grandjean, P. and Landrigan, P.J. (2014) 'Neurobehavioural effects of developmental toxicity.' *Lancet Neurology 13*, 3, 330–338.

Hendricks, D. (2010) 'Employment and adults with autism spectrum disorders: Challenges and strategies for success.' *Journal of Vocational Rehabilitation 32*, 125–134. doi:10.3233/JVR-2010-0502

Holwerda, A., van der Klink, J.J.L., Groothoff, J.W. and Brouwer, S. (2012) 'Predictors for work participation in individuals with an autism spectrum disorder: A systematic review.' *Journal of Occupational Rehabilitation 2*, 3, 33–52.

Holwerda A, van der Klink, J.J, de Boer, M.R, Groothoff, J.W. and Brouwer S. (2013) 'Predictors of sustainable work participation of young adults with developmental disorders.' *Research in Developmental Disabilities 34*, 9, 2753–2756.

Howlin, P., Goode, S., Hutton, J. and Rutter, M. (2004) 'Adult outcome for children with autism.' *Journal of Child Psychology and Psychiatry 45*, 2, 212–229. Accessed on 21/05/2018 at http://doi.org/10.1111/j.1469-7610.2004.00215.x

Howlin, P., Savage, S., Moss, P., Tempier, A. and Rutter, M. (2014) 'Cognitive and language skills in adults with autism: a 40-year follow-up.' *Journal of Child Psychology and Psychiatry 55*, 1, 49–58. doi:10.1111/jcpp.12115.

Jain, A., Marshall, J., Buikema, A., Bancroft, T., Kelly, J.P. and Newschaffer, C.J. (2015) 'Autism occurrence by MMR vaccine status among US children with older siblings with and without autism.' *Journal of the American Medical Association 313*, 15, 1534–1540. doi:10.1001/jama.2015.3077. Accessed on 08/08/2017 at http://jamanetwork.com

Keenan, M., Dillenburger, K., Röttgers, H.-R., Dounavi, K., Jónsdóttir, S.L., Moderato, P., *et al.* (2014) 'Autism and ABA: The gulf between North America and Europe.' *Review Journal of Autism and Developmental Disorders 2*, 2, 167–183. doi:10.1007/s40489-014-0045-2

Kielinen, M., Rantala, H., Timonen, E., Linna, S.L. and Moilanen, I. (2004) 'Associated medical disorders and disabilities in children with autistic disorder: A population-based study.' *Autism 8*, 1, 49–60.

Kim, Y.S., Leventhal, B.L., Koh, Y.J., Fombonne, E., Laska, E., Lim, E.C., *et al.* (2011) 'Prevalence of autism spectrum disorders in a total population sample.' *American Journal of Psychiatry 168*, 9, 904–912. doi:10.1176/appi.ajp.2011.10101532.

King, M. and Bearman, P. (2009) 'Diagnostic change and the increased prevalence of autism.' *International Journal of Epidemiology 38*, 5, 1224–1234.

Kopp, S. and Gillberg, C. (2011) 'The Autism Spectrum Screening Questionnaire (ASSQ)-Revised Extended Version (ASSQ-REV): An instrument for better capturing the autism phenotype in girls? A preliminary study involving 191 clinical cases and community controls.' *Research in Developmental Disabilities 32*, 6, 2875–2888.

Levy, S.E., Giarelli, E., Lee, L.C., Schieve, L.A., Kirby, R.S., Cunniff, C., *et al.* (2010) 'Autism spectrum disorder and co-occurring developmental, psychiatric, and medical conditions among children in multiple populations of the United States.' *Journal of Developmental and Behavioral Pediatrics 31*, 4, 267–275. doi:10.1097/DBP.0b013e3181d5d03b

Lord, C., Rutter, M. and Couteur, A.L. (1994) 'Autism diagnostic interview-revised: A revised version of a diagnostic interview for caregivers of individuals with possible pervasive developmental disorders.' *Journal of Autism and Developmental Disorders 24*, 659–685. Accessed on 21/05/2018 at http://doi.org/10.1007/BF02172145

Lord, C., Risi, S., Lambrecht, L., Cook, E.H., Leventhal, B.L., Dilavore, P.C., *et al.* (2000) 'The Autism Diagnostic Observation Schedule-Generic: A standard measure of social and communication deficits associated with the spectrum of autism.' *Journal of Autism and Developmental Disorders 30*, 205–223. Accessed on 21/05/2018 at http://doi.org/10.1023/A:1005592401947

MacDonald, R., Parry-Cruwys, D., Dupere, S. and Ahearn, W. (2014) 'Assessing progress and outcome of early intensive behavioral intervention for toddlers with autism.' *Research in Developmental Disabilities 35*, 12, 3632–3644. doi:10.1016/j.ridd.2014.0

Mannion, A. and Leader, G. (2013a) 'Comorbidity in autism spectrum disorder: A literature review.' *Research in Autism Spectrum Disorders 7*, 1595–1616.

Mannion, A. and Leader, G. (2013b) 'An analysis of the predictors of comorbid psychopathology, gastrointestinal symptoms and epilepsy in children and adolescents with autism spectrum disorder.' *Research in Autism Spectrum Disorders 7*, 1663–1671.

Mannion, A., Leader, G. and Healy, O. (2013) 'An investigation of comorbid psychological disorders, sleep problems, gastrointestinal symptoms and epilepsy in children and adolescents with Autism Spectrum Disorders.' *Research in Autism Spectrum Disorders 7*, 35–42.

Matson, J.L. and Shoemaker, M. (2009) 'Intellectual disability and its relationship to autism spectrum disorders.' *Research into Developmental Disabilities 30*, 6, 1107–1114. doi:10.1016/j.ridd.2009.06.003

Motiwala, S.S., Gupta, S., Lilly, M.B., Ungar, W.J. and Coyte, P.C. (2006) 'The cost-effectiveness of expanding intensive behavioural intervention to all autistic children in Ontario.' *Healthcare Policy 1*, 2, 135–151.

Mouridsen S.E., Rich, B. and Isager, T. (2010) 'A longitudinal study of gastrointestinal diseases in individuals diagnosed with infantile autism as children.' *Child Care Health and Development 36*, 3, 437–443. doi:10.1111/j.1365-2214.2009.01021.x

MRC (Medical Research Council) (2001) *MRC Review of Autism Research: Epidemiology and Causes.* Accessed on 02/08/2017 at www.mrc.ac.uk/documents/pdf/autism-research-review

NAS (National Autistic Society) (2016a) 'What is Asperger Syndrome?' Accessed on 02/08/2017 at www.autism.org.uk/about/what-is/asperger.aspx

NAS (2016b) 'Government must tackle the autism employment gap.' 27 October. Accessed on 18/10/2017 at www.autism.org.uk/get-involved/media-centre/news/2016-10-27-employment-gap.aspx

NAS (2016c) 'Recruiting an autistic employee.' Accessed on 24/01/2018 at www.autism.org.uk/professionals/employers/information-for-employers/recruitment.aspx

NHS Digital (2016) *Adult Psychiatric Morbidity Survey: Survey of Mental Health and Wellbeing, England, 2014.* Accessed on 21/09/2017 at http://content.digital.nhs.uk/catalogue/PUB21748

NICE (National Institute for Health and Care Excellence) (2012) *Autism: Recognition, Referral, Diagnosis and Management of Adults on the Autism Spectrum: Guidance and Guidelines.* Accessed on 18/10/2017 at www.nice.org.uk

NICE (2015) *Challenging Behaviour and Learning Disabilities: Prevention and Interventions for People with Learning Disabilities Whose Behaviour Challenges.* Accessed on 18/10/2017 at www.nice.org.uk/guidance/ng11

NIMH (National Institute of Mental Health) (2016) 'Autism Spectrum Disorder: Overview.' Accessed on 02/08/2017 at www.nimh.nih.gov/health/topics/autism-spectrum-disorders-asd/index.shtml?utm_source=rss_readersutm_medium=rssutm_campaign=rss_full

ONS (Office for National Statistics) (2005) *Mental Health of Children and Young People in Great Britain, 2004.* London: HMSO.

Orinstein, A.J., Helt, M., Troyb, E., Tyson, K.E., Barton, M.L., Eigsti, I.M., *et al.* (2014) 'Intervention for optimal outcome in children and adolescents with a history of autism.' *Journal of Developmental and Behavioral Pediatrics 3*, 4, 247–256. doi:10.1097/DBP.0000000000000037

Pequegnat, B., Sagermann, M., Valliani, M., Toh, M., Allen-Vercoe, E. and Monteiro, M.A. (2013) 'A vaccine and diagnostic target for Clostridium bolteae, an autism-associated bacterium.' *Vaccine 31*, 26, 2787–2790.

Peters-Scheffer, N., Didden, R., Korzilius, H. and Matson, J. (2012) 'Cost comparison of early intensive behavioral intervention and treatment as usual for children with autism spectrum disorder in The Netherlands.' *Research in Developmental Disabilities 33*, 6, 1763–1772. doi:10.1016/j.ridd.2012.04.006

Redman, S., Downie, M., Rennison, R. and Batten, A. (2009) *Don't Write Me Off: Make the System Fair for People with Autism.* London: National Autistic Society.

Reichow, B., Barton, E., Boyd, B. and Hume, K. (2014) 'Early intensive behavioral intervention (EIBI) for young children with autism spectrum disorders (ASD): A systematic review.' *Campbell Systematic Reviews 10*, 9. Accessed on 21/05/2018 at https://campbellcollaboration.org/media/k2/attachments/Reichow_EIBI_Review.pdf

Research Autism (2016) 'Interventions for Adults on the Autism Spectrum.' Accessed on 10/02/2018 at http://researchautism.net/autism/adults-on-the-autism-spectrum/interventions-for-adults-on-the-autism-spectrum

Richards, C., Moss, J., Nelson, L. and Oliver, C. (2016) 'Persistence of self-injurious behaviour in autism spectrum disorder over 3 years: A prospective cohort study of risk markers.' *Journal of Neurodevelopmental Disorders 8*, 21. Accessed on 21/05/2018 at http://doi.org/10.1186/s11689-016-9153-x

Rosenblatt, M. (2008) *'I Exist': The Message from Adults with Autism in England.* London: National Autistic Society. Accessed on 10/02/2018 at http://researchautism.net/publications/3528/i-exist:-the-message-from-adults-with-autism-in-england-

Rutter, M.L. (2011) 'Progress in understanding autism: 2007–2010.' *Journal of Autism and Developmental Disorders 41*, 395–404. doi:10.1007/s10803-011-1184-2

SEN Advocates (2018) 'Applied Behavioural Analysis.' Accessed on 01/06/2018 at www.senadvocates.co.uk/aba-applied-behavioural-analysis/

Smith, K.R.M. and Matson, J. L. (2010a) 'Social skills: Differences among intellectually disabled adults with co-morbid autism spectrum disorders and epilepsy.' *Research in Developmental Disabilities 31*, 1366–1372.

Smith, K.R.M. and Matson, J. L. (2010b) 'Behavior problems: Among intellectual disabled adults with autism spectrum disorders and epilepsy.' *Research in Developmental Disabilities 31*, 1062–1069.

Soke, G.N., Rosenberg, S.A., Hamman, R.F., Fingerlin, T., Robinson, C., Carpenter, L., et al. (2016) 'Brief report: prevalence of self-injurious behaviors among children with autism spectrum disorder – A population-based study.' *Journal of Autism and Developmental Disorders 46*, 11, 3607–3614. Accessed on 21/05/2018 at http://doi.org/10.1007/s10803-016-2879-1

Shattuck, P.T., Seltzer, M.M., Greenberg, J.S., Orsmond, G.I., Bolt, D., Kring, S., et al. (2007) 'Change in autism symptoms and maladaptive behaviors in adolescents and adults with an autism spectrum disorder.' *Journal of Autism and Developmental Disorders 37*, 9, 1735–1747.

Szatmari, P., Paterson, A.D., Zwaigenbaum, L., Roberts, W., Brian J., Liu, X.Q., et al. (2007) 'Mapping autism risk loci using genetic linkage and chromosomal rearrangements.' *Nature Genetics 39*, 3, 319–328.

Troyb, E., Orinstein, A., Tyson, K., Eigsti, I.-M., Naigles, L. and Fein, D. (2014) 'Restricted and repetitive behaviors in individuals with a history of ASDS who have achieved optimal outcomes.' *Journal of Autism and Developmental Disorders 44*, 12, 3168–3184. doi:10.1007/s10803-014- 2182-y

Tuchman, R. and Rapin, I. (2002) 'Epilepsy in autism.' *The Lance Neurology 1*, 352–358.

Wakefield, A.J., Murch, S., Anthony, A., Linnell, J., Casson, D.M., Malik, M., *et al.* (1998) 'Ileal lymphoid nodular hyperplasia, non-specific colitis, and regressive developmental disorder in children.' *Lancet 351*, 637–641. [Retraction in public statement published 2 February 2010.]

Waugh, I. (2016) 'The prevalence of autism (including Asperger Syndrome) in school age children in Northern Ireland.' Belfast: Department of Health. Accessed on 01/01/2016 at www.health-ni.gov.uk/news/prevalence-autism-including-aspergers-syndrome-school-age-children-northern-ireland-2017

WHO (World Health Organization) (1992) *The ICD-10 Classification of Mental and Behavioural Disorders: Clinical Descriptions and Diagnostic Guidelines.* Available from www.who.int/classifications/icd/en/bluebook.pdf

Wills, J. and Evans, Y. (2016) *Health and Service Provision for People with Autism Spectrum Disorder: A Survey of Parents in the United Kingdom, 2014.* A report for the Autism and Inflammation Project. London: Queen Mary University. Accessed on 21/05/2018 at http://treatingautism.org.uk/wp-content/uploads/2016/03/Health__Service_Provision_for_People_with_ASD_March2016.pdf

Zhao, X., Leotta, A., Kustanovich, V., Lajonchere, C., Geschwind, D.H., Law, K., *et al.* (2007) 'A unified genetic theory for sporadic and inherited autism.' *Proceedings of the National Academy of Sciences 104*, 12831–12836.

Chapter 7

ON-THE-JOB FUNCTIONAL ASSESSMENTS

Angelika Anderson

Problem behaviours represent a barrier to learning and participation, put individuals at risk of social exclusion and are predictive of poor developmental and educational outcomes, so preventing and addressing them is a priority. A critical first step is understanding their causes. Diagnosis and labelling tend to support the notion that the causes of problem behaviour reside exclusively within the individual, an assumption that does not readily lead to positive interventions.

A behavioural approach is based on a different set of assumptions: that behaviour is learned and serves a purpose for the individual. Successfully addressing problem behaviour in this paradigm requires determining its function. This is accomplished with a functional behavioural assessment (FBA), a systematic process to identify environmental events associated with the behaviours in question. A functional approach to addressing behaviours of concerns facilitates positive outcomes that do not involve restraint, seclusion or exclusion. Such positive approaches to managing behaviours that challenge are now widely supported, not only in schools, for example, in the US (IDEA 2004), but also in the context of disability services more generally, for example, Australia (Victoria State Government 2018) and the UK (PBS Academy 2016), including in the workplace (Kittelman, Bromley and Mazzotti 2016). Nonetheless, a research-to-practice gap exists and implementation barriers have been identified.

This chapter outlines the conceptual and philosophical underpinnings of a functional approach to addressing problem behaviour. It describes recent efforts to bridge this research-to-practice gap, and reviews recent methodological advances to facilitate a function-based approach to addressing behaviours of concern in community and employment settings.

Why conduct functional behavioural assessments?

Behaviours of concern, challenging behaviour, behaviour difficulties – these are some of the terms that are used to refer to behaviours that are problematic for individuals and those around them. Such behaviours are often associated with high levels of stress for everyone concerned, can compromise a safe and productive environment, and limit the extent to which the individuals concerned may participate meaningfully in the community, including in the workplace. Behaviours of concern are a major barrier to employment for individuals with disabilities (Nord *et al.* 2016). Unaddressed they are likely to lead to increasingly restrictive practices and placements. Dealing effectively with such behaviour is therefore important, and understanding its causes is a critical first step in developing effective interventions.

Problem behaviour is often associated with skill deficits, which is one reason why individuals with disabilities are at an increased risk for developing problem behaviours. But what are the skills critical to success in the workplace? As well as job-specific skills, more generic problems with time management, task engagement and low productivity have been identified. Similarly, deficits in social skills have been identified as a major barrier to workforce participation for some. Addressing deficits in social, communication and interpersonal skills, and enhancing task engagement and task completion could therefore be critical to improving employment outcomes. How is it, then, that skill deficits can lead to problem behaviour? Taking a functional approach helps us to understand this connection and leads to positive approaches for minimising the risk of problem behaviours to occur, and for dealing with them when they do.

The way we think about problem behaviours affects the way we approach such behaviour and the extent to which positive solutions are sought. It depends, to a large extent, on the conceptual framework we adopt. Two common and very different conceptualisations with relevance to a psychological discussion of problem behaviours are the *medical model* and the *educational model*. Outside of this there is then also a *correctional approach*, where the discussion focuses on the 'rights and wrongs' of behaviour and the need for justice and retribution.

Often the same words are used to describe phenomena from these different perspectives, making discussions potentially confusing. For this reason, I begin this chapter with a brief outline of these different ways of thinking about behaviour.

The medical model

The medical model is based on the assumption that the causes for problem behaviour reside primarily within the individual concerned, and are therefore somehow controllable by the individual or indicative of some dysfunction or disorder. Consequently, this approach focuses on *treating* the individual as a *patient* and is likely to under-estimate the contribution of the environment. Associated treatments tend to be clinical and include both medication and psychiatric services. Assessments commensurate with a medical model seek to identify individuals with specific deficits or abnormalities, leading to differential *diagnosis*. Assessment procedures within this paradigm typically focus on the topography and intensity of the behaviour in order to ascertain some kind of *pathology*.

The medical model is associated with a number of problems when it comes to addressing behavioural issues. Diagnosis typically involves identifying and describing a set of behaviours individuals exhibit, behaviours seen as deviant, maladaptive or beyond normative expectations in terms of their topography, intensity or frequency, and assigning a summary label to represent them. Conceptually, it is easy to fall prey to circular reasoning in this paradigm by ascribing causal properties to the summary label that was correctly used to describe a behavioural pattern. Ultimately, the assumption that people behave in a particular way because of some inherent deficits does not lead towards solutions, especially if the cause of the behaviour is ascribed to some facet of personality or a lifelong condition (e.g., they behave this way because they are an aggressive person or because they have autism), which cannot be changed. The process of diagnosis is often costly, and though useful for the purpose of allocating funding, its utility to inform intervention is limited.

From a correctional perspective some behaviours are judged as bad and in need of correction. Individuals are thought to have the capacity to behave appropriately but choose not to. Wrong choices therefore need to be dis-incentivised by punishment, which is also thought to serve as a deterrent to others. Dealing with problem behaviours from this perspective requires *discipline* and *correction*: there is a perceived need for retribution, reformation, restitution and deterrence. Individuals in need of intervention come to the attention of those in authority through their wrongdoings or *rule violations*. The purpose of the correction is not only to reform the individual, but also to set an example to others to signal that such rule violation will not be tolerated, a way to establish *boundaries*.

The educational model

In the workplace, maintaining a productive and safe environment for all is clearly most easily accomplished by excluding those who cause problems. Employers have no obligation to maintain employment for individuals who do not follow the rules and expectations of the workplace. This is probably one of the main reasons why problem behaviours are associated with difficulties in maintaining employment. In the school system this is different as in many countries now, equal opportunity laws exist that state that all individuals, including those with disabilities that include behavioural disorders, have a right to access to an appropriate education (e.g., IDEA 2004). Perhaps this is the reason why so much research on this topic has been conducted in the field of education. An alternative explanation is the general lack of research on employment in adults with disabilities, as lamented by Shattuck and colleagues (2012). I therefore draw heavily on school-based research in some of the following discussion. After all, there are significant similarities between schools and the workplace in that both are demanding environments where individuals are required to perform and have to manage socially complex situations. Once employed, similar to schools, participation in the workplace is not voluntary.

From an educational perspective problem behaviour is seen as a skill deficit: individuals are not thought to have learned appropriate behaviours, or to lack information regarding behavioural expectations in a given situation or context. In this model, the ecology of the behaviour is thought to be important and the contribution of the environment to the occurrence of the problem behaviour is in the foreground. It follows that procedures to address problem behaviours from this perspective include assessing and improving the environment. It is only when problem behaviour persists in spite of environments that are considered adequate for most individuals that more intense assessments and interventions are warranted. Assessment and intervention needs are therefore identified through a *response to intervention* approach: individuals who fail to respond to adequate environments are those who require more intense assessment and intervention. Even then, though, the focus is still on the interaction of an individual with the environment. The question a social approach asks is, how does the environment need to change to better meet the needs of this individual?

An educational conceptualisation of problem behaviour may be particularly apposite to the problem behaviour of children in schools, individuals in residential care facilities, or indeed, in the workplace. These places are complex and demanding environments, and individuals need to be prepared or equipped to meet these demands. They need to be familiar with all the rules and behavioural expectations, and have the social, communication, self-regulation and other skills required. Populations particularly at risk include minority ethnic groups, including refugees (Anderson 2004; Herz 2014), and individuals with developmental disabilities or delays, especially those associated with communication and social deficits such as autism (Shattuck *et al.* 2012).

Conceptual background

People have long argued for a move towards an educational, function-based conceptualisation of problem behaviour in schools (Church 2003; Meyer and Evans 2006; Moore and Anderson 2001), where the goals of intervention are less about discipline, justice and retribution, but more concerned with learning, training and shaping behaviour (Bear 1999). A move towards function-based approaches such as positive behaviour support (PBS) is evident in supporting adults with disabilities in the workforce (Kittelman *et al.* 2016). However, few employers have the resources or the incentives to engage in complex behaviour support planning. While in many places schools have an obligation to provide appropriate educational services to all students regardless of disability, including problem behaviours (e.g., Goodman and Burton 2010; Herz 2014; IDEA 2004), employers can simply dismiss people who experience difficulties performing well in the workplace. This kind of behaviour support is therefore generally the responsibility of disability support workers such as job coaches, with a particular focus on prevention and early intervention.

Like schools, the workplace is potentially a high-risk environment for problem behaviour: it is demanding in that individuals have to follow instructions and sometimes engage in non-preferred activities. Most workplaces are also socially complex and challenging places. Getting along with co-workers is critical, and good social communication and adaptive skills have been identified as barriers to employment. The lack of such skills is often associated with inappropriate behaviours, leading to a failure to maintain employment (Kittelman *et al.* 2016). A function-based approach assumes that all behaviour is learned and serves a purpose (function) for the individual concerned. In the presence of demands, for example, problem behaviour may escalate if it leads to escape from the demands. The solution therefore is to ensure that individuals do not encounter excessive demands and to teach appropriate replacement behaviours, such as requesting a break or asking for help.

As with the PBS approach common in schools and community facilities, it follows that prevention is often the best way to manage problem behaviour in the workplace. Two function-based, preventative strategies that arise from the discussion above are:

- Ensure the environment (workplace) is behaviourally safe.

- Ensure that individuals are work-ready and have the required social communication skills, as well as specific jobs skills.

If behaviours of concern do occur despite these prevention strategies, individualised interventions that are function-based may be needed.

Practical background

Research has shown function-based interventions are more effective than procedures that are not function-based (Horner *et al.* 2002). Further, the use of FBAs in the process of addressing problem behaviours has been validated by numerous research studies (see, for example, LaRue, Weiss and Ferraioli 2008), and is endorsed by professional organisations such as the Association for Behavior Analysis International (ABAI) and the National Institutes of Health (NIH). In 1997, the inclusion of an *FBA-informed* behaviour intervention plan to address challenging behaviour was legally mandated in the US (Yell, Drasgow and Ford 1997).

In order to implement function-based interventions one must first identify the function (or purpose for the individual) of the behaviour. This is accomplished with an FBA, that is, a systematic step-wise investigation to identify those environmental events that are reliably and causally associated with the problem behaviours.

It is important, though, to situate this technology clearly within an overall framework of prevention and early intervention. While clear descriptions of effective preventative interventions exist for schools (e.g., Brophy 1983; Kincaid et al. 2007), there is little research to inform the development of similarly 'behaviourally safe' workplaces.

Preventative approaches could seek to:

- improve the environment

- identify and address skill deficits for the individual concerned.

Common skill deficits associated with problem behaviour include a lack of leisure skills (Camacho et al. 2014; McDonald, Moore and Anderson 2012), compliance (Lui, Moore and Anderson 2014), academic skills (Moore, Anderson and Kumar 2005), and social communication skills (Anderson, Moore and Bourne 2007; Anderson et al. 2004). In addition, Hanley (2012) also identified recruiting and maintaining the attention of others, escaping and avoiding unpleasant situations, gaining and maintaining preferred materials and tolerating delays, denials and termination of preferred events as important skills. Teaching these skills and implementing environmental adaptations to simplify difficult or demanding tasks are therefore important preventative strategies that do not require an FBA, and are entirely aligned with the fundamental assumption that underpins a function-based approach: that behaviour is learned and serves a purpose.

In an innovative project targeting the successful employment of adults with autism, Rausa, Moore and Anderson (2016) successfully taught specific gardening skills to individuals with autism working in a commercial horticultural setting growing edible flowers using video-modelling procedures. These projects were embedded within a larger *frame* of preventative measures involving video-priming procedures, self-management strategies and technology-assisted prompting procedures (Menon 2014). Video priming was used to show participants how to safely travel to and from work, familiarise them with the workplace, and inform them of safety regulations and other behavioural expectations. The video format enabled a close link between the required skills and behaviours and the specific locations or context in which they should occur. All participants were provided with iPods and taught how to use them using direct instruction. The iPods were used to allow participants access to individualised prompts including conversation starters for social situations such as coffee breaks, and appropriate responses for other work-related conversations such as meetings. Participants were also taught self-recording procedures to check and monitor their own on-task behaviour. Video prompting was used to remind participants of the skills and tasks they had been taught and were required to perform.

Menon (2014) also implemented environmental adaptations including a clear structure of the working day that was communicated to all participants and posted on a board every day, and other environmental prompts and models for appropriate behaviour (i.e., signs to remind participants to put on safety gear, and ensuring that all staff always wore safety gear, including the researchers involved). Other staff were introduced to the participants and informed about such things as the importance of communicating clearly and stating requests positively. While Menon was able to demonstrate that participants acquired and used all the skills taught as part of the *frame*, it was not possible to evaluate the extent to which these strategies contributed to the success of the programme as a whole. Nonetheless, this project provides a model of how job coaches could work in collaboration with employers to identify specific job-readiness skills, and suggest and implement simple environmental adaptations.

If problem behaviours do occur in spite of work-readiness and behaviourally safe workplaces, individual interventions based on the assumption that all behaviour serves a purpose may be needed. Behaviours of concern often communicate important needs, such as the need for access to attention or desired objects or activities, or the need for a break or escape from demanding or unpleasant tasks or circumstances. Especially for people with social communication impairments, problem behaviours often have a communicative function. Interventions designed to reduce, limit or eliminate such behaviours without replacing them with socially acceptable alternatives further deprive these individuals of the capacity to control their environment and reduce behavioural repertoires. If problem behaviour serves a purpose for the individual, to address such behaviour we need first to determine its purpose or function. With this knowledge it is then possible to implement a positive (non-aversive or restrictive) intervention, enabling individuals to get their needs met in more acceptable and appropriate ways. This often includes teaching a functionally equivalent replacement skill and ensuring that the replacement behaviour is more efficient than the problem behaviour in meeting the individual's needs. In this way we render the problem behaviour unnecessary. The following section describes in some detail the FBA process, including recent innovations, along with a discussion of implementation issues.

Practical guide to functional behaviour assessments

The term 'functional behaviour assessment' is an umbrella term to describe a variety of procedures used in the process of identifying behavioural function. FBA technologies are based on early behavioural research that demonstrated functional relationships between distinct environmental events and problem behaviours (Hart *et al.* 1964). FBA procedures subsumed under the generic term FBA include a variety of descriptive and experimental assessments (Kates-McElrath *et al.* 2007). *Descriptive assessments* include both indirect procedures (e.g., questionnaires and interviews, but also the review of records) and direct observation procedures (such as contingency assessments and scatterplots). These procedures provide descriptive and correlational information about variables in the natural environment associated with the problem behaviours. *Experimental assessments* include functional analysis and, as the word 'analysis' suggests, these procedures involve the experimental manipulation of environmental events to establish a causal relationship between these events and the behaviour of concern. Other descriptive assessment procedures can usefully inform more detailed experimental assessments (functional analysis); however, there is evidence to suggest that they have limited reliability (Alter *et al.* 2008), and direct observational procedures can be expensive and time-consuming (for a more detailed discussion, see Hanley 2012; Thompson and Iwata 2007). Therefore, while descriptive procedures can make an important contribution by informing the intervention, a reliance on these non-experimental procedures alone is not generally recommended.

Brian Iwata and colleagues developed comprehensive, systematic functional analysis procedures in the early 1980s (Iwata *et al.* 1982). In their seminal study, they experimentally assessed the occurrence of self-injurious behaviour under four different conditions, each implemented for 15 minutes at a time, in a randomised multi-element design. The conditions were *academic (demand), alone, social disapproval* and *play*, based on the hypothesised potential functions of positive, negative and automatic reinforcement, with play as a control condition. The study demonstrated that the cause of a problem behaviour cannot be determined by consideration of its topography or severity alone, but rather by identifying its function. Iwata *et al.* (1982) provided a first detailed description of a set of experimental procedures that could be used to identify the functions of a behaviour.

Since then, the utility of function-based approaches has been widely demonstrated, and the standard functional analysis proposed by Iwata, Kahng, Wallace and Lindberg (2000) has proved robust in identifying behavioural function for different populations, behaviours and settings (Hanley, Iwata and McCord 2003). At the same time a number of limitations and barriers to implementation of the standard procedure have been identified, including the length of time it takes, the high level of clinical expertise required and the ecological validity of lab-based procedures (Dixon, Vogel and Tarbox 2012). In addition, conducting FBAs in community settings, including schools and the workplace, requires specific adaptations and special considerations (Ellis and Magee 2004; Filter and Horner 2009; Karsh *et al.* 1995; Larson and Maag 1998).

There is some disconnect between what research suggests is best practice in FBA and what is commonly undertaken (Kates-McElrath *et al.* 2007). FBAs conducted in community settings are generally limited to descriptive assessments and do not include experimental functional analysis procedures (Lloyd, Weaver and Staubitz 2015). A problem is that while FBAs are widely supported and even mandated in some places, such as in the US with the advent of the IDEA (Yell, Drasgow and Ford 1997), this mandate has not been supported with guidance regarding the kind of FBAs required and who should conduct them, or by the provision of adequate additional resources and training (Kates-McElrath *et al.* 2007; Sasso *et al.* 2001; Scott *et al.* 2004). Addressing implementation barriers might therefore be particularly important in developing FBA procedures that can be used effectively in community settings, with limited support from skilled professionals.

Refined methods of functional analyses

In order to address the limitations of original functional analysis procedures, researchers have developed and refined alternative procedures, including *brief functional analysis* (Northup et al. 1991; Wallace and Knights 2003), *discrete trial functional analysis* (Sigafoos and Saggers 1995), *latency-based functional analysis* (Thomason-Sassi *et al.* 2011), and *antecedent-behaviour models of functional analysis*, which differ from the antecedent-behaviour-consequence (ABC) contingency, in that only the antecedents or motivating operations are manipulated experimentally. Such refinements in the development of more efficient functional analysis variants require a parallel process whereby inefficient indirect and direct procedures are replaced by more informative procedures that yield specific and relevant information to inform targeted functional analyses.

An example of such a method that incorporates the adaptation of both indirect and direct methods to inform expedient functional analyses is the recently developed interview-informed functional analysis (Hanley *et al.* 2014). Here, an open-ended interview designed to identify specific and idiosyncratic variables that might be functionally related to the problem behaviour is followed by a brief direct observation of the behaviour under natural conditions. This information is then used to devise functional analyses, typically limited to comparing only two specific conditions, which can incorporate synthesised contingencies (i.e., more than one contingency is tested in one single condition), as indicated by the indirect assessment (Hanley *et al.* 2014). For example, the test condition might be *escape from specific demands to access preferred activities*, and the control condition would include both access to potentially very specific preferred activities and the absence of specific demands.

Barriers to functional behavioural assessments

Several reviews have discussed a range of barriers to the implementation of FBAs, highlighting practical concerns and calling for the development of adapted procedures that address these without compromise on rigour (Gable 1999; Reid and Nelson 2002; Scott *et al.* 2004). One important question is, who should be conducting FBAs in community settings? Though a number of studies have shown that FBAs can be conducted in community settings with good results (Mueller, Nkosi and Hine 2011; Reid and Nelson 2002), in most cases researchers or clinicians conducted the FBAs. Some argue that following FBA procedures accurately requires special expertise, or at least a basic understanding of the essential conceptual premises that underpin them (Hanley 2012; Larson and Maag 1998).

A recent systematic review focused specifically on this issue. Lloyd, Weaver and Staubitz (2015) reviewed the published research in which FBAs were conducted in public schools, including studies where only the school personnel implemented functional analyses. They identified 39 studies published between 1997 (the advent of IDEA) and 2013, involving a total of 88 participants. The main purpose of this review was to identify and describe the ways in which functional analyses were integrated into the FBA process in public schools, and to evaluate the extent to which these functional analysis procedures aligned with previous recommendations regarding addressing implementation barriers. An interesting finding was that although a variety of functional analysis approaches were utilised in the studies they reviewed, AB models were more frequently observed here than in other, broader reviews. The AB model may well be more feasible in public school and other community settings compared to the ABC model, as it is probably easier to control antecedent variables than it is to control the delivery of required consequences to individuals within such places. In addition, the AB model might be more acceptable in applied settings as it does not involve the temporary reinforcement of the problem behaviour (Lloyd *et al.* 2015).

Novel adaptations that avoid some of these barriers and limitations include the use of synthesised contingencies and the practice of embedding the functional analysis procedure into instructional contexts (Lloyd *et al.* 2015). These adaptations enhance the ecological validity of the functional analysis. Not only are the functional analyses adapted into classroom and school procedures; they also incorporate specific contextual variables likely to be of relevance. A clear advantage of integrating the functional analysis procedure into the regular classroom proceedings is that students do not miss out on instructional time during the functional analysis process. These adaptations are equally advantageous in the workplace for all the same reasons.

While these adaptations addressed some implementation barriers, other strategies were found to be under-utilised. Few studies limited the functional analyses to two conditions, while others recommended variations of functional analysis, although such trial- or latency-based functional analysis is rare. However, over half of the studies did use open-ended indirect assessment procedures and adapted and individualised functional analysis conditions, though how the interview data were used to inform these adaptations was generally not clearly described.

Further implementation barriers emerged from this review. Typically, it was the researchers who were the primary data collectors and who conducted additional assessments. Lloyd *et al.* (2015) argue that given the importance of data collection, better models are required where personnel are available and able to perform these functions. In the studies reviewed, the FBA process, primarily the functional analysis and the direct observations prior to the functional analysis, were very time-consuming, requiring several hours for each participant. The authors therefore generally conclude that abbreviated indirect assessment procedures and functional analysis require further evaluation.

Who should carry out functional behavioural assessments?

While some argue that in school and community settings teachers and similar professionals should be the ones to conduct FBAs (e.g., Larson and Maag 1998; Lloyd *et al.* 2015; Reid and Nelson 2002; Scott et al. 2004), Hanley (2012) argues that the FBA process requires sophisticated professional judgements and should therefore be conducted or at least overseen by professionals with sufficient training in these methodologies, such as Board Certified Behaviour Analysts® (BCBA). In employment settings, job coaches are well placed to conduct data collection for FBAs under the supervision of appropriately qualified behaviour analysts. Skills in observational data collection should therefore be in the repertoire of job coaches.

Regardless of who is involved in conducting FBAs, efficient and ecologically valid methods are required to achieve more widespread implementation and meaningful results. Enhancing the ecological validity of FBAs conducted in the workplace may require some level of involvement by relevant staff, but it does necessitate the involvement of specialists with a high level of expertise in FBAs. Addressing the identified barriers to implementation without compromising rigour and reliability might best be achieved within a model of a collaborative partnerships between professionals with special expertise such as behaviour analysts, and other stakeholders such as the individual concerned, and where appropriate, their parents and caregivers, disability support workers and job coaches.

Such a collaborative approach has been trialled by Hanley and colleagues in implementing the *interview-informed functional analysis* described above, first, in partnership with parents in an outpatient clinic (Hanley *et al.* 2014), and later, in two cases of severe problem behaviour, one in the home and the other at school, in partnership with teachers and parents (Santiago *et al.* 2016). In these investigations, the researchers not only monitored the effectiveness of the FBA, but also its efficiency in terms of time and costs. In both studies the interview-informed FBA led to clearly differentiated results able to inform effective function-based interventions. While in the 2014 study it was the researchers who primarily conducted the FBA, in the 2016 study all procedures were implemented by teachers or other service providers, though it should be noted that the implementers had significant background knowledge in behaviour analysis and were supervised by a BCBA.

The 2014 clinic-based cases were reported, on average, to take 11.3 weeks with 27 visits, and at a cost of US$6900 for the entire process, including intervention. The FBA itself only took on average 2.3 clinic visits and cost US$660. The cases reported in the 2016 study took an average of 26 hours across a period of four months at an average cost of US$4225. Again, the FBA only took three visits and cost US$475 on average. In conjunction these studies demonstrate that FBA procedures can be conducted in a relatively short time frame, requiring relatively little time and professional input, and in ecologically valid ways in relevant community settings and involving teachers and parents in the process.

Others have reported similar results. For example, a data-based summary of 90 FBAs involving 69 students, conducted in public schools by a behaviour consulting organisation where all consultants were Master's or Doctoral-level behaviour analysts, demonstrated the feasibility of conducting FBAs in schools (Mueller *et al.* 2011). These FBAs all included indirect, direct and experimental methods to determine behaviour function. The functional analyses were conducted along the general lines of those described by Iwata *et al.* (1982), except that only conditions indicated by interview and observation were tested, and the alone condition was replaced by an ignore condition for practical reasons. Of the 90 FBAs, the majority (61%) were conducted in the classroom by trained behaviour consultants (80%), although teachers often participated. The average duration of the functional analyses was 109 minutes (range 30–430 minutes), with 33 per cent falling in the 30–60-minute range. The majority of the functional analyses took 90 minutes or less and few (20%) took more than three hours. A clear result was achieved in 90 per cent of the FBAs. Of the entire FBA process, the functional analysis part was the least time-consuming element.

Conclusion

This chapter has summarised a substantial evidence base and presented an argument for an educational approach to addressing problem behaviour. The key ideas, that all behaviour is learned and serves a purpose for the individual concerned, underpin a function-based approach, which incorporates positive (preventative) behavioural interventions and systems, and the use of *functional behavioural assessments* (FBAs) to inform individualised interventions. These technologies, developed to reduce the use of aversive treatments of problem behaviour with disabled populations, are now widely considered best practice.

FBA is a set of assessment procedures designed to identify the purpose of problem behaviours in individuals and inform function-based interventions. Though a number of implementation barriers have been identified, significant advances and the potential benefits of this technology support its use to assess and address problem behaviours. Guidelines for best practice of this technology are emerging, making it more accessible.

Though some questions remain regarding who is best placed to conduct such assessments and what competences and qualifications such individuals require, the current state of research supports the following guidelines regarding the assessment of problem behaviours in community settings, at the level of the individual, in cases where such behaviour persists:

- Conduct an interview-informed FBA, as described by Hanley (2012), consisting of an open-ended interview, a brief baseline, direct observation and a functional analysis.

- Maximise the efficiency of this process by using the interview and observational data to inform a specific functional analysis testing only those conditions identified in the preliminary assessments.

- Maximise the social and ecological validity of these procedures by conducting them in the natural environment, where the behaviour typically occurs.

- Involve relevant people in the procedure, such as parents, carers or job coaches.

References

Alter, P., Conroy, M., Mancil, G. and Haydon, T. (2008) 'A comparison of functional behavior assessment methodologies with young children: Descriptive methods and functional analysis.' *Journal of Behavioral Education 17*, 2, 200–219. doi:10.1007/s10864-008-9064-3

Anderson, A. (2004) 'Issues of Migration.' In R. Hamilton and D. Moore (eds) *Educational Interventions for Refugee Children* (pp.64–82). London: Routledge Falmer.

Anderson, A., Moore, D.W. and Bourne, T. (2007) 'Functional communication and other concomitant behavior change following PECS training: A case study.' *Behaviour Change 24*, 3, 173–181. doi:10.1375/bech.24.3.173

Anderson, A., Moore, D.W., Godfrey, R. and Fletcher-Flinn, C.M. (2004) 'Social skills assessment of children with autism in free-play situations.' *Autism 8*, 4, 369–385. doi:10.1177/1362361304045216

Bear, G.G. (1999) *Interim Alternative Educational Settings: Related Research and Program Considerations.* Alexandria, VA: National Association of State Directors of Special Education.

Brophy, J.E. (1983) 'Classroom organization and management.' *Elementary School Journal 83*, 265–285. doi:10.1086/46131

Camacho, R., Anderson, A., Moore, D.W. and Furlonger, B. (2014) 'Conducting a function-based intervention in a school setting to reduce inappropriate behaviour of a child with autism.' *Behaviour Change 31*, 1, 65–77. doi:10.1017/bec.2013.33

Church, J. (2003) *The Definition, Diagnosis and Treatment of Children and Youth with Severe Behaviour Difficulties: A Review of Research.* Wellington, New Zealand: Ministry of Education.

Dixon, D.R., Vogel, T. and Tarbox, J. (2012) 'A Brief History of Functional Analysis and Applied Behavior Analysis.' In L.J. Matson (ed.) *Functional Assessment for Challenging Behaviors* (pp.3–24). New York: Springer New York.

Ellis, J. and Magee, S. (2004) 'Modifications to basic functional analysis procedures in school settings: A selective review.' *Behavioral Interventions 19*, 3, 205–228. doi:10.1002/bin.161

Filter, K.J. and Horner, R.H. (2009) 'Function-based academic interventions for problem behavior.' *Education and Treatment of Children 32*, 1, 1–19.

Gable, R.A. (1999) 'Functional assessment in school settings.' *Behavioral Disorders 24*, 3, 246–248.

Goodman, R. and Burton, D. (2010) 'The inclusion of students with BESD in mainstream schools: Teachers' experiences of and recommendations for creating a successful inclusive environment.' *Emotional & Behavioural Difficulties 15*, 3, 223–237. doi:10.1 080/13632752.2010.497662

Hanley, G.P. (2012) 'Functional assessment of problem behavior: Dispelling myths, overcoming implementation obstacles, and developing new lore.' *Behavior Analysis in Practice 5*, 1, 54–72.

Hanley, G.P., Iwata, B.A. and McCord, B.E. (2003) 'Functional analysis of problem behavior: A review.' *Journal of Applied Behavior Analysis 36*, 2, 147–185. doi:10.1901/jaba.2003.36-147

Hanley, G.P., Jin, C., Vanselow, N.R. and Hanratty, L.A. (2014) 'Producing meaningful improvements in problem behavior of children with autism via synthesized analyses and treatments.' *Journal of Applied Behavior Analysis 47*, 1, 16–36. doi:10.1002/jaba.106

Hart, B.M., Allen, K.E., Buell, J.S., Harris, F.R. and Wolf, M.M. (1964) 'Effects of social reinforcement on operant crying.' *Journal of Experimental Child Psychology 1*, 2, 145–153.

Herz, B. (2014) 'Inclusion: Accessibility – except for children and adolescents with behavioural disorders?' *Vierteljahresschrift für Heilpadagogik und ihre Nachbargebiete 83*, 3, 185–190. doi:10.2378/vhn2014.art16d

Horner, R.H., Carr, E.G., Strain, P.S., Todd, A.W. and Reed, H.K. (2002) 'Problem behavior interventions for young children with autism: A research synthesis.' *Journal of Autism and Developmental Disorders 32*, 5, 423–446. doi:10.1023/A:1020593922901

IDEA (Individuals with Disabilities Education Act) (2004) Accessed on 10/02/2018 at https://sites.ed.gov/idea/

Iwata, B.A., Kahng, S.W., Wallace, M.D. and Lindberg, J.S. (2000) 'The Functional Analysis Model of Behavioral Assessment.' In J. Austin and J.E. Carr (eds) *Handbook of Applied Behavior Analysis* (pp.61–89). Reno, NV: Context Press.

Iwata, B.A., Dorsey, M.F., Slifer, K.J., Bauman, K.E. and Richman, G.S. (1982) 'Toward a functional analysis of self-injury.' *Analysis and Intervention in Developmental Disabilities 2*, 1, 3–20.

Karsh, K.G., Repp, A.C., Dahlquist, C.M. and Munk, D. (1995) 'In vivo functional assessment and multi-element interventions for problem behaviors of students with disabilities in classroom settings.' *Journal of Behavioral Education 5*, 2, 189–210.

Kates-McElrath, K., Agnew, M., Axelrod, S. and Bloh, C.L. (2007) 'Identification of behavioral function in public schools and a clarification of terms.' *Behavioral Interventions 22*, 1, 47–56. doi:10.1002/bin.230

Kincaid, D., Childs, K., Wallace, F. and Blase, K. (2007) 'Identifying barriers and facilitators in implementing school-wide positive behavior.' *Support Journal of Positive Behavior Interventions 9*, 3, 174–184.

Kittelman, A., Bromley, K.W. and Mazzotti, V.L. (2016) 'Functional behavioral assessments and behavior support plans for work-based learning.' *Career Development and Transition for Exceptional Individuals 39*, 2, 121–127. doi:10.1177/2165143416633682

Larson, P.J. and Maag, J.W. (1998) 'Applying functional assessment in general education classrooms – Issues and recommendations.' *RSE: Remedial & Special Education 19*, 6, 338–349.

LaRue, R.H., Jr, Weiss, M.J. and Ferraioli, S.J. (2008) 'State of the art procedures for assessment and treatment of learners with behavioral problems.' *International Journal of Behavioral Consultation and Therapy 4*, 2, 250–263.

Lloyd, B.P., Weaver, E.S. and Staubitz, J.L. (2015) 'A review of functional analysis methods conducted in public school classroom settings.' *Journal of Behavioral Education*. doi:10.1007/s10864-015-9243-y

Lui, C.M., Moore, D.W. and Anderson, A. (2014) 'Using a self-management intervention to increase compliance in children with ASD.' *Child & Family Behavior Therapy 36*, 4, 259–279. doi:10.1080/07317107.2014.967613

McDonald, J., Moore, D.W. and Anderson, A. (2012) 'Comparison of functional assessment methods targeting aggressive and stereotypic behaviour in a child with autism.' *The Australian Educational and Developmental Psychologist 29*, 1, 52–65. doi:10.1017/edp.2012.9

Menon, S. (2014) 'The EdAble Project: A Pilot Study into Supported Employment Using Self-Management Techniques and Assistive Technology for Adults with ASD.' Unpublished Master's Thesis, Monash University, Melbourne, Australia.

Meyer, L. and Evans, I.M. (2006) *Literature Review on Intervention with Challenging Behaviour in Children and Youth with Developmental Disabilities*. Wellington, New Zealand: Victoria University of Wellington, College of Education.

Moore, D.W. and Anderson, A. (2001) *Effective Educational Practices in the Development of a Centre for Extra Support for Students with ongoing Severely Challenging Behaviours, Their Teachers and Families. Literature Review to Inform Best Practice*. Auckland, New Zealand: Auckland UniServices Limited, The University of Auckland.

Moore, D.W., Anderson, A. and Kumar, K. (2005) 'Instructional adaptation in the management of escape-maintained behavior in a classroom.' *Journal of Positive Behavior Interventions 7*, 4, 216–223. doi:10.1177/10983007050070040301

Mueller, M.M., Nkosi, A. and Hine, J. F. (2011)' Functional analysis in public schools: A summary of 90 functional analyses.' *Journal of Applied Behavior Analysis 44*, 4, 807–818.

Nord, D.K., Stancliffe, R.J., Nye-Lengerman, K. and Hewitt, A.S. (2016) 'Employment in the community for people with and without autism: A comparative analysis.' *Research in Autism Spectrum Disorders 24*, 11–16. doi:10.1016/j.rasd.2015.12.013

Northup, J., Wacker, D., Sasso, G., Steege, M., Cigrand, K., Cook, J., *et al.* (1991) 'A brief functional analysis of aggressive and alternative behavior in an outclinic setting.' *Journal of Applied Behavior Analysis 24*, 3, 509. doi:10.1901/jaba.1991.24-509.

PBS Academy (2016) Accessed on 06/02/2018 at http://pbsacademy.org.uk

Rausa, V.C., Moore, D.W. and Anderson, A. (2016) 'Use of video modelling to teach complex and meaningful job skills to an adult with autism spectrum disorder.' *Developmental Neurorehabilitation 19*, 4, 267–274. Accessed on 22/05/2018 at http://doi.org/10.3109/17518423.2015.1008150

Reid, R. and Nelson, J.R. (2002) 'The utility, acceptability, and practicality of functional behavioral assessment for students with high-incidence problem behaviors.' *Remedial and Special Education 23*, 1, 15–23. doi:10.1177/074193250202300103

Santiago, J.L., Hanley, G.P., Moore, K. and Jin, C. (2016) 'The generality of interview-informed functional analyses: Systematic replications in school and home.' *Journal of Autism and Developmental Disorders 46*, 3, 797–811. doi:10.1007/s10803-015-2617-0

Sasso, G.M., Conroy, M.A., Peck Stichter, J. and Fox, J.J. (2001) 'Slowing down the bandwagon: The misapplication of functional assessment for students with emotional or behavioral disorders.' *Behavioral Disorders 26*, 4, 282–296.

Scott, T.M., Bucalos, A., Liaupsin, C., Nelson, C., Jolivette, K., DeShea, L., *et al.* (2004) 'Using functional behavior assessment in general education settings: Making a case for effectiveness and efficiency.' *Behavioral Disorders 29*, 2, 189–201.

Shattuck, P.T., Roux, A.M., Hudson, L.E., Taylor, J.L., Maenner, M.J. and Trani, J.-F. (2012) 'Services for adults with an autism spectrum disorder.' *The Canadian Journal of Psychiatry/La Revue canadienne de psychiatrie 57*, 5, 284–291.

Sigafoos, J. and Saggers, E. (1995) 'A discrete-trial approach to the functional analysis of aggressive behaviour in two boys with autism.' *Australia & New Zealand Journal of Developmental Disabilities 20*, 4, 287–297.

Thomason-Sassi, J.L., Iwata, B.A., Neidert, P.L. and Roscoe, E.M. (2011) 'Response latency as an index of response strength during functional analyses of problem behavior.' *Journal of Applied Behavior Analysis 44*, 1, 51–67.

Thompson, R.H. and Iwata, B.A. (2007) 'A comparison of outcomes from descriptive and functional analyses of problem behavior.' *Journal of Applied Behavior Analysis 40*, 2, 333. doi:10.1901/jaba.2007.56-06

Victoria State Government (2018) *School-Wide Positive Behaviour Support.* Accessed on 06/02/2018 at www.education.vic.gov.au/school/teachers/management/improvement/Pages/swpbs.aspx

Wallace, M.D. and Knights, D.J. (2003) 'An evaluation of a brief functional analysis format within a vocational setting.' *Journal of Applied Behavior Analysis 36*, 1, 125–128. doi:10.1901/jaba.2003.36-125

Yell, M., Drasgow, E. and Ford, L. (1997) 'The Individuals with Disabilities Education Act Amendments of 1997: Implications for School-based Teams.' In C.F. Telzrow and M. Tankersley (eds) *IDEA Amendments of 1997: Practice Guidelines for School-based Teams* (pp.1–27). Bethesda, MA: NASP Publications.

Chapter 8

DEALING WITH CRISIS AND CHALLENGING BEHAVIOURS

Brian Fennell and Karola Dillenburger

While job coaches for adults with disabilities are not behaviour analysts or therapists, they may at times experience crisis and behaviours that are challenging and should therefore have basic knowledge and skills to support their employee in contexts that are challenging for them. In this chapter, the case of Brendan[1] is used as an example to look at positive behaviour support as an evidence-based process to either deal with or better, to avoid escalation and crisis.

— BRENDAN'S STORY

Brendan is a young man diagnosed with autism spectrum disorder (ASD). During his school career Brendan acquired basic reading skills and some maths, including telling the time, following a schedule and using currency. At 19 years of age, Brendan began a job at a local coffee shop with the support of a job coach.

Brendan's duties included clearing tables, brushing the floor, emptying bins, stocking cups and cutlery, and sales at the cash register. The shop owner had been pleased with Brendan's job performance, especially his efficiency with cleaning up and restocking, but the job coach was called in on several occasions when things were not so satisfactory.

On several days over the period of a few weeks, Brendan became agitated and began shouting at the customers. Usually, Brendan was pleasant to the patrons of the coffee shop, and they enjoyed

---

1 Not his real name.

exchanging greetings and chatting about the weather. After enquiries by the job coach, it seemed that each of these incidents occurred during Brendan's shift at the till. He had completed this task before, with the owner close at hand. The job coach was informed that Brendan had been asked to do this task on his own, while the owner was out of sight, in the office at the back of the shop.

Brendan had been handling the till successfully with the support of his supervisor and job coach. However, on the occasions that Brendan was asked to perform this job independently, he became anxious as customers grew impatient waiting for their change. While Brendan was able to handle money and count it accurately, his maths skills for adding and subtracting the sums involved were not fluent.

The coffee shop owner wanted to keep Brendan in the job, but this shouting behaviour was not acceptable, or the business would lose customers.

Behaviours that challenge

While given the right support most employees with disabilities adapt to their work settings and employer expectations, there are some who will find it more difficult and, at times, engage in behaviours that are not appropriate. Therefore, it is important that a job coach has the skills to deal with a crisis and understand the function and management of challenging behaviours. They may also have to advise employers and work colleagues on strategies to prevent these kinds of behaviours from occurring.

Dealing with a crisis and challenging behaviours effectively is difficult (Arbuckle and Little 2004; Thompson and Webber 2010), and service providers must consider employee stress and high levels of staff turnover (Joyce, Ditchfield and Harris 2001; Robertson et al. 2005). Understanding and addressing these issues begins with defining what is meant by 'challenging behaviour'. The most widely accepted definition is:

> Culturally abnormal behaviour(s) of such intensity, frequency or duration that the physical safety of the person or others is likely to be placed in serious jeopardy, or behaviour which is likely to seriously limit use of, or result in the person being denied access to, ordinary community facilities. (Emerson 1995, pp.4–5)

The definition of behaviour used by behaviour analysts is useful in understanding challenging behaviour. Behaviour is defined as any publicly or privately 'observable and measurable act of an individual' (Alberto and Troutman 2009, p.423) that can be tested via the 'dead man's test':

> If a dead man can do it, it ain't behavior. And if a dead man can't do it, then it is behavior. (Malott and Suarez 2004, p.9)

Thus, the definition of behaviour is inclusive of the thoughts and inner experiences of the individual as well as the outwardly observable activities of the person (Skinner 1974). In other words, observable and measurable activities include those that are observable by an individual themselves, privately, and by others, publically. This definition of behaviour is contrary to the popular use of the term that is commonly limited to adherence to or a breach of codes of discipline (Dillenburger *et al.* 2010).

Sometimes the identification of challenging behaviour relies on a topographical definition, that is, the mere description of the form of behaviour (Arbuckle and Little 2004; McCready and Soloway 2010). This approach provides a list of specific actions deemed problematic, for example, aggression, property destruction, theft, repetitive stereotypical movements and self-injury (Westling 2010). The topography does not provide information related to behavioural function (Dixon, Vogel and Tarbox 2012), and tends to lead to hypothesising the origin of the problem to be within the individual (Lyons and O'Connor 2006).

In contrast, a *functional definition of behaviour* allows for behaviour to be classified as challenging or otherwise by noting environmental causes and contingencies, including the role of other actors (Emerson 1995). Thus, a functional/operational definition will allow on-the-spot decisions by the job coach as to whether an observed behaviour needs to be addressed urgently to ensure it changes for better workplace outcomes.

In Brendan's case, there were many behaviours that meant he was a valued employee. However, he had had several episodes where he shouted at customers. To define this behaviour topographically, we would need to know what Brendan shouts, how loud his 'shouting' is, and whether there are other behaviours happening concurrently with the shouting. A topography of this behaviour may include shouting in response to customers in a very loud voice, shouting in the vicinity of customers or covering his ears and talking loudly at the till, for example. A functional definition of Brendan's behaviour (i.e., loud and aggressive shouting directed at the customer at the register because Brendan is not confident to work the till by himself, or shouting for the owner to help, blocking out the criticisms of the customer with his hands over his ears because he has oversensitivity about the loud noise in the coffee shop) will give an observer a complete understanding of the target behaviour and variations of behaviour that may occur in this situation.

In the work setting, a consensus of the definition of challenging behaviour may be difficult to achieve, but colleagues and supervisors are usually able to give examples of specific behaviours (Ofsted 2005). So, while topographical definitions of challenging behaviour may be agreed on, they have notable limitations. For example, minor disturbance behaviours in the workplace may be reported as significant (Arbuckle and Little 2004), yet they may not be classified as challenging behaviours – for example, a single incidence of the behaviour may have limited severity but repeated, it may have a major aversive impact. Therefore, focusing solely on the topography of behaviour limits the inclusion of novel behaviours, so even slight variations are technically beyond the scope of the intervention (Cooper, Heron and Heward 2007). These problems are avoided in a functional approach to challenging behaviours, where the function, rather than the topography, is the focus.

The development of problematic behaviours early in life, for example, during school years, may result in special education placements or diagnoses of emotional, behavioural difficulties/disabilities (EBD) (Department of Education and Science 2005; Macleod 2006; Ofsted 1999) that require sustained and specialised interventions (IDEA 1997). If these issues persist when the student progresses through education, transition programmes, and eventually, adult services, they will need job coaching when they reach employment.

The estimated rate of challenging behaviour in young people with intellectual disabilities is between 10–15 per cent (Emerson 2001). Challenging behaviours in students with autism far exceeds the rate of those with intellectual disabilities; in fact, children diagnosed with autism are four times more likely to have clinically significant maladaptive behaviours (Woodman et al. 2014).

Autism is a diagnosis determined by persistent behavioural differences in social communication skills and restricted and repetitive behaviours (APA 2013). Although challenging behaviour is not part of the autism diagnosis, it can include behaviours deemed inappropriate, excessive or disruptive of activities (Matson and Nebel-Schwalm 2007; O'Reilly *et al.* 2010).

Job coaches who work with individuals who behave in ways that are challenging will need to be skilled in strategies that reduce the likelihood of these behaviours occurring, and in dealing with crises when they do occur. The frequent and intensive nature of this kind of behaviour (Matson, Fodstad and Rivet 2009) makes a focus on evidence-based interventions an important issue for professionals in employment and community sectors (Matson *et al.* 2009).

Purely reactive strategies for dealing with challenging behaviour have resulted in a punishment paradigm (Maag 2001), oftentimes in a very uniform manner irrespective of the actual behaviour (Munn and Lloyd 2005; Thompson and Webber 2010). Usually, the person engaged in misbehaviour who causes a disturbance for the group (e.g., even low-level behaviours, such as talking out of turn) is removed from the situation – for example, in school a child would be sent to the principal's office (Martinez 2009), and in an employment setting the person may be sent to the staff room. This reaction is meant to be a punishment aimed at reducing the problem behaviour, but it often has an opposite effect in that it reinforces the behaviour, that is, it increases the problem behaviour because the person learns that challenging behaviour gets them a break from work (Woods 2001). Functionally/analytically speaking, removal from the setting can inadvertently reinforce the problem behaviour through allowing the difficult and non-preferred task to be avoided.

This process not only reinforces an employee's misbehaviour; it negatively reinforces the behaviour of the team and the job coach as well. The job coach and the team get respite from the offensive behaviour by removing the person who engaged in the challenging behaviour, and this makes it more likely that they will repeat this response, possibly for much less serious problem behaviours (Maag 2001). This *negative reinforcement trap* becomes even more problematic when a care provider, employer or job coach submits to the demands of the person who is engaged in challenging behaviour as a means of 'keeping the peace' or re-establishing order. This cycle can produce an escalation of problematic behaviours through an inadvertent shaping process in which increasingly intense or extreme challenging behaviours are needed to ensure that future demands are met (Emerson 2001). Another major problem with non-functional reactive and prescriptive procedures is that they obviously do not improve the behavioural repertoire of individuals who engage in challenging behaviours, that is, they do not teach the person any new appropriate coping strategies (Maag 2001; Osher *et al.* 2010). Thus, addressing challenging behaviour or crisis situations without due consideration to behavioural principles can have the unintended effects of actually perpetuating or even increasing the intensity of the challenging behaviour.

A range of behaviour analysis-based interventions alleviate the negative reinforcement trap and address the needs of these employees (Maag 2001; Osher *et al.* 2010). The science of behaviour analysis provides the basis of procedures and techniques used to build socially relevant behaviours in schools and other community settings (Carr *et al.* 2002). This has been utilised to teach all sorts of skills (e.g., academic, social, employability) to children as well as adults with and without disabilities (MADSEC 2000; US Surgeon General 1999).

Positive behaviour support (PBS), one of the most researched behaviour analysis-based interventions for challenging behaviour (Carr *et al.* 2002; Maag 2001), offers useful procedures for job coaches who support employees with challenging behaviours.

Positive behaviour support

PBS is a preventative approach to problem behaviour that makes use of many behaviour analysis-based intervention methods, including functional assessment and analysis, shaping, prompting and positive reinforcement contingencies. Within the PBS system, data collection and analysis plays a pivotal role in assessing individual needs (Horner, Sugai and Anderson 2010). Another significant benefit of PBS is the clearly defined behaviour policy (Sugai and Horner 2002).

Traditional disciplinary methods commonly rely on management-imposed sanctions, while in PBS, consistent rules and consequences throughout the environment mean that positive behaviours are identified early and reinforced (Center for Positive Behavior Intervention and Support 2014). This approach tends to increase the successful inclusion of employees with disabilities (Carr *et al.* 2002). PBS works proactively along a multitiered system (Sugai and Horner (2002) that includes primary, secondary and tertiary prevention tiers.

Primary prevention tier

The primary prevention tier entails key support strategies for the whole workplace and all community members. The support team includes job coaches, employers, mangers, peers and in some cases, outside behavioural experts, who determine the necessary structures and strategies (Sugai and Horner 2002). Acceptable behaviours are defined, expectations of the worker and other staff are outlined, and behaviour-monitoring systems are put in place (Center for Positive Behavior Intervention and Support 2014; Cooper *et al.* 2007). Positive reinforcement and, if necessary, response-cost procedures (Cooper *et al.* 2007) are discussed with all clients and staff (Center for Positive Behavior Intervention and Support 2014). The clarity regarding expected behaviours and the consequences that are to be expected for rule-adherence or rule-breaking behaviours provides a predictable working environment (Osher *et al.* 2010) and a clear focus on positive outcomes (Safran and Oswald 2003). Primary prevention tier strategies that support the employment of individuals with disabilities include the following:

- Environmental adjustments that help to either avoid or manage triggers for challenging behaviours.

Brendan was hypersensitive to auditory stimuli (i.e., loud noises in the workplace). An functional behaviour assessment (FBA) determined that this was a cause of Brendan's problematic behaviour. His job coach was able to select from several intervention options for reducing the chances the behaviour reoccurred.

  - The job coach could introduce 'sensory awareness' hours. These have become popular with shops, cinemas and restaurants adopting quiet environments to support inclusion, and could be implemented during Brendan's shifts at the coffee shop.

  - A 'closed door policy' could be used to isolate noises from the kitchen or appliances from the seating area of the café.

- On the other hand, specific non-aversive background 'noise' could be utilised to mask the aversive auditory stimuli.

- Brendan enjoyed music, and so music could be played at a volume loud enough to block the aversive noise but not so loud to be disturbing itself, or Brendan could use a wireless headset on one ear, although he would still have to be able to focus on customers.

• Employees can be given opportunities to make choices.

- Employees could be given a 'task list' that includes all activities to be completed during a shift, but the order of task completion would be left to the employee to decide, with the stipulation that all jobs are done by the end of the shift.

Brendan's task list included the cash register and other tasks. He was able to work the cash register at the beginning of his shift when he was not tired and therefore more tolerant to sensory over-stimulation.

• Job coaches use frequent and specific reinforcers.

- The job coach, supervisor and mentor could adopt a high-frequency reinforcement approach.

For appropriate customer interactions and other successfully completed job functions, Brendan received frequent verbal or activity reinforcers.

Secondary prevention tier

The secondary tier of preventative support is mainly based on group work. The interventions are based on the functional assessment of the individual's learning needs and employees with similar needs are grouped together (Freeman *et al.* 2006). The focus of the group work is on building skills necessary for employees to successfully participate in the work environment. Intervention methods include using positive reinforcement, shaping of behaviours and direct teaching of deficit skills (Center for Positive Behavior Intervention and Support 2014). For example, several individuals may be engaging in inappropriate behaviours that serve the function of escape from difficult tasks. For these clients, a peer group can provide support for skills development and improving behaviour. Peer support can include creating an employee peer mentor programme, with experienced workers acting as training partners. Obviously, it is important that mentor and mentee are well matched, and that support is available from job coaches and/or supervisors.

> Brendan was given a mentor who had been working in the coffee shop for a year and who was able to perform the tasks Brendan was asked to complete. In addition, Brendan and his peer mentor were given a list of activities for the day's shift. Brendan was able to do some jobs independently while being supported by his mentor for the more difficult tasks.

If behaviour change is resistant to interventions at the secondary prevention tier, individualised support is initiated at the tertiary level.

Tertiary prevention tier

The third tier includes intensive individualised behavioural support interventions. Full functional assessments, including experimental functional analysis, are used (Freeman *et al.* 2006) with the aim of reducing persistent problem behaviours that are resistant to methods used at primary or secondary prevention tiers (Sugai and Horner 2002). In addition, specialised systems (e.g., environmental accommodations, individual monitoring and intensive skills instruction) are implemented (Center for Positive Behavior Intervention and Support 2014) along with individualised behaviour change strategies (Freeman *et al.* 2006).

At the tertiary tier, family and community-based caregivers of the employee need to be included in the support team, to ensure that the intervention is person-centred (Carr *et al.* 2002) and leads to cooperative decision-making, consistent behaviour monitoring and effective interventions (Freeman *et al.* 2006). The tertiary prevention tier includes some of the following strategies:

• Visual communication devices are used to ensure the employee can communicate effectively.

Brendan had problems when becoming stressed while interacting with customers independently at the cash register. Being provided with 'break' request cards, Brendan was able to ask for a chance to leave the stressful circumstance for a brief respite before returning to complete his task. These requests were monitored and, over time, reduced to increase job performance as Brendan increased his tolerance of the stimuli involved in this activity.

- A task analysis is constructed that ensures that all steps are completed and the tasks are performed accurately and in a timely manner. The task analysis needs to include 'start' and 'stop' points ensuring that the employee is taught when they should start a task and how to recognise that the job is finished. It also needs to include 'safety steps' that cannot be excluded from task completion. Task prompts can be created with a series of visual cues for each step of the task process.

Brendan took on the new task of monitoring and taking out the rubbish as necessary over the course of his shift. Along with the necessary skills for this task, Brendan had to learn when to start this task (e.g., he had to empty the bin when it was nearly full but not overflowing) and when the task was completed (e.g., after he emptied the bin, put in a new liner, and put the bin back in its proper location).

- Visual schedule and prompts are used, if necessary. Large corporations use this system with franchises to ensure consistency and quality across a large numbers of sites. This strategy can include a schedule for the employee to indicate the order of activities for the entire shift, including breaks, meals and opportunities to use the toilet.

Brendan was provided with a visual task completion guide for each job activity that he had not yet mastered. Some of these guides were located at his workstation while he carried other ones with him. This allowed Brendan easy access to his individualised schedule of activities for each shift, and he was able to track his progress and be aware of time/tasks remaining before he was finished with his work.

By implementing programme-wide preventative interventions (i.e., for all employees in a workplace) rather than individual behaviour management strategies to address the problem behaviours, PBS harnesses resources that are not available under traditional disciplinary plans (Sugai and Horner 2002). The behaviour support team assists employees with disabilities, job coaches, line managers and co-workers as well as providing training for programme implementation (Cole 2003; Daniels *et al.* 1999).

Conclusion

Individuals with disabilities are more likely to be excluded from all types of community resources, including schools, social programmes and employment (Stevens and Martin 1999). Behaviours that challenge compound the difficulties experienced by these individuals and their support staff. Positive behaviour supports, including FBAs, have been shown to be efficacious in maintaining adults with disabilities in employment (West and Patton 2010). FBAs are essential for PBS methods to be effective (Sturmey and Didden 2014). PBS plans that are based on FBAs include organisation-wide adjustments, small group work and/or individual instruction (Kennedy 2002; Wehman *et al.* 2014).

Job coaches who have regular contact with adults with disabilities who engage in challenging behaviours need to be trained to implement PBS programmes (MacDonald, Hume and McGill 2010; McClean *et al.* 2005). Despite the success of PBS programmes in reducing challenging behaviours for employees with disabilities, however, these programmes have not increased access to employment to a significant degree (Sturmey and Didden 2014).

References

Alberto, P.A. and Troutman, A.C. (2009) *Applied Behavior Analysis for Teachers* (9th edn). Boston, MA: Pearson.

APA (American Psychiatric Association) (2013) *Diagnostic and Statistical Manual of Mental Disorders, 5th edition* (DSM-5). Washington, DC: APA. Accessed on 10/02/2018 at https://archive.org/details/DSM-5

Arbuckle, C. and Little, E. (2004) 'Teachers' perceptions and management of disruptive classroom behaviour during the middle years (years five to nine)'. *Australian Journal of Educational and Developmental Psychology 4*, 1, 59–70.

Carr, E.G., Dunlap, G., Horner, R.H., Koelgel, R.L., Turnbull, A.P., Sailor, W., *et al.* (2002) 'Positive behavior support: Evolution of an applied science.' *Journal of Positive Behavior Interventions 4*, 1, 4–20.

Center for Positive Behavior Intervention and Support (2014) *Positive Behavior Interventions and Supports in Schools.* Storrs, CT: University of Connecticut, Center for Positive Behavior Intervention and Support.

Cole, T. (2003) 'Policies for Positive Behaviour Management.' In C. Tilstone and R. Rose (eds) *Strategies to Promote Inclusive Practice* (pp.67–84). London: RoutledgeFalmer.

Cooper, J.O., Heron, T.E. and Heward, W.L. (2007) *Applied Behavior Analysis* (2nd edn). Upper Saddle River, NJ: Pearson Education, Inc.

Daniels, H., Visser, J., Cole, T. and de Reybekill, N. (1999) *Emotional and Behavioural Difficulties in Mainstream Schools.* Nottingham: Department for Education and Employment.

Department of Education and Science (2005) *Special Education Circular 02/05.* Dublin: Government of Ireland.

Dillenburger, K., Keenan, M., Doherty, A., Byrne, T. and Gallagher, S. (2010) 'Living with children diagnosed with autistic spectrum disorder: Parental and professional views.' *British Journal of Special Education 37*, 13–23.

Dixon, D.R., Vogel, T. and Tarbox, J. (2012) 'A Brief History of Functional Analysis and Applied Behavior Analysis.' In J.L. Matson (ed.) *Functional Assessment for Challenging Behaviors* (pp.3–24). Tarzana, CA: Springer Science and Business Media.

Emerson, E. (1995) *Challenging Behaviour: Analysis and Intervention in People with Learning Disabilities.* Cambridge: Cambridge University Press.

Emerson, E. (2001) *Challenging Behaviour: Analysis and Intervention in People with Severe Intellectual Disabilities* (2nd edn). Cambridge: Cambridge University Press.

Freeman, R., Eber, L., Anderson, C., Irwin, L., Horner, R., Bounds, M., *et al.* (2006) 'Building inclusive school cultures using school-wide PBS: Designing effective individual support systems for students with significant disabilities.' *Research and Practice for Persons with Severe Disabilities 31*, 1, 4–17.

Horner, R.H., Sugai, G. and Anderson, C.M. (2010) 'Examining the evidence base for school-wide positive behavior support.' *Focus on Exceptional Children 42*, 8, 1–14.

IDEA (Individuals with Disabilities Education Act (1997) Accessed on 10/02/2018 at https://sites.ed.gov/idea

Joyce, T., Ditchfield, H. and Harris, P. (2001) 'Challenging behaviour in community services.' *Journal of Intellectual Disability Research 45*, 2, 130–138.

Kennedy, C. (2002) 'Toward a socially valid understanding of problem behavior.' *Education and Treatment of Children 25*, 1, 142–153.

Lyons, C.W. and O'Connor, F. (2006) 'Constructing an integrated model of the nature of challenging behaviour: A starting point for intervention.' *Emotional and Behavioural Difficulties 11*, 3, 217–232.

Maag, J.W. (2001) 'Rewarded by punishment: Reflections on the disuse of positive reinforcement in schools.' *Exceptional Children 67*, 2, 173–186.

MacDonald, A., Hume, L. and McGill, P. (2010) 'The use of multi-element behaviour support planning with a man with severe learning disabilities and challenging behaviour.' *British Journal of Learning Disabilities 38*, 4, 280. doi:10.1111/j.1468-3156.2009.00602.x

Macleod, G. (2006) 'Bad, mad or sad: Constructions of young people in trouble and implications for interventions.' *Emotional and Behavioural Difficulties 11*, 3, 155–167.

MADSEC (Maine Administrators of Services for Children with Disabilities) (2000) *Report of the MADSEC Autism Task Force.* Augusta, ME: MADSEC. Accessed on 10/02/2018 at madsec.org

Malott, R.W. and Suarez, E.A. (2004) *Elementary Principles of Behavior* (5th edn). Upper Saddle River, NJ: Prentice Hall.

Martinez, S. (2009) 'A system gone berserk: How are zero-tolerance policies really affecting schools?' *Preventing School Failure 53,* 3, 153–158.

Matson, J.L. and Nebel-Schwalm, M. (2007) 'Assessing challenging behaviors in children with autism spectrum disorders: A review.' *Research in Developmental Disabilities 28,* 567–579.

Matson, J.L., Fodstad, J.C. and Rivet, T.T. (2009) 'The relationship of social skills and problem behaviors in adults with intellectual disability and autism or PDD-NOS.' *Research in Autism Spectrum Disorders 3,* 1, 258–268.

McClean, B., Dench, C., Grey, I. and Shanahan, S. (2005) 'Person focused training: A model for delivering positive behavioural supports to people with challenging behaviours.' *Journal of Intellectual Disability Research 49,* 340–352.

McCready, L.T. and Soloway, G.B. (2010) 'Teachers' perceptions of challenging behaviours in model inner city schools.' *Emotional and Behavioural Difficulties 15,* 2, 111–123.

Munn, P. and Lloyd, G. (2005) 'Exclusion and excluded pupils.' *British Educational Research Journal 31,* 2, 205–221.

O'Reilly, M., Rispoli, M., Davis, T., Machalicek, W., Lang, R., Sigafoos, J., *et al.* (2010) 'Functional analysis of challenging behavior in children with autism spectrum disorders: A summary of 10 cases.' *Research in Autism Spectrum Disorders 4,* 1, 1–10.

Ofsted (1999) *Principles into Practice: Effective Education for Pupils with Emotional and Behavioural Difficulties.* London: HMSO.

Ofsted (2005) *Managing Challenging Behaviour.* London: HMSO.

Osher, D., Bear, G.G., Sprague, J.R. and Doyle, W. (2010) 'How can we improve school discipline?' *Educational Researcher 39,* 1, 48–58.

Robertson, J., Hatton, C., Felce, D., Meek, A., Carr, D., Knapp, M., *et al.* (2005) 'Staff stress and morale in community-based settings for people with intellectual disabilities and challenging behaviour: A brief report.' *Journal of Applied Research in Intellectual Disabilities 18,* 3, 271–277.

Safran, S.P. and Oswald, K. (2003) 'Positive behavior supports: Can schools reshape disciplinary practices?' *Exceptional Children 69,* 3, 361–373.

Skinner, B.F. (1974) *About Behaviorism.* New York: Alfred Knopf.

Stevens, P. and Martin, N. (1999) 'Supporting individuals with intellectual disability and challenging behaviour in integrated work settings: An overview and a model for service provision.' *Journal of Intellectual Disability Research 43,* 1, 19–29.

Sturmey, P. and Didden, R. (2014) *Evidence-Based Practice and Intellectual Disabilities.* Chichester: John Wiley & Sons, Inc.

Sugai, G. and Horner, R. (2002) 'The evolution of discipline practices: School-wide positive behavior supports.' *Child and Family Behavior Therapy 24,* 1–2, 23–50.

Thompson, A.M. and Webber, K.C. (2010) 'Realigning student and teacher perceptions of school rules: A behavior management strategy for students with challenging behaviors.' *Children and Schools 32,* 2, 71–79.

US Surgeon General (1999) *Mental Health: A Report of the Surgeon General.* Accessed on 10/02/2018 at www.surgeongeneral.gov/library/mentalhealth/home.html

Wehman, P., Schall, C., McDonough, J., Kregel, J., Brooke, V., Molinelli, A., *et al.* (2014) 'Competitive employment for youth with autism spectrum disorders: Early results from a randomized clinical trial.' *Journal of Autism and Developmental Disorders 44*, 3, 487–500. doi:10.1007/s10803-013-1892-x

West, E.A. and Patton, H.A. (2010) 'Positive behaviour support and supported employment for adults with severe disability.' *Journal of Intellectual and Developmental Disability 35*, 2, 104–111. doi:10.3109/13668251003694580

Westling, D.L. (2010) 'Teachers and challenging behavior: Knowledge, views, and practices.' *Remedial and Special Education 31*, 1, 48–63.

Woodman, A.C., Smith, L.E., Greenberg, J.S. and Mailick, M.R. (2014) 'Change in autism symptoms and maladaptive behaviors in adolescence and adulthood: The role of positive family processes.' *Journal of Autism and Developmental Disorders 45*, 1, 111–126. Accessed on 22/05/2018 at http://doi.org/10.1007/s10803-014-2199-2

Woods, R. (2001) 'When rewards and sanctions fail: A case study of a primary school rule-breaker.' *Social Policy Report 5*, 3, 181–196.

Chapter 9

COLLABORATING WITH EMPLOYERS

— *Lucie Procházková and Helena Vaďurová* —

Job coaches have two primary partners in their work: people with disabilities and employers. To successfully support either of these groups, being aware of their expectations and opinions is vital. This chapter focuses on employers and offers an insight into the perspective of those who have experience with the employment of people with disabilities. The chapter begins by contextualising employers' attitudes and experience within European legislation and member states' approaches to the enhancement of the employment rate of people with disabilities, which remains rather low. The chapter then presents an analysis of employers' experiences in the Czech Republic, based on interviews with employers.

Background from an employer's point of view

Work and the possibility of self-fulfilment are basic human needs and the right of every human being. Yet only a minority of employers considers it a natural thing to employ people with disabilities. When describing their motivation, employers tend to use terms such as social responsibility, statutory duty or a type of charity. People with disabilities belong among those groups that are marginalised in the labour market, as they face a number of visible and invisible barriers that make finding and maintaining employment more difficult.

For people with disabilities, as for anyone else, an opportunity to work and earn a living is crucial at both a societal and individual level. Yet people with disabilities have an employment rate reaching only 50 per cent of that of their non-disabled peers, and for people with mental illnesses the rate is even lower, at only 25 per cent (Erickson *et al.* 2014; WHO 2011). At an individual level, work is, first, a source of economic independence, and second, a source of self-esteem and a means of establishing contact with other people (Vinzer and Roth 2013). At a societal level, employment supports the broader community and social inclusion of people with disabilities (Doose 2012), and helps to reduce negative beliefs towards people with disabilities (Bieker 2005; Procházková 2014). Unemployment – especially long-term unemployment – leads to financial problems, impaired perception of time, limited social contacts and gradual loss of identity and meaning of life (Jahoda, Lazarsfeld and Zeisel 1975). Furthermore, when taking account of the economic perspective, the loss connected with not utilising the workforce of people with disabilities has been calculated for The World Bank as a loss of GDP of US\$1.5–2 billion per year (Metts 2000).

European Union (EU) countries have implemented measures to remove the barriers encountered in the labour market by people from marginalised groups (European Commission 2010). The most important recent international document is the *Convention on the Rights of Persons with Disabilities* from 2006, which was a follow-up of far-reaching laws prohibiting discrimination in the workplace based on disability (European Commission 2012). The Convention sets goals for the level of general understanding and ethos around a wide range of issues, including employment of people with disabilities, it obligates the signing countries to combat any form of discrimination in the labour market, to promote the right of people with disabilities to work (UN 2006), and confirms the importance of anti-discrimination legislation adopted by many European countries during the 1990s (Garbat 2013). The way individual countries enhance employment opportunities for people with disabilities differs, reflecting in part, at least, different countries' political, social and economic histories that mirror the general attitudes of society towards people with disabilities as well as their opportunities to enter the free labour market. There is a range of approaches in Europe, from an emphasis on mandatory quota systems (e.g., Poland, the Czech Republic, Greece or Italy) to approaches relying on constitutionally guaranteed rights, including the right to work (e.g., the UK, Sweden, Finland, Estonia; see Garbat 2013).

Policy models of employment of people with disabilities

There are two main approaches to the employment of people with disabilities: the *civil rights approach* and the *employment quota approach* (Garbat 2013); a number of countries implement a combination of these approaches (Greve 2009).

The civil rights approach is based on such underlying principles as equality of opportunity, the right to work and non-discrimination. Employment of people with disabilities is not imposed by any strict regulation, but society recognises the right to work guaranteed to every one of its members as well as the right to equal opportunities. Mainly richer European countries with a longer democratic history have adopted this system, where the economy can 'easily absorb the labour force of people with disabilities' (Garbat 2013, p.48).

The promotion of employment of people with disabilities under the quota system uses a system of rules and obligations instead. These have to be met by employers and are mandated by legislation. Who qualifies as an employer with such an obligation and the number of mandatory jobs for people with disabilities per employer differs from country to country, but the aim is to ensure a certain percentage of employment among people with disabilities. However, as a result, people with disabilities find themselves in the undesirable position of being perceived as vulnerable and in need of help; their disability is perceived as a factor that negatively influences their job performance.

Many European countries have implemented a combination of the two approaches, with an emphasis on anti-discrimination legislation together with some form of mandatory quotas (OECD 2010). Garbat (2013) points out that a flexible system, having certain normative rules together with the high motivation of employers, high funding and technical support to adapt workplaces, seems to be the most effective.

The social and legislative environment in which employers operate influences their attitudes and willingness to employ people with disabilities. As no system has yet managed to 'provide satisfactory results' (Garbat 2013, p.48), established cooperation between employers and organisations that specialise in supporting people with disabilities is a crucial factor in ensuring the successful hiring of people with disabilities (Gewurtz, Langan and Sand 2016). These organisations and professionals (job coaches, work assistants, supported employment agencies, counsellors, etc.) have a good understanding of the strengths and needs of people with disabilities and also employers' needs and expectations. They can connect employers with candidates who are suitable for the particular position (Gewurtz *et al.* 2016; Procházková 2014).

Employer motivations

For people with disabilities, finding success in the labour market is influenced by several factors: their readiness and motivation, available opportunities, the attitudes of employers and society, as well as the suitability of the work environment (Procházková 2015). However, the willingness of employers to employ people with disabilities remains the key to the successful integration of people with disabilities in the labour market. An understanding of the motivation and reasons why employers employed a person with a disability helps job coaches reach and motivate other employers. At the same time, job coaches who are aware of employer concerns and who appreciate perceived barriers can offer appropriate support to both employers and employees with disabilities.

In looking at employer motivations, the following questions arise:

- What motivates employers to employ people with disabilities?

- From an employer's perspective, what facilitates the employment of people with disabilities?

- What are the barriers and concerns of employers when employing people with disabilities?

We asked employers for answers to these questions to allow us to understand, on a micro-social level, how they conceptualise their everyday behaviour (Patton 2002). The research sample consisted of employers in the Czech Republic having experience in employing people with disabilities. Semi-structured interviews were held with 15 employers and human resources (HR) specialists. The interview questions were determined beforehand, although the design of the interviews was such as to also provide room for emerging topics (Cresswell 2009). The data obtained were subsequently grouped into the categories that arose from analysis of the employers' answers (see Table 9.1).

In order to see the findings in context it is important to understand the situation of the Czech Republic. In terms of the social integration of people with disabilities, the Czech Republic has a similar history to other post-totalitarian countries (Slovakia, Poland, Romania, Hungary, etc.). Prior to the 1990s, people with disabilities were only integrated into the labour market to a very small degree. Since then, their potential became recognised and people with disabilities began to be employed in the free labour market. A lack of direct or mediated experience and few examples of good practice have implications for employers' attitudes, prejudice and stereotypes that are the most difficult to change (Bruyére, Erickson and VanLooy 2006).

Against this background, we expected different findings than those from countries with a longer history of a diverse workforce, especially in Western Europe and the US. However, when compared to international research into employers' experiences and attitudes to people with disabilities, we found many parallels with the situation in the Czech Republic, and the concerns of the employers were very similar.

Table 9.1: Overview of the sources of motivation, facilitating factors, concerns and barriers perceived by employers

Category 1: Motivation employers have to employ a person with disability	Category 3: Factors facilitating in hiring and employing people with disabilities
• Personal attitude – willingness to offer an opportunity • Economic aspect • Impetus from organisations supporting people with disabilities • Individuals and social network • Expertise	• Open and active approach of the employer • Provision of information and support at the beginning • Support for the employee with a disability and for the team • Tailored work/employee • Own experience
Category 2: (Initial) concerns about employing a person with disability perceived by employers • Frequent unfitness to work • Inability/limited ability to cope with working tasks • Negative attitude of the working team • Fear of the unknown	Category 4: Barriers and challenges in employing of people with disabilities • Micro level – people with disabilities, employer • Macro level – legislative environment, societal attitudes, labour market

Motivation of employers to employ a person with a disability

The analysis of the interviews confirms that there is usually more than one reason why employers hire a person with a disability. Most often the reason was a combination of the employer's personal attitude and economic factors. For some employers the initial impetus was external, from committed individuals at a corporate level, due to economic considerations, or from recruitment companies that sought to find a suitable candidate for available positions without regard to the person's health.

At the individual level, the personal attitudes of an HR manager, for example, were most important and defined their willingness to offer an opportunity to people with a disability, as evidenced by Employer 5: 'Partly there were my own reasons and reasons of my colleague at the time; we wanted to give a chance to a person like this.' At the corporate level, management commitment was an important initial impetus. As Employer 8 explained: 'We are a cultural institution and doing this is part of a culture and of our own setting... I see it as the right thing to do.' Others defined their attitude as a social responsibility and moral duty: 'We want to be a socially responsible company and offer an opportunity also to others' (Employer 10).

The economic aspect means financial motivation, including seeking to avoid penalties for non-observance of disability hiring quotas and a willingness to hire an employee with the expectation that the job would be subsidised for a period of time. In the former case the companies sought to reduce the costs of failure to meet the quotas: 'When the management saw the figures showing how much we were paying for not having the mandatory employment ratio, they saw it was important' (Employer 10). Some of the companies were motivated by free support from non-profit organisations in administering the hiring of an employee with a disability, as well as the possibility of having the new employee paid from external funds for a limited period of time (e.g., the salary was covered by the labour office). Employer 2 saw this as 'having the person help us free of charge'.

Support from non-profit organisations is partly intertwined with economic motivation because, as described above, some non-profit organisations provide their services free of charge. However, the non-profit sector is also active in the sphere of awareness-raising and actively searching for potential employers. Some employers employ a person with a disability on the basis of communication and cooperation with non-profit organisations, as evidenced by Employer 2: 'It appealed to us...that the possibility existed at all.'

Employers often begin to consider hiring a person with a disability on the initiative of the jobseeker's social network, that is, relatives and friends, who make enquiries. In many cases, these experiences increase employers' personal commitment in creating the job and arranging the conditions that result in hiring and successful integration.

The need to find a suitable candidate for a position is a less common motivation which, however, is rather important from the perspective of equality. Some companies do not look for a person with a disability in the first place, but rather, seek a suitable employee. The candidate's professional qualities are essential for these employers, as is obvious from the account of Employer 8: 'It is important here whether he is a good lawyer...it's irrelevant whether or not they're disabled when they are good experts.'

Concerns about employing a person with disability

Employers have certain concerns when considering whether to employ a person with a disability. These seem to exist at three different levels – personal, organisational and financial – and were intertwined in the employers' accounts and in the analysis. A separate category was 'fear of the unknown'.

At the personal level, employers may be apprehensive that the team would not accept a colleague with a disability or worried that hiring a person with a disability would adversely affect the climate in the team. The presence of such a person may be perceived as a burden: 'We obviously had concerns that we could make life difficult for our colleagues' (Employer 4). Frequent absence from work may be another reason for reluctance to hire a person with a disability. In this respect, the employers may be concerned about an increased burden on colleagues that could have implications regarding the degree to which the team accepts the employee with disabilities.

Concerns at the organisational level could be related to frequent absenteeism due to ill health. In their narratives, employers described this as a problem that they had to address and that had an adverse effect on the company's performance (financial level). Employer 10 saw this as a burden on the organisation and its human resources: 'When an employee is absent, we need a one hundred per cent replacement for him.' Concerns about increased sickness and absence rates was present in almost all the respondents' accounts, although in none of the cases did it become a real problem when the person was actually hired.

Financial concerns were related, in particular, to negative expectations of the ability of the employee with a disability to perform their working duties, whether due to the disability or difficulty of the work: 'Sometimes I feared he wouldn't handle the environment he was in as I was aware of his social phobia' (Employer 2). Some employers mentioned concerns about lower performance in general. This was closely related to the need to pay attention to finding a suitable employee for a certain position or suitable work content for an employee, which was an aspect emphasised by many employers: 'The important thing at the beginning is to find the right position and the right person for that position. It's quite a challenge to combine these two things' (Employer 10).

On the other hand, some of the employers rejected this concern, stating that the corporate general practitioner (GP) assessed the candidate's health and hence fitness for the job: 'When the GP gives him the go-ahead and we can be sure that it's OK on medical terms… which is something we do not really understand…then we have no more concerns' (Employer 6). Also falling into the financial category is the apprehension that significant and costly alterations of the working environment would be required, a concern that was voiced many times in the employers' accounts. Similar to the concern about frequent unfitness to work, this concern did not materialise in practice.

In their accounts, the employers repeatedly expressed the unspecified concern of a fear of the unknown, that 'complications can always occur' (Employer 8). These concerns were most likely related to stereotypes about people with disabilities. These negative expectations were present more often and more markedly in the narratives of employers who had their first experience with employing a person with a disability. Most employers noted that their initial concerns were not confirmed, as illustrated by the account of Employer 10: 'Managers with experience confirmed that it actually bonded the team and that it was a positive thing to bring a person like this into the team.'

Factors facilitating finding and employing people with disabilities

There are many factors that have an effect on the success of a person with a disability at work and their integration into the working team. Measures that the employers find facilitating are aimed at all stakeholders in the process – the employer, the team and the person with a disability.

The open and active approach of the employer is one of the main factors promoting the employment of people with disabilities. In our study, the employers talked about the importance of their personal commitment, willingness to create or adapt the job and the working conditions for the particular individual with a disability: 'He's doing well what he's doing now; he understands the job and he does it without errors' (Employer 2). In some cases, this involves structural alterations, in others, adjustment of working hours or a transfer to some other position: 'For example, we have a colleague with a weakened immune system who has been provided with her own office and is exempt from services where she would be bombarded by bugs' (Employer 4).

Support in the event of a change or worsening of the person's health also falls into this category: 'We have an employee with a hearing impairment that has got far worse so we had to get a special telephone for her' (Employer 7). Employers who are committed to hiring people with disabilities and building the image of a socially responsible company may also target their existing employees. Employer 10 launched a targeted campaign appealing to employees that they should not fear to disclose their disability: 'We did an internal campaign and lots of people disclosed their disabilities.' Nevertheless, large enterprises especially emphasised that taking a responsible attitude meant strengthening the HR department.

Employers in our study considered that up-to-date, relevant information was a key factor. They also agreed that while there were enough sources of information, the employer must proactively seek information and also take account of the constantly changing legislation. In this respect, the employers appreciated free support from non-profit organisations. As Employer 5 put it: 'This is a big benefit for me because they actually administered everything for me. This would be too big a challenge for me as we only have one such employee.'

Non-profit organisations offer support in the initial administration, and even more importantly, afterwards, when looking for the new employee and helping them to familiarise themselves in their new job. This is an important task for job coaches and work assistants.

Employees with disabilities frequently need support for settling into the new job or in changing routines for various reasons, such as their health, and this support is not always provided from outside the employment setting. Some of the employers referred to support provided by a designated peer mentor at the workplace: 'We have set up a normal adaptation process here, where every single worker has a mentor who helps new employees with orientation in the job' (Employer 10). The system where every new employee has a mentor is almost universal in large enterprises, but not always available in smaller firms. However, provision of information was seen as the minimum support, preferably through an appointed contact person, as described by Employer 2: 'I told everyone that they could come to me if they didn't know anything.'

The strategy of 'tailored work/employee' refers to the employers' endeavour to define accurately the requirements of a given position in order to find an employee with the right abilities. In particular, representatives of small companies emphasised the positive effect that the match between employee and job position had on both the employee (i.e., enhancement of skills, satisfaction) and employer (i.e., motivation to employ more people with disabilities). Employer 5 described his experience: 'We initially had a concept and Mr N. gave it great dynamics so he actually helped tremendously also the position itself…he began to enjoy it, which was unthinkable before.'

Last but not least, previous experience with people with disabilities is a strong facilitator for inclusive attitudes and practices, not just in the working environment. Employer 10 emphasised that having contact with people with disabilities from an early age makes society as a whole more aware, tolerant and open, which, in his opinion, has implications in employment: 'It surprised me as well because I did not expect such a commitment and performance.' In addition to employers whose attitude changed as a result of first-hand experience, there are also those who have many years of experience, and employing people with disabilities is a tradition in their company. Employer 6 described the setting in his company as follows: 'Records were kept even before the fall of communism…we always employed them.'

Barriers and challenges in employing people with disabilities

Factors that complicate the employment of people with disabilities can be divided into micro and macro factors. Micro factors are those relating to an employee with a disability, their views of their abilities and willingness to learn, as well as the employer's approach. Macro factors include the legislative environment, the labour market situation and the attitudes of the majority population.

The employers mentioned two complicating factors at the micro level. The first was inadequate or absent understanding of the person's own abilities. For example, Employer 4 described it as follows: 'We have a gentleman who was offered a disability pension but he refuses to take it...it's a bit of a problem for us because he simply doesn't perform, he doesn't make it.' The second was related to the fear of disclosing one's disability. Many employees hide their difficulties for fear of losing their jobs or being condemned by others.

The employers thought that societal attitudes were changing for the better; nevertheless, they still perceived a certain aversion, distance, lack of tolerance and social conscience: 'Society doesn't seek to motivate people but rather to place barriers in their way' (Employer 8). The attitudes of employers reflected societal attitudes, 'If they're present in society, employers definitely feel the same' (Employer 8). The effect on people with disabilities, if they feel rejection, is uncertainty and apprehension in their own attitudes and this, in turn, promotes passiveness and learned helplessness.

The employers saw systemic barriers and challenges, for instance, in legislation, that Employer 2 described as 'rigid'. And, according to Employer 11, 'Studying the constant changes and what they mean for our employees consumes much of the time we would need for other things.' Administrative complexities and insufficient support from the government were often mentioned in the discussions. Employers were critical about the discrepancy between declared and actual support for companies employing people with disabilities.

Similarly, support from government bodies such as labour offices was deemed insufficient. Obsolete and rigid procedures and lack of information were the main sources of criticism. According to Employer 2, the information provided was of poor quality: 'I expected the labour office to be more flexible...in fact I never got anything other than general information, quotations from the legislation, etc.'

Employers with long-term experience spoke about changes in the labour market related to modernisation and about losing jobs that were once given to people with disabilities often or almost exclusively (e.g., switchboard operators, receptionists). Low fluctuation, a positive indicator of workplace stability and satisfaction, inhibits the creation of vacancies, thus reducing job opportunities for adults with disabilities.

Discussion

The focus of this chapter has been the motivation (i.e., mandatory obligation versus personal commitment), opportunities and barriers for employers of people with disabilities. Findings from a small-scale interview study in the Czech Republic were used to illustrate the points made in the review of the literature. These employers spoke about a combination of reasons why they had decided to employ people with disabilities.

The employers whose initial motivation was to meet the mandatory quotas said that financial incentives alone did not provide sufficient motivation for hiring a person with a disability. The employers' previous experience played a role in whether or not the employee with disabilities stayed in the company for a prolonged period of time or not. This included not just the employee's abilities and effect of work on their development, but also their degree of integration and functioning in the team.

Employers motivated by personal commitment or the endeavour to build a socially responsible company appreciated financial support from the state and professional and need-oriented support, in particular from non-profit organisations. Consequently, the motivation to employ a person with a disability was not purely economic (quota system) or personal (rights-oriented), and legislation or financial support in itself was not sufficient to increase the employment of people with disabilities (Gewurtz et al. 2016), although smaller companies were more likely to consider financial support a motivating factor. Overall, personal experiences, attitudes and commitment were crucial factors in the employment of adults with disabilities.

Garbat (2013) has proposed a flexible system of support from the state that relies on social responsibility, while providing support to a range of activities that promote the inclusion of people with disabilities in the labour market. Erickson et al. (2014) recommended the identification of a 'disability champions' among senior management personnel whose role it would be to promote the employment of people with disabilities in society, while Vinzer and Roth (2013) also considered it important to establish diversity as a core value of a company.

Personal experience with people with disabilities was a primary factor. Morgan and Alexander (2005) point out that employers who have experience with people with disabilities recognise more advantages (but also more concerns) than those without such experience. Furthermore, most employers who have employed a person with a disability are positive about the experience (Morgan and Alexander 2005), and are willing to employ a person with a disability in the future. They realise that they can improve their company image by employing a person with a disability who contributes to the personal development of all employees and team bonding.

The barriers and concerns of employers appear to be common in all European countries, and include high sickness rates, necessary alterations of the working environment and related costs, as well as the person's failure to perform the assigned working tasks (Baumgartner, Greiwe and Schwarb 2004; Gewurtz et al. 2016). These fears often stem from a lack of personal knowledge and stereotypical notions about disability (Allport 1992; Unger 2002), which influence employer and colleague attitudes (Kaye, Jans and Jones 2011; Kleynhans and Kotze 2010). Research has shown that concerns about costly and demanding alterations of the working environment for employees with disabilities is unfounded (Jasper and Waldhart 2012; Morgan and Alexander 2005); half of people with disabilities do not need any alterations at all (Bruyére et al. 2006; Hrdá 2007). Also, the assumption that people with disabilities will be more often sick or unfit to work was not confirmed (Jasper and Waldhart 2012), and usually, failure to cope with work-related tasks can be avoided by minor adjustments to content of work and/or working hours (Gewurtz et al. 2016).

Personal experience and examples of best practice are also determining factors in relation to concerns about the competences and social skills of people with disabilities (Morgan and Alexander 2005). Awareness-raising can counteract prejudice and is recommended in the form of internship programmes in which employees with disabilities meet the employer and colleagues (Erickson et al. 2014; McDonnall, Zhou and Crudden 2013). This first step provides initial on-the-job training for the new worker, which facilitates orientation in the new workplace, helps the worker, reduces uncertainty and concerns and allows the team to become mutually acquainted.

Close cooperation with non-profit organisations can transmit required information and support all stakeholders. It is essential for employers to receive up-to-date information and keep track of the legislation, because a lack of awareness can produce concerns and 'leave employers feeling uneasy about employing people with disabilities' (Gewurtz *et al.* 2016, p.138). Concerns related to the administrative burden and the time needed for becoming acquainted with mandatory requirements may deter especially small employers without HR specialists. However, employers are generally very positive about cooperation with non-profit organisations, especially in the initial stages of employing people with disabilities (i.e., hiring, assessing skills deficits, making necessary accommodations and addressing training needs) (Bieker 2005; Gewurtz *et al.* 2016).

Conclusion

People with disabilities face numerous barriers in the labour market. Their employment rate is influenced by their own attitudes, the attitudes of employers and society as a whole. These are, in turn, largely influenced by their experience including the support they receive from job coaches. Positive personal experience with a job coach significantly contributes to greater openness, understanding and efficiency for people with disabilities in the working environment (Kleynhans and Kotze 2010; Švaříček and Šeďová, 2007).

Although European countries have introduced various systems for promoting the employment of people with disabilities, none of these provide optimum results. Non-profit organisations play a significant supportive role in the process and job coaches have proved to be beneficial for employees and employers who use their services; one-third of employers stated they would not be able to employ people with disabilities without initial support from job coaches in their company (Procházková 2009).

Job coaches provide support to all stakeholders (i.e., employers, team and employees with disabilities). They provide information, disseminate examples of best practice and motivate employers. They guide employers and employees with disabilities through the process of hiring and job orientation and provide follow-up support and counselling (Pančocha 2013). If they have a good understanding of employers' concerns and expectations, non-profit organisations are able to offer tailor-made support and counselling, which proves to be a powerful tool in supporting people with disabilities to succeed in the labour market.

References

Allport, G.W. (1992) *The Nature of Prejudice*. New York: Addison-Wesley Publishers.

Baumgartner, E., Greiwe, S. and Schwarb, T. (2004) *Die berufliche Integration von behinderten Personen in der Schweiz. Studie zur Beschäftigungssituation und zur Eingliederungsbemühungen (Kurzfassung)*. Forschungsbericht. Olten: FH Solothurn Nordwestschweiz.

Bieker, R. (ed) (2005) *Teilhabe am Arbeitsleben*. Stuttgart: Kohlhammer Verlag.

Bruyère, S.M., Erickson, W.A. and VanLooy, S.A. (2006) 'The impact of business size on employer ADA Response.' *Rehabilitation Counseling Bulletin 49*, 4, 194–206.

Cresswell, J.W. (2009) *Research Design: Qualitative, Quantitative and Mixed Method Approaches*. London: Sage Publications Inc.

Doose, S. (2012) *Unterstützte Beschäftigung: Berufliche Integration auf lange Sicht*. Marburg: Lebenshilfe-Verlag.

Erickson W.A., von Schrader, S., Bruyère, S.M., VanLooy, S.A. and Matteson, D.S. (2014) 'Disability-inclusive employer practices and hiring of individuals with disabilities.' *Rehabilitation. Research, Policy and Education 28*, 4, 309–326.

European Commission (2010) *European Disability Strategy 2010–2020: A Renewed Commitment to a Barrier-Free Europe*. Accessed on 10/02/2018 at http://eur-lex.europa.eu/LexUriServ/LexUriServ.do?uri=COM:2010:0636:FIN:en:PDF

European Commission (2012) *Discrimination in the EU in 2012*. Accessed on 10/02/2018 at http://ec.europa.eu/commfrontoffice/publicopinion/archives/ebs/ebs_393_en.pdf

Garbat, M. (2013) 'European policy models of employment of people with disabilities.' *Journal of Social Research and Policy 4*, 1, 47–63.

Gewurtz, R.E., Langan, S. and Shand, D. (2016) 'Hiring people with disabilities: A scoping review.' *Work 54*, 135–148.

Greve, B. (2009) *The Labour Market Situation of Disabled People in European Countries and Implementation of Employment Policies: A Summary of Evidence from Country Reports and Research Studies*. Academic Network of European Disability Experts (ANED). Accessed on 10/02/2018 at www.disability-europe.net/

Hrdá, J. (ed.) (2007) *Zaměstnávání Lidi se Zdravotním Postižením [Employment of People with Disabilities]*. Praha: JÚŠ.

Jahoda, M., Lazarsfeld, P.F. and Zeisel, H. (1975) *Die Arbeitslosen von Marienthal. Ein Soziographischer Versuch über die Wirkungen langandauernder Arbeitslosigkeit*. Frankfurt am Main: Verlag Suhrkamp.

Jasper, C.R. and Waldhart, P. (2012) 'Employer attitudes on hiring employees with disabilities in the leisure and hospitality industry.' *International Journal of Contemporary Hospitality Management 25*, 4, 577–594.

Kaye, H.S., Jans, L.H. and Jones, E.C. (2011) 'Why don't employers hire and retain workers with disabilities?' *Journal for Occupational Rehabilitation 21*, 4, 526–536.

Kleynhans, R. and Kotze, M. (2010) 'Bestuurders en werknemers se houding teenoor persone met fisieke gestremdhede in die werksplek' ['Managers' and employees' attitudes towards people with physical disabilities in the workplace']. *Tydskr. Geesteswet 50*, 3, 404–418.

McDonnall, M.C., Zhou, L. and Crudden, A. (2013) 'Employer attitudes towards persons who are blind or visually impaired: Perspectives and recommendations from vocational rehabilitation personnel.' *Journal of Rehabilitation 73*, 3, 17–24.

Metts, R.L. (2000) *Disability Issues, Trends and Recommendations for The World Bank.* Accessed on 10/02/2018 at http://siteresources.worldbank.org/DISABILITY/Resources/280658-1172606907476/DisabilityIssuesMetts.pdf

Morgan, R.L. and Alexander, M. (2005) 'The employer's perception: Employment of individuals with developmental disabilities.' *Journal of Vocational Rehabilitation 23*, 39–49.

OECD (Organisation for Economic Co-operation and Development) (2010) *Education at a Glance 2010: OECD Indicators.* Accessed on 01/06/2018 at www.oecd.org/education/skills-beyond-school/45925258.pdf

Pančocha, K. (2013) *Postižení Jako Axiologická Kategorie Sociální Participace [Disability as Axiological Category of Social Participation].* Brno: Masarykova univerzita.

Patton, M.Q. (2002) *Qualitative Research and Evaluation Methods.* Thousand Oaks, CA: Sage.

Procházková, L. (2009) *Podpora osob se zdravotním postižením při integraci na trh práce [Support of People with Health Disabilities during Integration to the Labour Market].* Brno: MSD.

Procházková, L. (2014) *Možnosti pracovního uplatnění lidí s postižením – současné trendy v České republice a v zahraničí [Opportunities at the Labour Market for People with Disabilities – Current Trends in the Czech Republic and Abroad].* Brno: Masarykova univerzita.

Procházková, L. (2015) 'People with physical disabilities on the labour market – abilities required for work self-fulfilment.' *e-Pedagogium 201*, 2, 114–122.

Švaříček, R. and Šeďová, K. (eds) (2007) *Kvalitativní výzkum v pedagogických vědách.* Praha: Portál.

Unger, D.D. (2002) 'Employers' attitudes toward persons with disabilities in the workforce: myths or realities?' *Focus on Autism and Other Developmental Disabilities 1*, 1, 2–10.

UN (United Nations) (2006) *Convention on the Rights of Persons with Disabilities.* Accessed on 10/02/2018 at www.un.org/disabilities/convention/conventionfull.shtml

Vinzer, Y. and Roth, M. (2013) 'General attitudes towards employment of individuals with mental disabilities in Israeli society: The employers' perspective.' *Revista de Asistenta Sociala 12*, 3, 95–110.

WHO (World Health Organization) (2011) *World Report on Disability.* Geneva: WHO. Accessed on 10/02/2018 at www.who.int/disabilities/world_report/2011/en

Chapter 10

BEING A JOB COACH: INSIDER PERSPECTIVES

—— *Lyn McKerr and Marea de Bruijn* ——

This chapter provides an 'insider perspective' of what it means to be a job coach. A number of job coaches from across Europe offered their views and experiences in relation to their work, the successes and challenges, and their feelings about the employees they support, the organisations in which they work, the importance of their role and the future of their work. The job coaches who agreed to share their views responded to questions based on Appreciative Inquiry methodology. Given that all of these job coaches worked in the European Union (EU), their work was generally based on the supported employment model outlined in Chapter 1 and summarised in Chapter 11. For reasons of confidentiality, we do not name the organisations or the job coaches themselves, but simply present their comments under the relevant themes.

Appreciative Inquiry

Appreciative Inquiry (Cooperrider, Barrett and Srivastva 2013) is a strengths-based model that is mainly used for the management of organisational development or change and an individual coaching method (Bouwen and Meeus 2011; Subirana 2016). It was developed in response to the overuse of a problem-solving approach that had focused on challenges and problems. Based on principles of self-determined change, it offers an alternative focusing on and giving attention to strengths in an organisation. Giving attention reinforces positive behaviours and increases their probability (Cooper, Heron and Heward 2007). The primary aim of Appreciative Inquiry is to gain new knowledge, models or theories, while also resulting in a productive allegory that induces a positive proactive and constructive approach to management (Bushe and Kassam 2005). The job coaches who contributed to this chapter offered their comments in response to questions that were based on the Appreciative Inquiry model. Their comments are an illustration of the real work of job coaches rather than being a theoretical model, so they should be read as samples of the working lives of job coaches, not as guidance or 'how-to' notes.

Being a job coach in practice

As a job coach for people with disabilities, Jakub supports his employees through a number of stages, with an introductory phase where he gets to know the person, calling on the expertise of psychologists, job advisors and legal professionals when appropriate, and running group meetings. This allows him to build up a picture of their skills. Once the employees are in employment, Jakub keeps in contact to ensure the continuing success of the placement:

> My name is Jakub and I am originally from a small town. From an early age I was into social work. I was a volunteer in several NGOs and cultural institutions. I majored in Business and Technology, but production engineering wouldn't be my career choice. For nearly a year, I have been supporting people at risk of social exclusion in finding a job and staying in the labour market. I work for the project called 'A'. Our aim is to test the model of employment contract in several districts in [the country] and then implement it in larger cities. In the project, we work with a group of ten people who are over 50 years of age and have problems finding a job. What is crucial, our work is not just limited to finding a job offer for the unemployed – we are called 'guardians' by them.
>
> We begin our work with the participants by getting to know each other, and sessions with a psychologist, a job advisor, a lawyer and other professionals whose expertise may be of interest for the unemployed. Then, for several weeks, we run group meetings, where we can get to know each other even better, and first and foremost, we create a passport of competence. This is a document that describes participants' knowledge, skills and experience, based on which we can help them search for a job. At present, the majority of participants

work in various businesses, but for me the work is not over yet. I am in constant contact with the formerly unemployed and their employers, supervising the process, helping to solve problems and ensuring that their cooperation will last. (Jakub)

Pat has a background in providing support for young people with learning and behaviour problems in a residential setting. Employees with autism can face specific challenges in relating to others in the workplace (cf. Chapter 6). The job coach often has to act as liaison officer, for example, between employee, family and employer. Pat enjoys his work as a job coach and sees the role as wider than just supporting the person in employment:

I have been working as a job coach for 13 years. Before that I coached young disabled people with everything in their life (they lived in a group with eight to ten other young people with learning and behaviour problems as they couldn't live at home because of their problems). I like my work and try to help people with autism with their work and in their life. When a person with autism works he often has problems with how other people understand him, why he does what he does and what not. I am often the translator for colleagues and I try often to explain why things go as they go. (Pat)

Rebecca has been involved in working with adults with disabilities since she left school. She finds the work extremely rewarding but admits it has its challenges. While Rebecca works full-time, this needs to be flexible to meet the needs of the employee's job, and so her schedule can include weekends and evenings. In Rebecca's setting, the employee's placement begins with a referral. Rebecca has time to get to know the individual and, where appropriate, their family. As with the other job coaches, Rebecca occasionally seeks advice from a number of other professionals before she undertakes an informal situational assessment with the employee. Once the employee is placed in a job, she provides ongoing support, with the aim of developing natural supports through workplace integration by building relationships with colleagues. When the employee is established in the job, Rebecca steps back a little, but continues to monitor the situation, usually with meetings every four to eight weeks depending on the needs of the employee:

Well, I'm in my early thirties, I'm a farmer's wife and I have four young children. I've been working in learning disability and autism since I was 16 years old, and I've been a job coach for 11 years now, which I thoroughly enjoy. It's extremely rewarding, but it has its challenges too. You have to find the right job match, the right employer. It pushes me out of my comfort zone, things like having meetings with employers. I'm very comfortable, for example, with working in the learning disability area, but you also have to go to business meetings, carry out job matching, etc. Overall, I do enjoy it. It's fascinating, you see such a variety of employment, cafés, farms, offices…as you know, no two people are the same, so different jobs suit different individuals.

I work full-time, sometimes that might include weekend or evening visits depending on the job; you have to be flexible to the needs of the service user. It starts with a referral. I'd meet with the individual and the family, there would be multidisciplinary meetings to find out the individual's likes and dislikes, their strengths and difficulties, any medical information etc. to build the best support you can. Then we'd have a situational assessment – that could be one-to-one, if that was considered suitable – it would be very informal, like going for a tea or coffee, getting to know each other. It also gives me an idea of things like timekeeping, if they are comfortable out and about in public life, ordering, dealing with money – it gives a bigger picture of how they cope, of their communication skills. Then there's pre-employment training – their skills and expectations, interview skills, getting a CV prepared – putting together a plan for the future. In some ways, this is the most vital part – that preparation side of things.

Then there's the job-finding stage – job centres, preparing for interviews, job sampling, the 'job carving' role where essentially you're 'selling' the service, the individual's skills – and yourself! Just to get people on board. Not every employer is initially sure; you're persuading people to 'buy in', promoting the positives. Once people are in a job, the ongoing support is the unique feature of this position. It's about 'building their confidence', to make it easier, to learn the job with them, so it's as smooth a process as possible and develops natural supports in the workplace. So they end up integrating without even knowing, and colleagues have built a relationship as well. Then you're stepping back a bit, but we never leave – we'll monitor maybe every four or six or eight weeks, depending on the situation – it's very person-centred. (Rebecca)

Jordan really enjoys working with employees who have learning disabilities, cognitive disabilities, behavioural issues, autism, attention deficit hyperactivity disorder (ADHD) or acquired brain injury:

> I have worked as a job coach for more than ten years now. I coach people with specific needs in finding their talents for work, finding a job where they can use their full potential and coach them to stay in the job. I love my job. It is wonderful being able to help people find their talents and help them create a work environment where they can use their talents and get appreciated therefore. (Jordan)

Jenny began working as a job coach in 2009, immediately after graduating from university, attracted by the social values and challenges of the work:

> I decided to submit an application to [name of organisation] because I liked the social mission of the company in relation to the needs of disabled people in the labour market and their attempts to become independent in their work environment. The beginning was not easy since neither the cooperating companies nor disabled people knew how to handle many situations at that time. Therefore, the role of a coordinator was crucial in the relations between them and it is still necessary, both in supporting disabled people and in communication between disabled people and the people who employ them in the open labour market. (Jenny)

Contribution to the life and wellbeing of employees

The majority of job coaches felt that they had made a significant contribution to the wellbeing of the employees. This was mainly centred round the impact of a successful job placement, which helped with confidence and happiness in other aspects of the employees' lives. The job coaches talked about the amount of preparatory work that was necessary before someone who had been unemployed for a long time felt able to take the steps into employment. Making this step offered a profound sense of achievement, both for the employee and the job coach:

During my work there were many moments when I could see that my work made sense. During the first sessions most of the unemployed were rather scared and withdrawn. I can definitely say that these people were not ready to go back to work. Most of them declared readiness to take up a job but these were just their good intentions. It was only our sessions, individual and group conversations that let them open up enough to really change their lives and get back to work. A moment that I will never forget was a conversation with one of the participants held two or three weeks after she had taken up a job. From a scared, intimidated person she had become a self-confident, strong woman, who knew her value and knew what she wanted. It was evident the project team's actions had changed her attitude to life. (Jakub)

Sometimes these were small things, and sometimes requiring quite a lot of decisions, a lot of talking, and a great deal of time. Many issues I solve, I consult with an appropriate person in the company to whom our worker is assigned. I try to always keep positive relations with both a disabled person and a contracting party and to listen to both of them. I am never rash in judging something after talking only to one of them. I try to get a good understanding of a situation and to explain it. I do my best to improve the situation of people who I supervise whenever I can, thanks to which I know that, one day, in many cases I will be able to count on them. (Jenny)

Preparation for employment takes time and depends on the individual employee's specific situation. While the initial processes may be slow, once someone has settled into employment the job coaches noticed how quickly other aspects of their lives improved. For one young employee, her social life was restricted to sitting in front of the television before she took the first tentative steps to finding employment. This quickly opened up new horizons, to the delight of her job coach. Another employee decided to catch up with a deferred qualification, which was a very rewarding experience:

A young lady who only sat in front of the TV was looking for volunteer work, for two days a week. She excelled, started to do sport, met friends, lost a lot of weight and then received a paid job in cleaning. (Kim)

I coached a man with autism to work at his own speed. It took us a year but now he is at work in a company where he has completed his interrupted study programme. (Pat)

Very simply, to see the individual achieve their own goals, whatever those might be, for example, getting paid work, or if they have been very shy, building their confidence, see them getting new experiences, doing things they wouldn't have been doing without the support. I've been with some people for 11 years – over time you can see the progress, the positives and also negatives and offer support to get them back on track. (Rebecca)

The sense of achievement and pride in their own capabilities is reflected in the client's success in the workplace, something that is recognised and valued by the employer:

After a month, [my client] was not the same any more, he was funny, cheerful and smiling. He works with people where he does not hide behind a machine. The change is big, both in [his] perception of the surrounding reality and in his appearance and disposition. When I see him, I feel satisfaction that we managed to achieve so much. I feel that I did my job well. What is more, the company in which [he] works hopes that I will find them 'another [name of client]' during further recruitment. They even stress that [he] is even better than many of their able-bodied employees. This is a big distinction and satisfaction for me that my intuition proved right. (Jenny)

For other job coaches, resolving workplace issues was a significant moment in their relationship with their employee. Jordan coached an employee who was in work and a training placement. The employee frequently did not turn up for work, which indicated that there were problems. Jordan was able to identify the issues, for example, one of the teachers was not providing adequate feedback, and they found a way to resolve these:

I have an employee who worked as a painter and got lessons in school at the same time. It is a combination, where they go to school one day a week and work for four days a week. He had the best teacher, but it wasn't the best teacher for him. The teacher didn't say much, although my employee needed frequent confirmation and regular checks; so he felt alone and misunderstood.

At some point he got angry, he tried to fix this by himself but it didn't work. There were more and more issues for being sick, or for some other reason, being unable to work. I stayed in close contact with him and suggested a conversation with the secretary and planner of the organisation. So, we did [this] together [and he got a new teacher].

Working with a new teacher was a great experience and it gave him back the motivation for the work. Otherwise he would not have stayed there much longer. He would have been demotivated so much that he would have probably stopped his lessons as well [because] he felt alone and misunderstood. (Jordan)

Making job coaching a success

For all the job coaches, knowing and listening to the employee, working at their pace, were major factors in a successful outcome, whether this was securing a job placement, enhancing skills or resolving workplace issues:

You have to act out of the box, and become more than just a career advisor or a work agent. An average person is not aware of their competences. Most people whom I have supported thought that they would work in the same field as they used to, even though it might have been 20 years ago. The passport of competence is a powerful tool that shows a person how many things they are not aware of. A job coach is just a signpost that shows a proper way for development and opportunities that a job from a different sector may bring. But remember that no one can be forced to get a job. That is why individual and group sessions are crucial. Only after a couple of weeks, or even months, the unemployed become convinced that they are ready to take up a job. Even if it's part-time, it's still a big step forward. (Jakub)

I made connections with him and his way of making commitments and his speed of doing things. No pushing!!!!!! Staying in contact with him and being open and positive and honest and clear. Listening to the wishes and interests of the employee and inquiring together how to get the most out of work. (Jordan)

I talk a lot to my clients in order to establish their goals and capabilities, I devote a lot of time for meetings and I confront both of them. I care for creating a good relationship in which both parties are able to feel comfortable in expressing their needs. I try to delve into an issue to achieve a goal. I explain my decisions to the people I supervise if there is a need to do so. (Jenny)

I think it's down to being very person-centred, so that my support is tailored to that individual, they know I am there for the 'long haul', being there through each step in the journey, and helping them become more independent. It's this that makes the success, the rapport you have. It's not always easy but it pays off. (Rebecca)

Sometimes success was about thinking differently, building confidence and highlighting aspects of skills or experience that the employee had not previously considered. Where possible, resolving issues together, rather than the job coach taking control, meant strengthening the relationship. This led to positive outcomes for both the employee and their employer:

I listened to my employee and I left the direction as long as possible with him. I suggested something else at a time when he was ready for it, not because I wanted to tell him what the best thing to do was for him. We went together to the secretary and planner. My employee was a participant in this conversation although he was very happy that I did the talking for him. When the planner talked about 'occupational therapy' I was happy anyway. It was fine by me, as long as my employee got this opportunity. It was the best step ever! (Jordan)

Facilitating and maintaining effective communication between the employee and employer was also an important factor in job coaching success, especially where there have been workplace problems, and this can extend to all those concerned with the wellbeing of the employee, including family and co-workers:

Providing information and creating trust between the employee and key role players (team leader, co-worker, parents) together with my colleagues. (Alex)

The attention of many of the job coaches focused on matching the employee with a suitable job. The relationship between the job coach and prospective employer was of key importance. Any networking capabilities of their organisation were an advantage:

> Being open, in real contact, being with him and his fear of failing and at the same time also positive and looking at the chances that there are (however small they may be). (Pat)

For the employee, obtaining paid employment was important and significant, but this was not a 'one-way street', and there were also real economic benefits to an employer:

> For the wellbeing of my employee and of the employer. I knew what kind of an employer he was, where his heart was, so I found that for my employee. Besides that, I was also aware of the commercial facts of a company. It was not about 'occupational therapy' so I focused also on the fact that my employee was an employee who needed to show his productivity. He would [do so] by this change. (Jordan)

For some, the initial stages of job coaching required most of their attention, including thorough preparation for work, involving a number of professionals, continuing contact and the process of listening and examining each opportunity with the employee, and was an important part of the process:

> For our participant gaining self-confidence was a milestone. Sessions with a psychologist, where they worked on traumatic events in her life, were essential. Thanks to them and the meetings and creating the passport of competence our participant declared that she was ready to take up a job, proposed what this job could be, justified her choice and started looking for a job. Owing to our good relationship with the employers she managed to find a job almost overnight. At the moment she is still working there. Even though she is fast approaching retirement age, she is not willing to retire yet. She wants to keep the paid job and do some community work as well. (Jakub)

> I focused primarily on striving to increase the self-esteem of a worker, to make him believe in himself. This is the only way he can overcome

social barriers. A worker's correct perception of himself means a great deal. (Jenny)

Once the employee was in employment, it was important to ensure that they had the resources to cope with the demands of the job, building independence through careful task analysis, and this could take a lot of planning:

> After securing the placement it was about learning alongside the individual, the job analysis – so if you weren't there, they coped with the day-to-day demands – breaking the job down into steps so it wasn't so daunting – providing a schedule and visual aids to give them security, allowing them to keep on track. It's about making sure they know what they are doing, that they wouldn't panic if you weren't standing beside them! (Rebecca)

When they were discussing successes they had with and for employees with disabilities, all job coaches emphasised the importance of trust in the relationship with their employees that was built up over a period of time, with patience and care. Job coaches recognised that good understanding of the function of challenging behaviour allowed for developing strategies, and carrying out a task analysis helped an employee work though their problems:

> The three most important things were: trust that was earned during sessions; making a person become fully aware that they are ready to take up a job; [and] being in touch before, during and after their taking up a job. (Jakub)

> For example, with my employee with autism who was working in an admin position, she had really good qualifications but couldn't answer the phone – it took a long time to get her to talk about why this was, it went back to 'practising' interviews at school where a teacher had overloaded her with questions. We developed strategies, broke down the tasks, drafted some 'key phrases' which helped her cope with phone calls and avoid panic. (Rebecca)

Trust was achieved through listening to the employee's concerns, and through offering tailored solutions that considered individual strengths and challenges. Keeping in touch at all stages of the relationship was crucial. Continued contact, even after a successful placement, offered the opportunity for discussion and resolution of any issues. As part of building a network of personalised support, getting the involvement of other significant people in the employee's life, such as close friends or family, had positive outcomes. Developing the employee's confidence was a major step in achieving success in a job placement, even if this took time. As well as offering positive reinforcement, resolving issues that challenge the employee was also an important part of building individual confidence:

> Understanding, if it comes to problems that are a limitation for the person. Willingness to listen to a person and time devoted, in order to show that the person you work with is important for you. (Jenny)

> Being person-centred, with the support tailored to the individual... Getting to know that person, not only the family but [also] other people involved in their life. Knowing their strengths and also their difficulties, and working with them to resolve those (Rebecca)

> Building trust, give compliments and to challenge. (Kim)

Most of the job coaches thought that employment stability, along with economic viability and job satisfaction, were the best indicators of successful job coaching, and they continued to keep in contact with their individual employees:

> As I am still in touch with people who can make a living due to our joint work, I know that they are satisfied, they do work and not try to avoid it. I believe that this pro-work, positive attitude is crucial, because, even if, for whatever reason, you become unemployed again, you will be able to get a new job somewhere else. I consider developing this proactive attitude as my biggest success as a job coach. (Jakub)

> ...When a person talks to me willingly and openly – I know that he/she trusts me and shares observations with me concerning a job. (Jenny)

> Life became meaningful to her again. (Kim)

It is successful when the employee and team leader are both satisfied in the long term (one to five years after the contract has been signed). (Alex)

If my employee is happy in his job and is grateful to me about him getting there…[in this instance] he is still working there, and he and the employer are both very happy. (Jordan)

For some job coaches, success was also measured by the employee's positive attitude to their own employability, something that contrasts with the negative self-image many had when they initially met:

If my employee is happy in his job and is grateful to me about him getting there. In this case, the company went bankrupt, but together we found a new job right away. With our experience of the first job we were able to tell what would work for my employee. He could tell by himself what it was he needed in the coaching from his colleagues and teacher on the work floor. It was great to notice how good his experience had been with his former employer and how it helped him in his new job. He is still working there, and he and the employer are both very happy. (Jordan)

Some of the job coaches knew their work had been effective when success in employment was reflected in the employee's attitude to their life outside work, and when co-workers admired and supported an individual's personal growth. Some of the employees had led very restricted social lives, perhaps because they felt their disability created barriers, and their workplace confidence greatly increased their ability to engage with others:

When goals are met – you see the results, and the progression in an individual – they grow and develop, you notice the impact of so-called 'soft outcomes' like confidence etcetera, the difference it makes to their lives. With my autism referrals, for example, we would find there are fewer opportunities, fewer things to attend than there are for people with learning disabilities. So they would be doing almost nothing else all week, and the job gives them that self-determination and sense of self-worth. When you see someone open up, when staff members say to you 'She's a different girl now to when she first started', you know it's all worthwhile. (Rebecca)

Valuing the work as a job coach

Most of the job coaches valued the personal successes and effectiveness as a job coach, in particular the ability to bring people from different backgrounds together to improve the financial and social aspects of life for their employees. The ability to successfully manage communications with potential employers was a valued aspect of job coaching:

> Being the one who is capable of getting all the relevant members of the system together in one room if necessary for the success of the match between employee and employer. (Jordan)

> Managing the relationship between the employee, co-worker and team leader. (Alex)

> I also appreciate the cooperation with employers. They are the other party of this partnership. Employers become increasingly aware of the seriousness of the labour market situation: the change from employer's market to employee's market. They continue to select the best candidates for specific positions, and thanks to a job coach it is possible to quickly fill in a vacancy with an appropriate person. (Jakub)

> I see that, very often, there is lack of courage in a relationship between an employer and an employee with regard to expressing their own needs, and a job coach fills this gap. He acts as an intermediary between an employer and a worker who is able to solve many disputed matters. (Jenny)

The job coaches valued getting to know the employees well and watching them take on and enjoy new responsibilities. The complexity of the role, while challenging, was also very rewarding, and the depth of knowledge and empathy required of a job coach was important:

> Again, it's the positive impact on the service user – you have the knowledge that someone's life is better because they have a job coach and a job that meets their employment needs. (Rebecca)

Contact with employees and letting them take a step in the positive direction. (Kim)

Getting the chance to learn about all the people I accompany and to learn a little bit of all these working environments where they find their jobs. (Jordan)

First and foremost, I must emphasise that a job coach is neither a work agent nor a rigid employment officer. It's a whole new dimension. It's a person who not only helps to find a job but also gets to know people, their approach to life, their skills and weaknesses. The ability to work with a human being and for a human being is crucial in this profession. (Jakub)

The job coaches gained energy from seeing the employee's personal happiness in their new occupation. Some elaborated on how their employee's success had given them a real sense of achievement. This was particularly true when the initial situation looked unpromising for the employee, whose skills and confidence were then brought out through the expertise of the job coach:

When an employee is happier than our first meeting. (Kim)

When the employee is satisfied and happy in the specific organisation. (Alex)

I get the most positive energy from the smiles of people I work with. And they smile because my work is adjusted to their skills and needs. I am happy when someone thanks me for help and says how their new job has changed their lives, why they are happy and how their family relations have improved, etc. (Jakub)

I would say that most energy comes from the thrill of success – when someone not only achieves but [also] maintains their employment – definitely! (Rebecca)

Being able to accompany people in finding their strength and their talents to work to their full potential. To bring out these strengths and talents of my employees brings a lot of energy to the coaching sessions. It's nice to see how the original 'hidden' situation can change to see possibilities and the steps to take for getting to work. (Jordan)

Positive solutions, people to whom I matter and who are happy to see me, who are always willing to talk to me, to share their joy with me. People supporting my work are also very important. (Jenny)

Dreams for 'miracles' for the future of job coaching

For most of the job coaches, their dream for the future of job coaching was a radical change in employers' attitudes so that they would actively seek out employees with disabilities. Job coaches hoped that in the future agencies that provide employment support and job coaching would be approached for help in finding suitable employees to fill posts rather than having to 'carve out' worthwhile positions for employees with disabilities:

That all employers have a passion for workers with a disadvantage in the labour market. (Kim)

I think the miracle would have to be the employers wanting the service, coming along and saying, 'Who have you got?' and automatically seeing the need, all being of the same mindset. That it would be the norm in employment – considering us when filling job vacancies, asking us to send people along for interview – and they would all know about our services already! (Rebecca)

Employers are open to all. I can come up with an employee and apply for a job and the employer is able to see the talents of my employee and how they could fit in the job or part of the job or the company. If this happens, will we still speak of people with a work restriction? (Jordan)

Alex was self-critical, saying that for her the miracle would be that, overnight, job coaches would have an instant insight into the employment needs of individuals, a position that normally involved a lengthy and sometimes challenging journey for everyone involved:

When I am able to fully understand my employee. (Alex)

Jakub thought that the most welcome miracle would be if the specialist approach involved in job coaching was applied much more widely to everyone who required support finding employment:

> In my opinion, job coaching should be implemented in the Employment Services system. If I woke up one morning and saw that in the Employment Office the employees talk to people, conduct group activities and various groups visit psychologists, then I would know that a miracle had happened. (Jakub)

Perhaps more pragmatically, Jenny felt the most miraculous event would be that all issues would be easily resolved without her, but happily acknowledges that continuing contact (even out of hours) is an indication that her role is important and worthwhile:

> I think that it would be a miracle to see no missed calls on my phone from a worker and no emails from a contracting party saying that a company needs support in some issues… However, if I did not see them, I would feel that I am not needed any more, which would mean that my job is done, and everyone is doing just fine without me. Every day, even on my days off, there are some missed calls and emails, it means that I always have to be alert and someone on the other side is waiting for me and counting on my support – whenever there is a need for it. (Jenny)

Conclusion

This chapter has offered a brief glimpse into the life and work of job coaches from an insider perspective. Using Appreciative Inquiry-based questions, a number of job coaches from across Europe described their experiences, their work setting, their successes and their dreams. It soon becomes apparent that these job coaches are highly committed and caring individuals. Their personal strengths and experience as well as their training enabled them to support employees with disabilities to prepare for employment, find jobs and maintain their contributions to the labour market. This chapter has shown that job coaches as well as employees benefit from successful job coaching.

References

Bouwen, G. and Meeus, M. (2011) *Vuur Werkt. Met Talent Toekomst Maken.* Houten, NL: Lannoo Campus.

Bushe, G.R. and Kassam, A.F. (2005) 'When is appreciative inquiry transformational? A meta-case analysis.' *Journal of Applied Behavioral Science 4*, 2, 161–181. Accessed on 22/05/2018 at http://doi.org/10.1177/0021886304270337

Cooper, J., Heron, T. and Heward, W. (2007) *Applied Behaviour Analysis* (2nd edn). Upper Saddle River, NJ: Pearson Prentice Hall.

Cooperrider, D.L., Barrett, F. and Srivastva, S. (2013) 'Social Construction and Appreciative Inquiry: A Journey in Organizational Theory.' In D. Hosking, P. Dachler and K. Gergen (eds) *Management and Organization: Relational Alternatives to Individualism* (2nd edn) (pp.157–200). Aldershot: Avebury.

Subirana, M. (2016) *Flourishing Together: Guide to Appreciative Inquiry Coaching.* Alresford: O-Books, John Hunt Publishing Ltd.

Chapter 11

TRAINING JOB COACHES: FRAMEWORK, PRINCIPLES AND PRACTICAL ILLUSTRATIONS

Marea de Bruijn

This chapter focuses on useful principles for training job coaches in a European framework. In most of Europe, job coaching is based on the supported employment model (see also Chapter 1), including engagement of the person with disabilities, vocational profiling, job finding, employer engagement and on-/off-the-job support. Within the support strategy the situation of the employee with disabilities is central to ensure opportunities to work in the open labour market. These opportunities are created and utilised, while focusing on the strengths and needs of the individual. The involvement of the support network, including family, therapists and employers, is important for successful and sustainable labour market participation. This multidisciplinary approach needs to be integrated into the training of job coaches.

The chapter starts with a brief review of the supported employment model within the context of a changing labour market, and elaborates on the changing role of the job coach. This is followed by a general outline of training programmes that ensure job coaches are prepared for best possible service delivery as well as their own occupational needs. Finally, some methodological examples are presented; while these serve as illustrations and practical guidance, they need adaptation to individual situations and respective cultures and social care system frameworks.

Framework for training job coaches: supported employment model

Job coaching is based on the supported employment model devised by Wehman and Kregel (1995), who looked for alternatives to the sheltered workshops that were prevalent in the mid-1980s. According to the European Union of Supported Employment (EUSE 2010, p.9), supported employment is defined as 'providing support to people with different disabilities...to secure and maintain paid employment on the open labour market.' This definition is generally accepted (with some modifications) and has three levels of supported employment:

- paid employment

- employment on the open labour market

- employment with ongoing support.

People with disabilities who strive to access the job market may require the support offered by job coaches. While the role of job coaches is described and defined throughout this book, 'there is a lack of consistency, guidance and training materials for professionals and service providers employed in the field of Supported Employment for disabled/disadvantaged people' (EUSE 2010, p.3). This chapter focuses mainly on the training of job coaches within the supported employment framework (cf. Noloc 2018).

In order to implement the values and guiding principles of supported employment, in accordance with EUSE's standards of good practice, a process of support for people with disabilities has been adopted that typically includes the following stages:

1. Employee/client engagement

2. Vocational profiling

3. Job finding

4. Employer engagement

5. On-/off-the-job support (EUSE 2010; PFON 2015).

1. Employee/client engagement

Job coaches for people with disabilities aim to build a constructive employee–job coach relationship that corresponds with the employee's competences and contributes to their personal and skills development. Within this employee–job coach relationship, the interaction of the job coach is characterised by a respectful and reciprocal attitude towards the employee. In general, the job coach aims to stimulate the interest of the employee in employment by introducing them to the aims, principles and stages of supported employment, explaining the role of the job coach in the process, and ensuring that opportunities are opening up for the employee (Noloc 2018).

2. Vocational profiling

From the very beginning of the vocational profiling process, the intake and assessment activities of a job coach must be person-centred, and should reflect the employee's individual characteristics, fully respecting of their needs and wishes (Noloc 2018; PFON 2015). In line with principles of self-determination, empowerment and choice, the job coach and the employee together determine goals and a plan of action (Maastricht University 2018). During the whole process, and in particular when it comes to formal and legal conditions related to employment, the employee's social and professional network should be involved (PFON 2015).

3. Job finding

On the basis of the employee profile, the job coach helps the employee to find a suitable job (PFON 2015). A job coach may also assist in creating a curriculum vitae and writing applications or elicit assistance from other public agencies or other institutions, for example, for job interview skills training. In order to identify potential employment settings, the job coach needs to be familiar with local services that offer support in labour market integration and company disability and social responsibility policies (these vary locally or nationally, from pay cheque subsidies to supportive workplace technology and various models of job coaching).

4. Employer engagement

An important element of the role of a job coach is engagement with potential employers to encourage them to see the benefits of employing someone with a disability. This activity can be more general, such as talking more widely about employees with disabilities, or it can be specific 'job carving', such as creating a new job or customising job duties in relation to a particular employee (BASE 2018).

Of course, the job coach has to be knowledgeable and realistic about the skills, motivation and abilities and challenges of the employee. In other words, the job coach identifies realistic employment opportunities within the context of necessary supports, including job coaching and other professional, technical, infrastructural, logistical provisions for the person, the employer and other colleagues. The conditions of the employment, the funding, as well as the most effective communication and workplace integration strategies need to be negotiated. Finally, the job coach should ensure that the information about the agreements between the employer and the employee are shared with the relevant social and professional support network. Here, the fundamental principle of autonomy dictates how much of the employee's medical etc. situation is shared with the employer, colleagues and other third parties. In practice, this may lead to suboptimal solutions from a labour market integration perspective. For example, an employee with epilepsy will not be able to work with fast-moving machines and drive vehicles, and a diagnosis of schizophrenia imposes restrictions on shift work. If an employee decides not to allow communication about their medical condition, a work placement may not be realised. These outcomes are undesirable and there may be cases in which close cooperation, for example, with therapists, might alleviate disclosure-associated fears, opening communication and thus opportunities. However, individual autonomy must be respected. The job coach's role and responsibility is to assess an employee's preferences and to proactively avoid or minimise frustration on both sides.

5. On-/off-the-job support

Finally, the job coach and the employee have to agree a coaching plan that is based on the core qualities and specific support needs of the employee, taking into account job tasks, practical necessities of the workplace, as well as the corporate culture of the employer (i.e., standards, values and unwritten rules). This plan should contain goals that are specific, measurable, attainable, relevant and time-based (SMART), with attention to the specific needs, talents and challenges of the employee (BASE 2018), for example, planning and securing transport to and from work, choosing the right attire for work, using support staff and technology, preparing the daily schedule and communicating with colleagues and managers. Setting SMART goals and outlining a clear plan on how to achieve them, including all practical parts of the job, makes it possible for the employee to be responsible for their own progress as much as possible. Furthermore, it provides predictability for colleagues and employers and achieves better labour market integration of people with disabilities.

On-the-job coaching also includes job-related skills training and may include the design and implementation of a clear task analysis. While this methodology has its origins in the scientific discipline of Applied Behaviour Analysis (ABA) (Cooper, Heron and Heward 2007), it is widely used in training and management (Usability 2018). A hierarchical task analysis is a list that identifies step-by-step the necessary skills to complete a task. This must be developed and agreed on by the job coach, employer and employee, keeping in mind the individual's condition. Thus, they allow the employee to develop the necessary skills to become a productive member of the team.

On-the-job coaching also means that the job coach may help to identify a co-worker who can act as a mentor for the employee, thus organising a natural support system within the employment setting and identifying and reinforcing the employee's social skills that are necessary to adapt to the workplace. In some cases, companies already have a mentoring system for new employees in general, and existing structures can be used and adapted by job coaches.

Off-the-job coaching means that the job coach may also have a role in supporting the individual in reconciling their new role as employee with other activities, such as attending a support centre or additional classes, or developing their hobbies and interests. As this also touches the functions of other professionals who may be better qualified or who have a defined mandate, the job coach has to know the limits of their role.

By adhering to these five guiding principles of supported employment, the job coach constitutes a pivotal role of bridging between the employee, colleagues, employer and social support network in a changing labour market (cf. BASE 2018; EUSE 2010; Noloc 2018).

Principles of training job coaches

The adoption of the United Nations Convention on the Rights of Persons with Disabilities (CRPD; UN 2006) has ensured that employment is one of eight major strategic goals with regards to people with disabilities in most countries across the world. Consequently, it provides the guiding principles that underpin the work and training of job coaches. Initially, many countries introduced a quota arrangement aimed at behavioural change at employer levels (Sargeant, Radevich-Katsaroumpa and Innesti 2016); however, the aim is that inclusion becomes the norm rather than the exception (see also Chapter 9 of this book). A job coach needs to be knowledgeable and skilful in securing effective support, not only in the workplace, but also in the local and national bureaucratic and administrative environment.

While policy and procedures for the employment of people with disabilities differ in each country, the European Commission has set out the overarching principles of equality and rights:

> Everyone has the right to timely and tailor-made assistance to improve employment or self-employment prospects. This includes the right to receive support for job search, training and re-qualification... People with disabilities have the right to income support that ensures living in dignity, services that enable them to participate in the labour market and in society, and a work environment adapted to their needs. (European Commission 2018, pts 4, 17)

People with disabilities are employed in all professional areas. However, the level of formal qualification and the work they perform often differs from the tasks of those without disabilities. People with disabilities frequently experience lower levels of autonomy and are allocated work that is judged as less varied and innovative as work that is allocated to non-disabled people (Maastricht University 2018). As the labour market shifts towards a more inclusive pattern of employment, the focus of the job coach shifts from matching and coaching the jobseeker and the employer to ensuring sustainable employment relationships and achieving inclusion and equality for people with disabilities. With more equality for people with disabilities comes more pressure to perform, driven by employer-led concerns related to profitability and economic principles. Those may be partially or totally counterbalanced by state-funded measures to support the employment of people with disabilities.

These developments require complex adaptations to the role for the job coach that need to be reflected in their training. The job coach must be able to take an organisational perspective that requires expertise in relation to social enterprise and/or business management. The role of the job coach thus tends to evolve more and more in the direction of recruiter or relationship manager, alongside that of on- and off-the-job coaching. The overall context surrounding the employee and the employer may become the main focus, including bringing on board stakeholders and developing a support social network for the employee.

The job coach who is dealing with these tensions takes on more of the role of consultant in employee relations in the network (around the client) than individual coach. Being able to act sensitively and yet assertively, within such a dynamic context and at so many different levels requires a good insight, knowledge, values and skills. Having successfully completed higher vocational training ensures that the job coach is a professional who can take the 'helicopter view' as well as being able to apply theory in practice at the individual level.

The importance of training

The changing role of the job coach in an increasingly complex working environment means that there now is a distinction between three levels of job coaching:

- Entry-level: the job coach implements the development plan and the set goals in practice

- Senior-level: the job coach combines the development of guidance and coaching on the job

- Expert-level: the job coach takes the role of organisational advisor and HR professional.

In the Netherlands, this tiered training and employment of job coaches has been institutionalised by distinguishing between the *internal job coach*, coaching directly in daily operations, and the *external job coach*, whose role is to have a wider field of vision, take a broader market perspective and keep up-to-date with helicopter-view knowledge and skills. The distinction between the different roles of job coaches includes a lifelong learning perspective that allows for the professional progression of job coaches (Noloc 2018). Thus, the definition of the job coach expands:

> [Job coaches] provide methodological support to people with occupational disabilities on a professional basis, aimed at finding and keeping a job on the regular labour market. The activities of the job coach for this purpose include an inquisitive attitude to employee support in finding answers to questions, learning to exploit opportunities, optimizing the independence in performing work, teaching (work) activities and in the development of knowledge and skills. If necessary, the job coach collaborates with a supportive social network. The job coach works in his support towards a time when the remaining guidance needs of the employee can be taken by the employer. (Noloc 2018)

Appropriate training lies at the centre of a job coach's knowledge, values and skills, and thus determines their effectiveness in supporting people with disabilities. Across Europe and further afield there are some recognised job coach courses. While they differ to some degree in the detail of how they are delivered (e.g., online vs. on campus or on-the-job) and duration, European standards for job coaching are available (Matuska 2016). In most cases, job coach training programmes are structured in a didactic dual-track approach, where theoretical learning and practice go hand in hand. Enrolment in these courses requires availability of a relevant workplace environment, where theory can be applied directly in practice, and skilled supervision is available. In addition, continuous professional development training courses are available.

The underlying vision and goals of job coach training are that training should enable the job coach to generate the process together with the employee in such a way that it corresponds with the employee's competences and contributes to expanding their skills. This process should be shaped together with the employee, ensuring that it is characterised by an equal, reciprocal, respectful and open attitude. The job coach needs good communication skills and knowledge of behavioural processes in order to effectively support learning by creating adequate conditions (see Appendix 1).

Furthermore, the job coach needs profound knowledge with regards to local laws and all relevant regulations, subsidies or funding criteria and available facilities. The job coach should know the regional labour market and understand the social map of local services so that they can manage effectively any tensions that may arise. In addition, the job coach should be able to report fluently, verbally and in writing to a variety of stakeholders, including the employee and the employer. Importantly, the job coach should be able to manage their own time and caseload, including planning, maintenance of relationships and networks, and recognise lead times for certain tasks, as well as being able to formulate concrete and measurable objectives and identify corporate boundaries and their own limitations. Last but not least, job coaches need health- and disability-related knowledge (covered in some of the chapters in this book; and see also Appendix 2).

The Polish Forum of Disabled People (PFON 2015) developed one example of a practical skills-based framework for job coach training), outlining the tasks and competences of job coaches:

1. *Recruitment,* including conducting individual and group recruitment meetings.

2. *Presenting,* including building the job coach–employee relationship and taking into account employees' needs and interests by introducing them to the aims, principles and stages of supported employment.

3. *Collection of initial, basic employee data,* including collecting information about the employee's preferences, motivation, interests, expectations, predispositions and family background from the employee and their social network.

4. *Developing and agreeing a contract,* including introducing the person with disabilities to the formal and legal conditions related to employment; recognising and overcoming challenges; building confidence; and ensuring mutual understanding regarding roles, limitations, rights and obligations. Finally, the job coach supports the employee in signing an employment contract.

5. *Intake and assessment,* including being able to conduct an efficient intake and assessment interview within the framework of a customer and organisation; assess employee needs, wants,

motivation and capabilities; ensure that the employee remains in control as much as possible; coach the employee in a way that is consistent with the process, procedures and their learning approach; translate the data from interviews and other assessment activities into goals and a plan of action; create together with the employee a profile that contains the core, the qualities, and take into consideration the concerns of the employee that serve as starting points for an appropriate job. Finally, the job coach ensures that the relevant network is part of the employees' network in the assessment, and makes the connection between the regional labour market and the profile of the employee.

Ultimately, the creation of an individual vocational profile includes strengthening the employee's motivation to participate in the supported employment process by inspiring them, reinforcing their aspirations, presenting attractive examples, indicating how their needs could be fulfilled through professional activity, establishing with the employee whether there is a need to cooperate with people from their environment (family, close relatives and partners) or professional supporters (doctors, therapists) in the course of the planned employment process, obtaining their consent and starting cooperation.

The subsequent action plan should include an individual plan on how to acquire necessary social competences, a strategy to support the employee in the further development of their career. The individual vocational profile and action plan are completed with final approval from the employee and/or their guardian or mentor (where appropriate). Appropriate training enables the job coach to engage in all of the above activities and to use their knowledge and experience to help the employee have a successful employment experience.

While the concepts presented above serve as a valuable blueprint, the details and categorisation of job coach activities vary between countries and/or employers (for further practical ideas, see Appendix 1). Yet most job coach training courses entail five to six modules, each focusing on a distinct area of theory, policy or practice. Each module is assessed through a professional assignment, in which the acquired knowledge, skills and values are integrated into a specific professional context.

Tables 11.1 and 11.2 offer possible outlines of curriculum content for a six-module job coach course. This is in no way meant to be prescriptive, but could be used to develop appropriate curricula for basic-level job coach training.

Table 11.1: Curriculum content for an online job coach training course

Module 1: Supported employment: An overview	Module 2: Context of supported employment
Define employment	Employment legislation
The history of services for people with disabilities	Context of supported employment
Work and employment for people with disabilities	Convention on the Rights of Persons with Disabilities
The importance of being employed	
Working when you have a disability	
Previous work options for people with disabilities	
Sheltered workshops	
Factors that influence the emergence of supported employment	
Module 3: Development of supported employment	**Module 4: Core values and underlying principles of supported employment**
Supported employment: the beginning	Ideological cornerstones of supported employment
Evolution of the model of supported employment	Underlying principles of supported employment
Individual placement models	
Supported employment in the present	
Trends for the future development of supported employment	
Module 5: Essential employment facilitator skills	**Assessment**
The role of the employment facilitator	Complete a project that involves working with an employee who is seeking work and supporting them through the process of supported employment. Write up the theory and the practice
Skills for effective communication	
Person-centred planning	
The role of person-centred planning in supported employment	
Career planning	
Marketing	
Job analysis	
Analysis of the work site culture and the environment	
Preparation for the first day at work	
Guidelines for facilitating decisions about supported employment strategies	
Systematic instruction	
Evaluation outcomes and supports	

Source: IASE (2016)

Table 11.2: Curriculum content for on-campus job coach training

Module 1: Employee engagement and labour market approach	Module 2: Knowledge of clinical issues
The core of this module involves contracting with the client and building a collaborative working relationship, getting to know the client, reflection and giving direction, and attention to the job context. Crucial skills for the job coach are highlighted, such as engaging in quality dialogue, questioning and active listening, to enable the job coach to guide the employee towards their best possible future, giving full attention to the employee: Methods and assessment Effective communication and conversation techniques: listening, summarising, appreciative questioning Give and receive feedback Dealing with resistances Theories of lifelong learning/lifelong development Drafting the employee's profile	Specific clinical disorders and related problems; help employers and social care professionals learn about job-related solutions in working with people with specific disorders. Specific target group knowledge in the field of: Mental limitations Learning disabilities ASD (autism spectrum disorder) Mental health complaints (depression, anxiety, OCD) Developmental and behavioural characteristics Meaning of this for work Employee presentation based on what is there, real possibilities Practical translation to the workplace and real expectation coaching
Module 3: Labour market approach	**Module 4: Job analysis and Job finding**
Job coaching aims to contribute to an inclusive job market. Job coaches need to be familiar with the labour market, workplace analysis, governmental policies and all relevant contexts. This requires input from a multidisciplinary team that includes local experts to share the latest developments in regional policies and job market developments, how to acquire jobs for the employee and how to engage their network of support: Acquisition, networks, workplace analysis, social media Regional labour market and social map Labour market prospects Social business administration and organisational science Legislation and regulations, current developments in social security Benefits and subsidy guidance Reintegration instruments Effective interventions	The job coach needs to learn how to place clients in a working environment and be able to assess the employee's capabilities in order to identify what kind of job is best suited, i.e., job carving: Employer approach Create a matching plan Presenting employee to the employer Job carving and job matching Employer's attitude and how to change positively towards inclusion of people with disabilities

Module 5: On-the-job coaching	Module 6: Attitude of the job coach and educational support
Placing an employee in a job and ensuring that the employee is able to stay in the job and find job satisfaction:	This module challenges the job coach in their own professionalism and teaches methods of self-reflection and values and attitudes of the job coach:
Create a coaching plan with goals	Vision and professional attitude
Coordinate the coaching plan and translate it into learning activities	Job coaching
Role of the employer in the job coaching process	Background method
	Supported employment
Writing a plan and conducting a task analysis	Formulate learning objectives
Coaching styles and methods: e.g., solution-oriented coaching, appreciative research attitude, formulating SMART goals	Professional attitude of the job coach
Reporting	
Assessment portfolio	
Complete a portfolio that involves describing and reflecting on your work with an employee who is seeking work and supporting them through the process of supported employment. Write up the portfolio including theory and the practice and present it to your colleagues on the course.	

Note: The content outlined here originated from a number
of different job coach education programmes.

Source: ELAN Training & Development (2018); Grone Schulen (2018);
Saxion University of Applied Sciences (2018); Combo (2018)

In addition to direct contact with the tutor, job coach trainees usually have to work on a portfolio. Commonly, this includes a portfolio with a personal development plan and a personal action plan to ensure that trainees discover and reflect on their actions, both personally and professionally. During the process of compiling the portfolio the job coach reflects on the competences, cooperation, planning and organising skills they have learned as part of the course. The portfolio itself serves as documentation of the development of theoretical knowledge and behavioural competencies, including empathy, analytical ability, effective communication, advice and coaching.

Conclusion

Job coach training has to ensure that participants are enabled to effectively assess and support the employee with disabilities in a given situation. The work of the job coach is based on the supported employment model that includes, but is not limited to, five stages: employee/client engagement, vocational profiling, job finding, employer engagement and on-/off-the-job support (EUSE 2010; PFON 2015). Therefore, training has to ensure that the learning needs of job coaches are met. Most courses, regardless of whether they are offered online or on-campus, entail at least five to six modules, aiming to meet the standards for job coaching (Matuska 2016). Some courses are approved by accrediting bodies and some countries have registers of job coaches, although this is not universally available, and the title 'job coach' remains largely unprotected.

References

BASE (British Association for Supported Employment) (2018) 'Job carving.' Accessed on 03/02/2018 at www.base-uk.org/employers-recruitment-jobcarving

Combo (2018) 'Welkom bij Combo Emonomy.' Accessed on 07/02/2018 *at www.combo.nl*

Cooper, J., Heron, T. and Heward, W. (2007) *Applied Behaviour Analysis* (2nd edn). Upper Saddle River, NJ: Pearson Prentice Hall.

ELAN Training & Development (2018) Accessed on 07/02/2018 at www.elantraining.org

European Commission (2018) *The European Pillar of Social Rights in 20 Principles.* Accessed on 04/02/2018 at https://ec.europa.eu/commission/priorities/deeper-and-fairer-economic-and-monetary-union/european-pillar-social-rights/european-pillar-social-rights-20-principles_en

EUSE (European Union of Supported Employment) (2010) *European Union of Supported Employment Toolkit.* Accessed on 01/02/2018 at www.euse.org/content/supported-employment-toolkit/EUSE-Toolkit-2010.pdf

Grone Schulen (2018) *Job Coach für Menschen mit Behinderungen.* Accessed on 07/02/2018 at http://ec.europa.eu/programmes/erasmus-plus/projects/eplus-project-details-page/?nodeRef=workspace://SpacesStore/7a7122ee-ff52-4835-8bc6-3099bb004a5d

IASE (Irish Association of Supported Employment) (2016) 'Certificate in Supported Employment.' Dublin. Accessed on 10/02/2018 at www.iase.ie/

Maastricht University (2018) *Research Centre for Education and the Labour Market.* Accessed on 02/02/2018 at www.maastrichtuniversity.nl/research/research-centre-education-and-labour-market

Matuska, E. (2016) 'European qualification profile of job coach for persons with disabilities.' Accessed on 07/02/2018 at http://ec.europa.eu/programmes/erasmus-plus/projects/eplus-project-details-page/?nodeRef=workspace://SpacesStore/7a7122ee-ff52-4835-8bc6-3099bb004a5d

Noloc (2018) *Erkende Jobcoachpleidingen* [Professional Association for career professionals and job coaches]. Accessed on 02/02/2018 at www.noloc.nl/jobcoachopleidingen

PFON (Polskie Forum Osób Niepełnosprawnych) (2015) *Polskie Forum Osób Niepełnosprawnych 2015–2020.* Accessed on 01/02/2018 at infobrokerstm.blogspot.co.uk/2015/09/polskie-forum-osob-niepenosprawnych.html

Saxion University of Applied Sciences (2018) Accessed on 07/02/2018 at www.saxion.edu

Sargeant, M., Radevich-Katsaroumpa, E. and Innesti, A. (2016) 'Disability quotas: Past or future policy?' *Economic and Industrial Democracy.* 0143831X1663965. Accessed on 23/05/2018 at http://doi.org/10.1177/0143831X16639655

UN (United Nations) (2006) *Convention the Rights of Persons with Disabilities.* Accessed on 03/02/2018 at www.un.org/development/desa/disabilities/convention-on-the-rights-of-persons-with-disabilities.html

Usability (2018) 'Task Analysis.' Accessed on 07/02/2018 at www.usability.gov/how-to-and-tools/methods/task-analysis.html

Wehman, P. and Kregel, J. (1995) 'At the crossroads: Supported employment a decade later.' *Research and Practice for Persons with Severe Disabilities 20,* 4, 286–299. Accessed on 23/05/2018 at http://doi.org/10.1177/154079699602000405

JOB COACHING CURRICULUM AND SKILLS: PRACTICE EXAMPLES

The central principles of job coach activities, knowledge and skills presented below are derived largely from the job coaching guidance developed at Arbeidsdeskundig Kennis Centrum Nijkerk, the Netherlands (AKC 2017), and include assessment, job finding, job analysis, job matching, job redesign and on-the-job coaching.

Assessment

Learning outcomes: being able to draw up an employee profile describing the employee's strengths, what inspires them in the field of work, what functional and social skills they have already, how and under what conditions they learn best, and in what type of (social) context their strengths and skills can best be further developed.

Table A1.1: Questions to be considered for assessment

Context/network	Job coach relationship
The job coach should explore the employee's strengths, talents and possibilities; investigate the needs of the employee; leave decisions and direction as much as possible up to the employee by inviting them to learn based on their own existing knowledge and experience. Some examples of useful questions to ask are as follows:	With respect to the relationship with the job coach, some of the following questions may be useful:

Context/network

- When is your work environment in an optimum state? And when is it too intense? What is an example you can tell us about?
- What has been an environment where you have felt lots of energy in doing your work? What moment of positive energy in your work can you describe?
- What interests you most in your work and why?
- What gifts and talents do you have and hold dearly? What would you really like to be able to use in a new work environment?
- Who are the most important people in your supporting network? What makes these people important for you?
- How have the people in your network supported you in making work and life choices?
- When have you really felt inclusive to your team and workplace?

Job coach relationship

- What are specific interests or things you are extra motivated for to work on?
- Do you have experiences with other consultants or coaches (sports coach, therapist, piano teacher)? What worked for you in those relationships?
- How did any past relationship with a job coach end?
- How can I help you to work effectively towards your goals based on former experiences?
- What responsibility do you think you have in making this relationship successful? What may the job coach expect from you?
- Have important developments occurred that could potentially affect the success of your employment (think of home location, health problems, drug use)?
- Are there any practical or medical issues that need to be taken into account regarding transport, physical needs, debt, addiction, legal issues?

These issues can affect the coaching process towards successful, sustainable labour participation. If one of these topics seems relevant, it may be useful to address the issue first before continuing to work towards work placement or accompanying work. Here, close cooperation with doctors and therapists or social care services is crucial.

Work-related aspects

To gain insights into a number of work-related aspects, the job coach may ask explicit questions about successes in the work placement. Going to a new workplace may cause resistance. Asking for moments when the employee went to new environments and situations and what worked in it help to prevent resistance because the change is linked to a previous (own) experience:

- What can you remember about going first to a new environment or situation (e.g., leaving parents' house, starting high school)?
- Can you describe such a moment?
- What helped you to get into this new environment or situation?

Cognition

Examples of questions for inquiry into cognition:

- How does learning and remembering work best for you?
- How do you proceed if you want to learn something?
- What are you doing easily and what demands more attention and concentration?
- Can you tell me what a work plan means? Do you have an example that you can share of your own experience in former practical or work environments?
- How do you deal with switching times in the day/at school or work?
- Is that easy for you? Or does it help if you get prepared for these switching moments?
- How do you deal with unexpected facts or situations?

Social functioning

Examples of questions for inquiry into social functioning:

- What do you value most about yourself?
- In relationships you have had for a long time, how did you make them work?
- Can you describe an example of when you have been assertive at school or in your work?
- What works for you in contact with others?
- How do you handle criticism?
- How do you rate yourself critically?
- What does working alone mean to you?
- What does working in a team mean to you?
- How do you make it work (working alone or working in a team)?

Work execution

Examples of questions for inquiry into work execution:

- Can you focus on one task for a long time? How long is this time? Did you succeed in attending normal school hours?
- How do you continue after setbacks?
- How do you create discipline in your work?
- How do you deal with tools?
- How do you deal with working arrangements?
- Can you keep your promises?
- How much guidance do you need in your work?
- How can a manager best address you?

The job coach should ask questions that invite the employee to talk about successful situations and how they addressed them. It is important to get as concrete a picture as possible about the situation and why this situation has just been experienced as successful. These successes can be used as 'building blocks' for future work and for strengthening the positive self-image of the employee.

Table A1.2: Assessment conclusions

With the information obtained from the questions in Table A1.1, the job coach should be able to answer the following questions:	Important data to support career choices are:
• Talents, competencies ('I can do this well') • Have fun ('I like to do this') • Ideal terms, context ('I need this') • Values and goals ('Here I believe I'm in favour of it') • Desire to self-development ('I want to learn') • Inspiration sources ('From which I do what I do')	• Interest in specific activities • Previously made choices • Strength analysis/development opportunities • Competences • Understand the working atmosphere • Required working conditions • Characteristics of working environment and degree and form of guidance needed
What dream does the employee have about the future? • What would your life look like if you can use your talents every day? • What are you doing? • Who do you work with? • Where is your work? • What do you like about your work?	The employee profile includes: • A general description of the employee • Depicting capacities: the strengths and qualities of the employee • A description of the way of learning, learning opportunities and conditions for learning • A general idea of the social context, background and network of the employee • Meaning and identity, atmosphere and personality of the employee • Desires, motives and real perspectives

Source: Adapted from Bouwen and Meeus (2011)

Job finding

The job coach sessions provide a workplace profile that best suits the employee. This should be compared and matched to the workplace options available.

Table A1.3: Workplace profiling

Individual workplace profile assessment: • Which of the strengths described do you like to see in your work? • What do you want to achieve in your work? • What would a workplace that focuses on your strengths look like? • Do you know workplaces where these strengths can be utilised?	Look for appropriate workplaces on the open market: • What do you do? • What is your responsibility? • What is my responsibility?
Building a network of jobs in the regional labour market: • Creating and maintaining a network of (potential) employers • Conducting orientation talks with potential employers • To inform the employer about employing an employee with a disability, the benefits of this and the job coaching provision • Supporting the client at job interviews	

Job analysis and job matching

The job coach should set up a work profile that indicates in what way the proposed workplace can be optimally deployed for maximum business performance. It is important for the employer and the employee to assess the employee's development and what supports are necessary. Job matching is about matching the employee profile and the work profile.

Table A1.4: Questions to be address in job analysis and job matching

The profile of the workplace must meet the employee profile: • What job skills etc. does the workplace require? • What are the development/career opportunities in the workplace? • What values and norms are in the workplace? • How does the workplace match the client's values and standards?	Matching • Both profiles are compared to look at similarities and differences • Look for the differences, whether they can be coached or possibly adjusted • Discusses mutual expectations with the employer and client • The employee should be able to work optimally and not to the maximum

Job redesign and on-the-job coaching

When agreements are reached with the employer about any adjustments to the workplace, the job tasks or the working environment, the core activities for practical job coaching consist of introduction into the workplace; training on the job/job coaching; support outside the workplace; and ongoing support.

Job redesign occurs if the job matching analysis shows that the workplace is suitable with a number of (minor) adjustments. These should be discussed with the employer and employee openly. Any necessary adjustments should be recorded, with possible evaluation times for adjustment.

Table A1.5: Job redesign and on-the-job coaching

Topics that ensure the effectiveness of job training:	If a match seems appropriate and the employee and employer agree, a coaching plan is drawn up together with the employee and employer that formulates concrete SMART goals:
• First place, then train • Integrated plan/supervision and mediation • Support sources are sponsored wherever possible across multiple lines, such as the employer, direct colleagues at work, family and acquaintances and professional support • The chosen workplace must provide sufficient stability and support to provide basic conditions for workplace performance • The employee is guided to a level of skills appropriate to the job and the company • The employee works as much as possible at the level that reflects their ability, training, experience and ambitions • The workplace and the related tasks are arranged in such a way that the employee can learn the skills for the job, as much as possible • When functional questions remain, they are secured through support from the immediate environment and colleagues in the workplace or through the job coach support • Abolish any additional burden for the employer • The employee is assisted in arranging transport to the workplace and home again	• Each goal indicates which activities will be carried out for this purpose and how the support will look in practice • For each goal, more than one activity is possible • When goals have been achieved, a new goal can be chosen. In the meantime, the importance of goals can change • Outline activities of the employer to ensure a suitable workplace and a suitable working environment • Make clear and explicit arrangements for guidance from the job coach (when, how, where)

References

AKC (Arbeidsdeskundig Kennis Centrum) (2017) 'Eigen regie bij opleiding en werk bij ASS.' Accessed on 26/02/2018 at http://docplayer.nl/50296192-Eigen-regie-voor-opleiding-en-werk.html

Bouwen, G. and Meeus, M. (2011) *Vuur Werkt. Met Talent Toekomst Maken.* Houten, NL: Lannoo Campus.

JOB COACHING EMPLOYEES WITH SPECIFIC DISABILITIES

The job coach, in collaboration with the employee and employer, needs to plan ahead as far as necessary, making sure that changes in the time plan are always made together with the employee. Special attention needs to be given to transition times. For some employees it can be useful to visualise 'building blocks' from the start using visuals or written text, making sure that the employer supports the guidance given to the employee. Make use of the Five Ws to clarify tasks: *What, How, When, Where, Who, Why* (de Bruin 2009).

The employee needs to know as clearly as possible:

- what's going to happen

- what the employee may or must do

- how the employee starts the task

- how the employee must continue the work

- what the desired behaviour is in a given particular situation

- how the employee can do their job efficiently

- how much time the employee has for a concrete task

- what to do if a task is finished

- how the transition moment from one task to another is organised.

There are various forms of guidance that may differ in intensity, that is, guidance for a limited period of time; intermittent guidance, for example, only necessary for changes; and continuous supervision.

- *Supervision:* An employee may need supervision. *Direct supervision* is about functional management, where the shop floor supervisor or the job coach occasionally/regularly 'keeps an eye' on whether the employee is performing the work appropriately. In *permanent supervision,* a specially trained person is present at all times to intervene immediately in an emergency situation. *Permanent supervision* is typically only available in sheltered workplace situations and unrealistic on the open labour market.

- *Job coaching:* The employee gets feedback on their behaviour at regular intervals. The job coach is not permanently present at the workplace.

- *Training:* Employee training is about learning job-related skills and knowledge and maintaining these on the job.

In principle, guidance is aimed at coaching the employee to perform a task or job function independently. The time and cost necessary to learn new tasks obviously depends on the learner's aptitude, the employment context, as well as the complexity of the task. It is therefore often necessary that an employee benefits from a long-term accompaniment, especially for employees for whom learning labour-related social skills is particularly time consuming (AKC 2017).

Key aspects of job coaching related to specific disabilities

The following tables outline some key aspects of job coaching employees with a specific disability. These serve as brief 'checklists' and are not necessarily exhaustive or comprehensive; they should be read in the context of the respective chapters of this book.

Table A2.1: Employees with intellectual disabilities

Assessment	• Depending on the employee, use adequate, not-complex, language wording, grammar and syntax • Use positive and clear communication, and be creative in distilling workable elements together • Express expectations explicitly; invite the employee to explore the meaning of what is being said • Recognise egocentric experiences, and help the employee to see more perspectives • For some employees social adaptability needs to be assessed • Support the employee to think first before acting, and then review the effects of certain steps
Job analysis	• Assess levels of available support for the employee's different needs
Job match	• Find a job in the region or within the employee's own network
Job redesign	• Allow time and facilities for experiential learning, 'learning by doing' • Job carving may be necessary to ensure adequate positions by combining less (academically) demanding aspects of work
Job coaching	• Ask open questions, make use of the Five Ws • Use visual support where necessary • Use different approaches, i.e., in some cases it is possible to enhance skills, in others it may be necessary to simplify tasks

Table A2.2: Employees with autism spectrum disorder

Assessment	• Be explicit with instructions and questions • Ask for the specific meaning of words • Use positive communication • Ask about the employee's personal resources and experiences (their own bike, computer, house) • For many (not everyone), visual information (written or pictorial) is useful or necessary (make sure you assess – do not assume all employees with autism need visuals!) • Are there environmental factors (sounds, smells, lights) that the employee is sensitive to? How do they usually deal with these? • Job skills assessment including motivation, perseverance, discipline and quality • Too many choices can be stressful and lead to poor, overly quick decisions to avoid 'choice stress' • Support self-reflection and self-awareness with regards to skills and challenges through targeted interventions; if necessary or available, consult caregivers, guardians and/or a therapist

Job analysis	• Use work visits or short-term plans to get to know workplaces • Explain 'tricks' or shortcuts explicitly
Job match	• Find a job in close proximity to the employee's home or within existing networks, and ensure familiar and professional support is available
Job redesign	• Make use of experiential learning, 'learning by doing' • Use phased introduction to work • Use behavioural methods such as task analysis, chaining and shaping to teach workplace processes • For some, a single workplace may be preferable to open workspaces
Job coaching	• Link new skills to the employee's own concrete, visual experiences • Visual support may help to transfer information from one context to another • Use the concrete questions (i.e., the Five Ws) • Jokes and informal procedures at work should be explained clearly • Some employees may need single instructions (one instruction at a time rather than multiple instructions in once sentence)

Table A2.3: Employees with mental health issues (e.g., schizophrenia)

Assessment	• Use positive communication (do not talk about failure) • Be aware that mental health problems are not a reflection of level of intelligence (do not 'talk down') • Be consistent and clear • Ask for initiative-rich moments • Pay attention to withdrawn behaviour
Job analysis	• Ensure Individual Placement and Support (IPS) is available • If necessary, refer to cognitive and/or behaviour interventions • Remember, the job coach is not a therapist • Increase the employee's self-esteem by including activities appreciated by others • Avoid complex and emotionally aversive social situations
Job match	• Ensure the work is stimulating, offering possibilities for the employee's development • Be aware of necessary limitations and safety arrangements in the work environment
Job redesign	• Customise tasks to different phases of the employee's health status (i.e., there may be periods where the employee has difficulties in concentrating) • Create a retreat for the employee • Avoid shifting work rhythms and night shifts

Job coaching	• Utilise Individual Placement and Support (IPS)
	• Ensure the employee experiences regularity in the job environment
	• Avoid stress or multiple deadlines and ensure continuity
	• Provide alternation between effort and rest (possibly with additional breaks)
	• Use self-management strategies
	• Ensure financial support is provided
	• Use colleagues in a multidisciplinary approach

References

AKC (Arbeidsdeskundig Kennis Centrum) (2017) 'Eigen regie bij opleiding en werk bij ASS.' Accessed on 26/02/2018 at http://docplayer.nl/50296192-Eigen-regie-voor-opleiding-en-werk.html

de Bruin, C. (2009) *Geef me de 5: een praktisch houvast bij de opvoeding en begeleiding van kinderen met autism.* Uitgever: Graviant Educatieve.

ABOUT THE CONTRIBUTORS

Angelika Anderson is an Associate Professor at the University of Waikato, New Zealand. She is a Board Certified Behaviour Analyst®-Doctoral™ (BCBA-D™) working at the interface of developmental psychology, Applied Behaviour Analysis and educational psychology. Her research focuses largely on developing and trialling efficient, often technology-based behavioural interventions, able to be implemented in low-resource environments, targeting diverse populations. She publishes widely in peer-reviewed journals and seeks to promote evidence-based practice through her research, teaching and community engagement.

Marea de Bruijn is a Board Member of the Professional Association for Job Coaches in the Netherlands, and played an important role in the merger of the professional association with the Professional Association for Career Professionals (Noloc). Marea has a Master's of Science in Educational Sciences and has been a teacher in special education for many years. She has extensive experience in job coaching people with various disabilities in preparation to work and into work and employment. Marea works from a strength-based appreciative perspective with her clients. She is a trainer in Appreciative Coaching.

Karola Dillenburger is Professor of Behaviour Analysis and Education and Director of the Centre of Behaviour Analysis at Queen's University Belfast, Northern Ireland. She is a Board Certified Behaviour Analyst®-Doctoral™ (BCBA-D™) and registered Clinical Psychologist (HCPC), and has worked extensively in childcare, education and therapeutic settings before being called to Queen's University Belfast. She has published widely, in print and multimedia electronic formats. She has authored over 80 academic peer-reviewed papers and is frequently invited to teach or deliver international keynote addresses in the US, India, Europe and Australia.

Brian Fennell is Assistant Principal (Personal Development, Welfare, & Behaviour) at Ambitious College, London, UK. He received his PhD from Queen's University Belfast. With many years as an educator of students with special educational needs in Ireland and the US, he has recently moved into higher education where he works with students training to become teachers. His research interests are autism spectrum disorders, intellectual disabilities and challenging behaviours.

Trish MacKeogh is an AssistID Post-doctoral Fellow at Dublin Institute of Technology (DIT) in Ireland funded through RESPECT and the European Union (EU) People programme, Marie Curie Actions. As Information and Research Officer she has longstanding experience in the field of in assistive technology. She was a project officer on four EU-funded projects including 'Inclusive Learning through Technology, Keeping Pace with Technology', ATIS4All and Cardiac. She has co-authored four online training programmes in assistive technology. Trish has a Master's in Library and Information Science.

Ewa Matuska is Assistant Professor and Chief of the Management Department, Faculty of Management and Safety Sciences at Pomeranian University in Słupsk, Poland. She is a psychologist, human resources specialist and project manager. She has worked in managerial positions in business support and educational organisations, and occasionally, in therapeutic settings, alongside her longstanding academic career. She has authored over 70 academic peer-reviewed papers and regularly attends international educational and regional development projects in Europe.

Lyn McKerr is a Research Fellow at the Centre for Behaviour Analysis, Queen's University Belfast, Northern Ireland. She is a qualified teacher and the parent of a young adult diagnosed with Asperger's Syndrome and attention deficit hyperactivity disorder (ADHD). She was a founder member of the autism charity Parents' Education as Autism Therapists (PEATni.org) and chair of a local pre-school/social skills group for children with autism. After bringing up her own family, she returned to university to study anthropology and archaeology and received her doctorate. She undertakes voluntary work with children with autism and has published widely, in books, reports and peer-reviewed journals, with co-authors from many other disciplines.

Caterina Metje was diagnosed with autism spectrum disorder (ASD) as a young adult and, as a result of her former engagement in self-help groups for young adults with autism, has a keen interest in ensuring that the 'insider' view is included fully in research. She has a degree in politics, history and economics from the University of Münster, Germany. She worked as a journalist (salaried and freelance) for several years before being appointed as a Research Assistant at the University of Applied Sciences in Münster, where she contributes to the research, consults students and works as an exam assistant. She represented the university as a partner in the Erasmus+ project 'Job Coach for People with Disabilities'.

Blazej Piasek is the Vice-chair of the Warsaw Initiative for Non-Governmental Support in Poland and was an officer for the State Fund for Rehabilitation of Disabled Persons (PFRON) and Member of the Project Approval Commission for the European Social Fund (ESF). He is the founder of the Toto Animo Foundation for people with autism, and has implemented more than ten social and vocational rehabilitation projects funded by ESF. He was a project specialist at the Association for the Disabled for the Environment (EKON), one of the leading social enterprises in Poland, supporting approximately 1500 people with disabilities in 'green' (that is, environmental protection) and other jobs in the open employment market throughout the country. He has an MA in Political Science from Warsaw University with a specialisation in Social Policy, and worked for the United Nations as electoral specialist in East Timor and Nepal and as an election observer for the Organization for Security and Cooperation in Europe (OSCE).

Lucie Procházková is a Senior Lecturer at the Institute for Research in Inclusive Education, Faculty of Education, Masaryk University (MU), Czech Republic. Her research focuses on the employment of people with disabilities, support during vocational education and integration into society. She runs courses in education and the support of adults with disabilities. Before entering the Faculty of Education at MU, she worked as a researcher in Vienna, Austria.

Hanns Rüdiger Röttgers is Professor of Social Medicine and Health Care Sciences and Head of the Autism Research Unit at the University of Applied Science (UAS), Münster, Germany. He is a certified medical specialist in psychiatry/psychotherapy, public health and environmental medicine, and has additional Masters' grades in Ethics and Political

Sciences. He has worked in different hospital and healthcare settings before being called to UAS Münster. His publications cover clinical as well as juridical, political and ethical issues in autism and mental healthcare, and he works as an expert for courts and public institutions.

Marcia J. Scherer is the founding President of the Institute for Matching Person and Technology. She is Professor of Physical Medicine and Rehabilitation at the University of Rochester Medical Center, USA, where she received both her PhD and MPH degrees. She is a past member of the National Advisory Board on Medical Rehabilitation Research, National Institutes of Health, and is Editor of the journal *Disability and Rehabilitation: Assistive Technology*. She is co-editor of the book series for CRC Press, Rehabilitation Science in Practice Series. Marcia is Fellow of the American Psychological Association, American Congress of Rehabilitation Medicine and the Rehabilitation Engineering and Assistive Technology Society of North America (RESNA). She has authored, edited or co-edited nine book titles and has published over 75 articles in peer-reviewed journals as well as 30 book chapters on disability and technology. Others have cited her research more than 4500 times.

Norman Sterritt is Chair of the Northern Ireland Union of Supported Employment (NIUSE) and a Board Member of the European Union of Supported Employment (EUSE). He is the Progression to Employment Services Manager for Triangle Housing Association in Northern Ireland. He is a strong advocate for the inclusion of people with intellectual disabilities within society, and has been involved in the development of employment services for many years. He played a role in having the right to support for employment incorporated within the Northern Ireland Department of Health Service Framework for Learning Disability, and has contributed to the development of revised UK National Occupational Standards for Supported Employment. Norman holds a Diploma in Management Studies (DMS), a Master's in Business Administration (MBA) and an Advanced Diploma in Social Enterprise.

Helena Vaďurová is a Senior Lecturer at the Institute for Research in Inclusive Education, Faculty of Education, Masaryk University, Czech Republic. Her research focuses on inclusive principles at all levels of education, social inclusion and the quality of life of people with special educational needs. She studies Applied Behaviour Analysis, both theoretically and practically.

SUBJECT INDEX

AUTHOR INDEX